From
Trigger
to
Happy

Free Yourself from Toxic Relationship Patterns
Forever!

ELLEN MALAN

ISBN: 978-1-955622-45-5

Published by

Fideli Publishing, Inc.
119 W. Morgan St.
Martinsville, IN 46151
www.FideliPublishing.com

All names, identifying details, and personal characteristics of the individuals involved have been changed. People mentioned in the book are also composites of more than one individual in the author's life, and sibling or friend references have been changed to protect and preserve the privacy of individuals and connections, both present and past.

Dedication

To the open-hearted woman
searching for the one
and falling short time and time again,
my words are for you.

For the committed woman
fed up with relationships and the pursuit of love,
may my message bring you clarity and freedom from the chase.

To the unsuspecting recipient of narcissistic abuse
who feels elated by a man
and yet confused, unsure, and self-blaming
within the connection, may this book bring you peace.

For my inner child, the youngest form of me,
who had no idea of the wounds she carried in her heart
or the intensity of the damage accumulated over time.
This book is for you and for all the women ready to overcome the past
and be the person they were meant to be.

About This Book

This book is based on the stories we tell ourselves and the truths and misconceptions that we all weave into our relationship storylines. The personality traits and characters depicted in this book exist in this world and are likely to visit each and every one of us to varying extents.

The interpretation of accounts and people carry immense lessons of growth for both the readers and the author. These struggles, the clash of perspectives, and any perception of abuse is a gift resulting in an intentional life filled with freedom, awareness, strength, independence and inter-dependence that we all have access to live out. Without life's trials, we would not become the humans that we are meant to be. Read on with gratefulness for the lessons learned from any and all relationships from the past.

All names, identifying details, and personal characteristics of the individuals involved have been changed. People mentioned in the book are also composites of more than one individual in the author's life, and sibling or friend references have been changed to protect and preserve the privacy of individuals and connections, both present and past.

Table of Contents

Preface

Trigger Happy is intended to be poignant. I hope that readers will find it relatable and that they will be drawn in by both fear and hope. It was only out of my own fear that I was lured to a place so disconnected from myself and my dreams.

I idolized a narcissistic man and put my own desires for love and family aside. I spent decades with emotionally unavailable and distant men believing that my love for them would change their ways. I sympathized with men and their difficult personal situations rather than opening up to lasting love that may have been available.

Have you stayed too long with abusive, dangerous, or distant men? How will you change this tendency and transform your love life?

In this book are the lessons of self-empowerment, self-love, healing, and discovery that I have learned to escape unhealthy relationships.

The purpose of this writing is to be a living, breathing apparatus for you. I hope that it comes to life with the power of my voice and all voices that have forged a path out of psychological abuse. Your voice, whether on the surface or hidden within a deep trance, needs to awaken. Step up for yourself now, and show up here.

Fear left me diminished, devalued, and misused. Fear had me holding on to toxic relationships and aching to find true love. One must know that kind of abandonment of self to truly be moved to act.

You must have a risk-it-all and there-is-nothing-left-to-lose kind of attitude to benefit from this book. When you do, this book will be life-altering in the most positive way and worth far more than the price tag. This is your beautiful life that we are talking about here. There is no turning back and no giving up.

If you understand the depth of the pain unraveled in my story, I am certain that you have thrown away a significant amount of money already. Perhaps you drank it away in evenings out or carelessly inhaled it into your lungs. If you relate to the consistent attempts to push away the trauma and the relationship anxiety, then you most certainly have thrown your hard-earned savings at mind-numbing entertainment, too much chocolate, or new apparel that brings a temporary respite and a high to get you to the next work day.

I experimented with all of these outlets and more. I did anything for an escape from thoughts, the day, the person, this life.

I spent more money than I can count to save myself. I don't want you to do that, and this is why everything I know about my recovery from narcissistic abuse, anxious-avoidant relationships, and dangerous men is in this book and the one to follow.

You don't have to have dated or married a person with Narcissistic Personality Disorder to benefit from this book, although this was a part of my journey. The SOULutions found here will help anyone who has been manipulated, cheated on, physically or mentally abused, lied to, or corrupted in any way. If you suffer from low self-worth, co-dependency, fear of intimacy, or mistrust in yourself or others, this book will benefit you as well.

May my words deliver peace to your heart and a calmness to your mind and body. Please stop driving yourself deeper into exhaustion and fatigue and save yourself now.

You may read this book while you're In It, meaning in the grip of a noxious relationship with yourself or another. It will help change you and gift you with an awareness that your soul wishes for you to see. I will speak to the layer that lies beneath your conscious restraints, the motherboard of all of your patterns (your subconscious mind).

You must stand up and take radical responsibility for your life. You have a story to write and a life to create that is unique to you. Remember this as you read. There isn't a simple way in or an easy way out of toxic binds. However, you may walk in power with your head held high, or you may be kicked alongside those trapped in suffering. Who do you want to be? The help offered in this book is yours for the taking, a choice to say yes to you.

Depending upon where you are in the internal chaos, my words will either fall upon you as a whisper of wisdom from an eternal love, tingle your soul with an ethereal awakening, or they will strike through your heart like a lion's roar.

Due to the inner tumult of recovery, you may feel that I skip around from memories to present day trials. This is a part of the post-traumatic stress response, and my linear timeline may be skewed. Please be compassionate towards my symptom. My instincts tell me that you will relate and not even notice. In fact, you may pay yourself the same kindness as you investigate your own memories down the road.

Regardless, I hope that you will step into your true authentic self, or that your shoulders will shift toward the possibility of a new year, or that the sparkle that lives in your eyes will be reflected back to you in the mirror once again. Your purchase of this book is your ticket in, but this is not a show. Your participation is required. I know that these words are Soul-y true, so together we will get on with it, dive right in, heart first.

My Pledge to You:

I will be here for you the whole way out. I have walked, crawled, and sprinted down this path. I have at times lost my direction, my voice, and my mind. You may have or will too, but you will not and cannot fail yourself completely. Your heart will hurt, and bleed, and pound, but it will not break, and it will not quit. Your mind may turn inside out and still be untangled by your loving, knowing hands. Your lungs will fill with the breath of life again. Your face will light up, and your heart will dance.

You will learn to trust, and you may practice by trusting me. I hope to guide you to believe in yourself and build your self-worth. It can be done. It will be done!

PART I
In It

CHAPTER 1

Trigger

When you can't sit still, you gasp for air, and your heart races, recognize that a trigger is set.

When your mind is fixed on an impossible mission to figure out a confusing interaction, keeping you tossing and turning through the night, know that your internal weapon of your mind is firing.

When you whisper to yourself, *What's wrong with me? Am I going insane?*, you are in the grip of a psychological ambush.

When you feel under attack with no apparent threat or no text back from your crush, trust that your nervous system has been detonated by fear.

When you can't stay present, you can't relate in a loving way with those around you, and your mind is fixed on thoughts of the past and predictions for the future, the part of your brain called the amygdala has captured your senses and is holding you hostage.

Trigger: A benign stimulus that causes distress, fear, anxiety, sudden shifts in mood, and physical changes, such as sweating hands and a racing heartbeat, as a result of arousing feelings or memories associated with a particular traumatic experience. Also known as *losing your mind for no good reason.*

We call it *losing our mind* because we physically do lose function of our sound ability to reason and flip into survival mode.

Every human being experiences triggers. From your new computer crashing to being physically or emotionally deserted by a parent or suffering the death of a loved one, triggers are natural physical reactions to difficult life events. However, the reoccurrence of triggers during safe, everyday circumstances is a human condition that we should strive to overcome, not a life sentence to endure. Your reactive state may be keeping you locked in unsatisfactory relationships. This stress response cycle can be stopped. It is possible to overcome.

In this fast-paced world, you face and respond to everyday life events that may trigger an overactive nervous system. At times, one trigger may ignite a strand of dormant trauma points trapped in your body and your memories from the past. Living under these circumstances is exhausting and may take a heavy toll on intimate relationships and your precious life.

Tiny t and Capital T Triggers

You forgot to set your alarm, and work begins in fifteen minutes. You rocket out of bed in a panic. The first domino falls and kicks the nervous system into high gear. Your mind races in a frantic state to all of the possibilities for your day. The sheer embarrassment of walking into the meeting late and earning a spot on your boss's radar is nerve-racking and energy-depleting.

Triggers produce risky behavior and spur us to make poor decisions in life and in love. Before you know it, you're flying down roads past suburban homes (in a school zone, no doubt) driving fifty miles per hour in a twenty-five-mile-per-hour zone importuning the fates to allow you to add a few seconds of recovery time. You make subtle attempts to relax, slow down, and all the while you clench the wheel and grind your teeth. Dare I say it, but you may even text a colleague to cover for your tardiness as you are driving!

As soon as you take a breath, the catastrophic thoughts rush in. *I bet I'll be observed today. What if I get fired from my job? Wait, is this really happening? Am I dreaming? Am I late? Maybe my clock is broken.* The whole day follows in this manner from this ominous beginning.

This is a soft trigger, or a lowercase *t* trigger. You are a few minutes late. This problem is not life or death, so why such an elaborate physical response?

Here we are with this simple, everyday trigger. Being launched into anxiety and over-analysis may be troublesome. On the other side of the spectrum lies the capital *T* triggers. Meeting the eyes of your rapist at a court hearing, the smell of burned rubber and gasoline after realizing that you're the sole survivor of a fatal car crash, or a sudden bang after returning from war where you were forced into combat all qualify as capital *T* triggers.

These life-threatening traumas put a late start to shame. Yet, here we are bolted to excruciating patterns, spinning our wheels, reaching for help over meager *t* terrors. The body doesn't know the difference between an attack on your life, an attack on your soul, or an attack on your fragile ego.

All triggers feel devastating to the person involved. Remember the feeling of the rejection trigger when he didn't call? Most of us have been there. All triggers need our attention and should neither be maximized nor minimized based on the interpretation of the event that caused them. It is time to normalize ourselves with resilience. It is time to stop grasping for quick fixes that continue the trigger cycle and have us holding on to harmful relationships.

For most human beings, a trigger develops after a traumatic event occurs in their lives. For a rare population, trauma and triggers go together like the chicken and the egg. It is a mystery as to which came first due to the bedeviling nature of life events, such as childhood abuse, suppressed memories, or even a difficult birth experience. Some of us feel triggered with no awareness as to where this feeling derived. How many of us feel that we were born anxious and sensitive and later realize that our environment shaped such conditions?

My Big T Memory

The first trauma that left a lasting impression on my mind, my heart, and my body happened in 1996 during my sophomore year of college at Rhodes College in Memphis, Tennessee. I, along with other Midwest-raised teens, set off to find ourselves at a quaint university that provided our parents with peace of mind, since it was a Christian school, and offered us a short commute home for breaks and holidays.

However, as a *highly sensitive person* (one who feels every emotion, nuance, and undertone of an exchange), I struggled to find my way. My parents may as well have dropped me in a war zone in an exotic foreign country.

My censored and Catholic upbringing armed me with no guide for protection in this unmonitored setting. As a young, naive college freshman, who wore her heart on her sleeve, college exposed me to alcohol, drugs, sex, and recklessness on the part of my peers and me. Needless to say, we either sank or swam. My new college friends and I had to swim, which resulted in a bond on this journey of experimentation, soul-searching, and the making of mistakes.

I thought that I held my own sufficiently. At least, my reliable ego led me to believe this. I played soccer, partied, and kept my grades up. Instead of establishing thoughtful boundaries, I used my quick wit and sarcastic defenses to keep others at bay. I functioned and survived my first year of college. Life felt manageable, until a shocking event changed everything.

On November 9, 1996, my close friend, Angela, suffered a fatal car accident after leaving my apartment and driving two miles to her home. An elderly woman's vehicle broadsided the jeep that Angela's boyfriend, Drew, drove. For the woman, the road dipped down and then back up at the exact point of Drew's crossing. No matter how cautious the drivers had been, two lines collided.

Angela made it halfway home that day, or all the way home, depending upon where your spirit lies.

Angela had a child-like wonder about her. She stole hearts with a glance, and she danced and sang with abandon. Her sudden absence rippled out in waves, washing the smiles off of the faces of her family members and friends for miles.

For me, as an acutely sensitive teenager far from home, the last day of Angela's life unfolded in a profound way.

Nothing important happened in the morning. I attended my classes, and I didn't see her. I don't recall any particular pull or desire to visit that day.

That all changed when I saw her later that afternoon. I sat at the dining table in my apartment, my face buried in school work, when Angela flung open the door, showered me with a flirty smile, and lit up the room with the twinkle in her bright brown eyes. Her boyfriend, Drew, strolled in behind her and shut the door.

She belted out the words of a song. "Just call me angel of the morning, angel. Just touch my cheek before you leave me, baby!"

As happy as a meadowlark, she hopped onto the couch and continued her song and dance on her make-shift stage.

Suddenly, the energy in the room veered in another direction for me, and then for her. We both seemed to feel a shift in the air. Maybe this change is why the rest of the story altered my life forever.

I raised my eyes from my textbook, peering at her over the carafe of hot coffee there to keep me going.

My gaze became obvious to her.

She questioned me, interrupting her own song. "Why are you staring at me?"

Every movement, every word, and every sound evolved in slow motion around me.

Bewildered, I spoke. "I have no idea."

I tried to break out of the trance and shake the feeling. I directed my eyes toward the book in front of me. After all, I had been ignoring my intense subtle energetic nuances and feelings for two decades, why pay attention to them now?

The command to re-focus on the school work didn't last. I gawked at her. Something was going on, a certain air compelled me to notice her. I felt a thickness in the room, a presence. Every moment felt like a video recording in my memory. I struggle to make sense of this, and yet the heightened experience felt undeniable and distinct.

My next vivid memory is of my boyfriend, Brian, calling. He lived in a house off-campus with other members of the football team, but he spent most nights with me, and I assumed that he was calling to let me know that he was on his way.

"Hey, Ellen, my throat hurts. I don't want your friends to catch whatever I've got. Why don't you come to my house?" Brian coughed.

The habitual, appeasing caregiver in me normally would have rushed right over and delighted in nursing him back to health. I resisted the invitation.

For some unexplainable reason, I did not want to leave my place. While I spoke to him from my bedroom, I sensed the happenings in the living room, where Angela and Drew greeted my roommate, who had just arrived.

As I sat on my stiff, single-sized bed trying to persuade my ill boyfriend to come over, we both decided that my logic was skewed and that I should go to his house. Once we made this decision, I slipped out the side door in haste and left Angela and Drew to an evening with our mutual friend, my roommate.

My friends and I never utilized a practice of formal good-byes, as a come-and-go philosophy had been established among us. I also knew that Angela would have convinced me to stay had I announced my exit, and Brian had already tested my willpower. We made eye contact as I slid past the living room to the kitchen and out the door. I remember the moment like it was yesterday. As if playing on a movie screen, I watched Angela lean forward with an attentive ear, her glass swinging on the tips of her fingers as her elbow rested and rocked on her knee. I feel our glance captured as a snapshot in my memory even today.

I can't say that I was even decent company at Brian's house. Something felt off. My energy and attention were scattered. We eventually retired to bed.

While deep in sleep, my 1990s cellphone rang at 1:00 a.m. Neither I nor anyone else in the house heard the call come in.

Up until that moment in my life, I had had no conscious trauma that would have triggered a heightened sense of alertness. What came next changed all of that.

Through the fog of sleep, I did hear the faint knocking on the front door, or did the banging of my heart wake me? It all happened in a flash. I heard commotion in the hallway and a familiar voice in anguish. The voice belonged to a girlfriend, Alyssa, whom I had helped out of a jam in the middle of the night a number of times before.

After all, my college crew did a great deal of partying, and interruptions to sleep felt like the norm in my early college years. *It's okay, my friend is drunk.* Alyssa broke through the hallway guards of Brian's football team roommates.

She cried, "I need to see Ellen."

This time her voice sounded different. She appeared frantic, and yet her deathly serious words cut through the alcohol-induced euphoria that she had looked to achieve that night.

She made it to Brian's bedroom, where I had bolted upright in bed. The sudden flood of lights blinded my vision, her words pierced my ears, my blood congealed. I stood up on the bed just as Angela had stood on my apartment couch stage. The closer Alyssa stepped toward the bed, the further I scrambled away from her words, her agony.

Backed against the wall, I muttered. "No, that's not true! You're drunk! She's at my house. I saw her there. She is fine."

With that, I thought back to moments before as I slept, and I knew that I had been dreaming of Angela.

"Angela's fine. She's not dead. It's not true." I reiterated my incoherent belief.

The most intense ten seconds of my life played out like a never-ending story set on repeat for days, then weeks, then months.

I peeled myself off of the wall.

I heard a whisper outside of me. "It *is* true."

The switch inside me flipped.

I dropped down from the bed. "Okay, okay, okay."

I then did what I do best. I took charge of the situation. I escorted Alyssa into the kitchen, where she dropped to her knees and relayed the story between drunken sobs. I stood still with my arms crossed in front of my chest and leaned against the cabinets for support. Holding an energetic space for her grief and for the collected towering assemblage of football guys, I remained quiet and composed.

Among the members of the crowd stood Brian, who was no stranger to the terror of unfortunate events. Brian's brother's car had been hit head-on by a truck on his way to volunteer at a basketball camp for the local boys' club. As a sixteen-year-old, he had been the first one to answer the dreaded knock on the door of the police officer carrying the news of his brother's death. He attempted to shield his mother from the decimating announcement. To his dismay, the officer's words penetrated right through him and landed like a brick on his mother's chest.

He also held an empathic and noble pose for the space of Alyssa's despair, with a keen eye aimed toward my well-being. Then silence prevailed.

A slow, deep, and heavy methodic trance enveloped me that lasted for days.

Instead of attending to my personal tragedy, Alyssa swept me off to Drew's parents' home.

I learned that Angela had been ejected from her seat and that the side of the jeep fell on top of her. From what I know, this tore her aorta, and she bled out at the scene. This precious life, this incredible being so full of love and light, died of a broken heart.

Standing in a suburban home with parents whom I had never met before felt like a deleterious hallucination. Alyssa's reactive intention to be there for Drew negated our own needs. I felt invisible among these strangers, and my own parents were hundreds of miles away. Curled up in his bed gazing out into a far-off land and trembling, Drew used blankets to hold himself in place. Nothing could console him.

Apparent to those present, we had to get home. In the dark, cold, wet night, we returned to my apartment, driving past the scene of the accident, the final spot where Angela's body had rested in the grass.

"Ellen, Angela mumbled to me that she felt cold." A college soccer player named Steven, from my psychology class, later informed me.

He didn't know why, but he needed me to know that he had arrived upon the accident that night and that he had seen Angela lying on the ground. He had been there and couldn't do anything to control the outcome.

My heart cracked in the agony of her death. I felt it all. I felt her fear, her lips shivering and wet with the taste of iron from her blood. I felt her terror and her final release. I felt Steven's helplessness and Drew's disbelief, the maelstrom at the scene, and the repose that only comes when extreme heaviness is in the air. I felt it all as if peering down from above, somehow suspended in a dome overhead. It felt like I had been there.

I disappeared the night after we returned from Drew's. I refused to go inside my apartment as I felt her there. I wandered to campus and sat on the stairs of the liberal arts building that Angela and I had visited a multitude of times. In the middle of the night, I sat there with my head in my hands, my heart weeping, the campus sound asleep around me.

To my surprise, a single snowflake drifted down from the sky. Then more followed. Before I knew it, I stared up in awe at the street lights watching fluffy flakes of glistening white snow waltz from the southern sky and melt on the street. This felt like nothing short of a miracle, an early November snow in Memphis and perhaps a good-bye from my departed friend.

To my dismay, I didn't see miracles then. I felt alone. My Catholic upbringing hadn't prepared me for this trauma, as I had listened in my youth to sermon after sermon of the concept that God would always be there for me. I felt disjointed. No God arrived to help me. My world no longer made sense, and the fragile support system of pure faith with which I had grown up crumbled. I believed in nothing, and I wanted an escape. I wanted to disappear.

Brian was concerned about my whereabouts, and he appeared in front of me on the campus sidewalk. "Where have you been? I have been looking all over for you."

I mumbled like a zombie in a trance, "I don't know."

I became possessed by the purgatory in which I found myself. The morning after Angela's fatal accident, I packed my school bag and headed off to class like any other school day. I cut through the crowded hall of students, all of whom had learned of Angela's passing. I felt people gaping at me, but I didn't make eye contact. I walked into the empty classroom, sat down in my seat, and saved the desk in front of me for Angela, as I always did.

She wasn't there yet. My denial evident, I waited. *That's okay. She always scrambles in at the last minute.*

Today, no other student entered the classroom. Old-school desks lined up in tight rows on a faded and worn wooden floor. All of the earth-made natural material was reassuring. It seemed to have a pulse, as if it breathed around me. I felt embraced, and the earthy oak beckoned me to inhale and exhale with it.

A classmate interrupted my daze. "Ellen, class is cancelled. Angela died last night."

He thought that he imparted news that I didn't know.

"Oh, yeah, that's her seat." Hiding my face, I slid my backpack onto my shoulder and ducked into the hallway, past the crowd, and out of the building.

I learned to make this type of exit throughout my life, as a fear of good-byes developed after this crippling event.

During the weeks following Angela's death, I felt every footstep. My feet sunk into the ground on heavy legs weighed down by the immense calamity in my heart. I avoided people, as I had no energy to interact with others. I had no words or thoughts to share. Idle chitchat proved of no significance now, and surface conversation enraged me. Not only am I a highly sensitive person, I have also since discovered that I am an empath. An empath can be defined as a person who senses and feels the emotions of others as if having the same experience. This term is argued, explored, and unexplainable to most. Let's tread lightly around terminology as we will do the same with the term narcissist. We are all trying to find our way.

The empath's dilemma is when she feels the feelings of others and has no plan of defense or coping skills in place. I remained trapped in the sorrow of Angela's accident for ten years. Only then did I claw my way out of the wreckage.

If you feel like you are not the same after a big T trauma, if you are not yourself, know that you are right. Actual brain changes occur that contribute to anxiety, depression, and addiction.

I was depressed, but I couldn't put a name to it. I disengaged from my college friends and spent most of my time in bed. Later, I became so entrenched in relating to my triggers related to Angela's death that I identified myself as an anxious mess who needed to subdue herself with adrenaline-inducing sports, a drink, or late-night dancing. I became the Queen of Self-Medicating.

Somehow I appeared as if I had managed this loss, as I pulled it together on the outside and moved through the motions of life.

Though I was completely wrecked, I never saw a counselor concerning Angela's death. Angela departed this earth in November, and I don't remember the rest of that school year.

Summer arrived, and I returned to my parents' home in St. Louis to work and nurse my broken heart.

To my everlasting dismay, I received a phone call during that time from the same friend, Alyssa, who had informed me of Angela's car accident. "Adam overdosed on Angela's birthday."

The hits kept on coming. I recalled Adam sitting next to me in art appreciation class. A classmate and friend, Adam possessed a deep, perceptive, and humanitarian soul. The weight of Angela's death crushed him as well, or perhaps his own personal circumstances influenced his fatal overdose. Perhaps it was intentional or nothing but an accident. I will never know.

I had nightmares about Adam after this news. I didn't want to be awake, and I didn't want to fall asleep. I saw him in my dreams and heard his voice while awake. I felt under attack from all quarters.

Adam liked to tease me in art class in a loving way, and in my dreams this became terrifying. I felt him in my room when alone, and this scared me. Sharing this with friends or family fell nowhere on my radar. If I was heading toward crazy, I was going to go there alone.

To combat the stress, I stayed in my bedroom painting an old table of my mother's. With precision and redundancy, I tapped the brush against the wood until I fell asleep. The dreams haunted me night after night, and it felt as if Adam lingered in the bedroom or in my mind somewhere unable to escape. One night, I dreamt that he called me on the phone.

"I'm fine. Please don't worry." He offered me a weird kind of strength.

"Where's Angela?" I pleaded for answers.

"She's not here anymore. She didn't stay here for long." He conveyed to me what he knew in this dream state.

My instincts led me to believe that I knew what he meant. Angela's soul was safe.

My Catholic upbringing related to suicide, purgatory, heaven, and hell allowed me to interpret my dream of Adam in accordance with those teachings. Later, a traditional therapist named Sharon claimed that I had processed my pain through my dreams. She explained that I had made up all of my sensing and precognition after the traumatic events.

My biggest mistake, and what took years away from me being able to move in the direction of my desires, was that I believed Sharon and trusted her judgment over my own intuitive knowing.

A gift of strong intuition mutated into mistrust, self-doubt, and two decades of misguided trigger responses. I lived in a constant state of alertness and fear. This heightened state was evident in all areas of my life and caused severe anxiety and a potent insecurity. My vulnerabilities and anxiety surfaced as torment and fear of abandonment in my intimate relationships. As an intelligent woman, I hid these emotions from partners the best that I could, which caused more internal damage.

Unaware of the extreme impact of Angela's death, I developed co-dependent tendencies and suffered with associated separation anxiety. I stayed in relationships well past the expiration date because (since my partner was still alive) I believed that we could manage any problem together. I also loved deeper than ever after experiencing the magnitude of the loss that I did.

Though my story is a long and treacherous road to healing, I did survive college and graduated with a teaching degree. The loss of a close friend and distraught relationships produced a woman susceptible to pain and a magnet for abuse.

Why We Can't Shake the Triggers

While I noticed hidden gifts and lessons after Angela's death, I could not relate to them then. Instead, my life focused on the triggers.

And I now know that there is more to understand about these pesky reactions.

For one, a trigger is an experience that presses play on a recorded memory within our mind. A sudden flashback transports a person to a single traumatic event, and the physical body responds as if the trauma is reoccurring. Hence, the reason why it took me ten years to pull myself out of this. Angela's death played on a repeated loop in my mind, my heart, and my body. I re-traumatized myself by discussing the events ad nauseam.

In addition, triggers are specific to each individual. My friends and I all reacted in our own way. I developed a compulsion about answering the phone, even in the middle of the night, after missing the call about Angela. My mind took hold of the concept that I could have prevented her death had I answered the phone. These displaced coping strategies are typical of a traumatized mind. If you have developed any tendencies like this, know that this is common and is also an inclination that you want to be aware of in order to heal. What are you doing to avoid pain from the past?

Avoidance is another strategy that the mind promotes after trauma. Whether one is avoiding a scene similar to the trauma, the type of person who attacked her, or even a time of day when problems occurred, the mind does whatever it takes to move away from the crisis. This may lead to isolation and years of depression.

Now, all triggers are received through one of the five senses: sight, sound, smell, touch, or taste. In the case of empaths, such as myself, I will add another sense, which is heightened sensory perception, and which I struggle to articulate into words at times. I am here to honor this phenomenon, which some readers might recognize as a gut feeling or a knowing. I call it a sixth sense. Truth be told, I labeled it my curse most of my life.

Below are some examples of how trauma and abuse triggers may be manifesting in your life through your senses.

Sight: Someone who resembles the abuser or who has similar traits or wears specific clothing, has the same body features, or who has distinct mannerisms may elicit a trigger response. Likewise, witnessing someone being abused or an accident, whether in real life or on a screen, is risky for the nervous system of a traumatized person. Any object associated with the trauma or abuse, be it a common household item, the presence of drugs or alcohol, or even the time of year, could cause a reaction in the nervous system. Specific locations, events, and holidays may be problematic to the abused mind.

Sound: A raised voice, sudden bangs, or something breaking may shock and overwhelm a person more than would usually be expected. In addition, the sound of a muffled whisper or crying may evoke terror. Sounds from before or after a traumatic event may also be implanted deep in one's emotional wiring. A song, a cheerful good-bye, or a door closing may imprint on the mind, sending fear messages out when these sounds are heard again.

In the case of abuse, footsteps, keys hitting the table, or the pop of a bottle opening may cause one to panic. Put-downs may cause alarm. If an abuser used terms of endearment like sweetie or honey while engaging in physical or mental abuse, these words no longer sound safe and loving. When common sounds ripple through the body with agitation, we have serious problems attending to everyday life.

Cellphones ringing and text tones sent shivers down my spine, and my heart ceased to beat when a manipulative ex called me or texted me. I resisted looking at my phone out of fear when I heard a text alert, and still the ground moved beneath my feet guiding me along like the walkways in an airport straight to my phone to read the message. In the moment when I read the text, my trigger either exploded, or I dodged a bullet, and relief swirled through my body.

Smell: From perfume to tobacco, any smell may ignite a trigger. If an odor smells like the assailant or a place where a boundary invasion occurred, the body may react as if the trauma is occurring again. The most pleasant of smells may stop a person in their tracks and fear may abound with every inhale.

Touch: A light caress or a caring hug may send chills of alert after physical abuse. Standing too close to someone or the way that another person approaches may send the nervous system into high alert.

Throughout my own healing, I noticed that I could not receive a hug without pulling away. I avoided people and was even rude to others to ensure that they wouldn't approach me or move too close at points in my life. In time, I covered my chest with my arms as a shield while someone hugged me. Even a pat on the hand or the shoulder sent up a flare of alert that my physical boundaries had been crossed. Unsolicited touch may cause retreat and isolation for those who have been injured in one way or another.

Taste: A specific food may trigger a traumatic memory, whether it occurred before, during, or after a harrowing event. If a child is given ice cream every time his dad goes into an abusive rage, the adult may then have a strange aversion to the delicious treat. Alcohol and tobacco are also common taste triggers associated with trauma and abuse.

The Empath's Sixth Sense: Anything that causes an energetic shift in the environment, pressure in the chest or the awareness of the fight/flight/freeze response when only yourself or others are present, may be a red flag of abuse or trauma. Picking up on subtle clues in the environment and even developing a sudden and overwhelming sense of anxiety or fear of another individual hits the radar for an empath.

Empaths may be bemused by the underlying motives of a person. They may know what others are feeling, even if their words do not match that feeling. Empaths are like human lie-detectors, but it is difficult to convince others of their intuitive knowing and this may create self-doubt. Self-doubt is a green light for an abuser, and he may seek out this trait in those whom he wants to manipulate.

These heightened senses of an empath also expose a need to escape a scene with no sensible explanation as to why or avoid certain people whose actions are not aligned with their words. These people are deemed unsafe for the empath, whereas an average person may find the empath rude or unreasonable to make such judgments.

As a result, I have left parties without saying good-bye after an odd interaction. I have fled to the restroom to collect myself in order to quiet my nerves and slow my heart rate.

There is no defined empath *sense* with an accompanying outward, visible body part or organ. The empath sense defies logic. Hence, I have yet to meet one empath who hasn't felt like a lunatic or been selective about with whom they discuss this heightened sense to avoid being labeled insane. It is common to have intuition, but it is unusual to have an extreme heightened empathic sense.

The drawback to this sense is that experiences are elevated and difficult to move through at a fast rate. Feelings are intense and prolonged, and the ability to read another person's misalignment (their subtle lies) makes for dubious experiences in intimacy. After all, who wants a partner who shines the spotlight on his vulnerabilities or discrepancies? I learned the hard way that it is best to not conclude without evidence that others understand this sixth sense. It took me thirty-eight years to realize that not everyone felt the way I felt.

I honestly believed that all people experienced the world as I did. During my early childhood, instead of feeling different, I believed that all individuals felt the same and that we all had this sixth sense. I was happy and enjoyed life and the company of others...until the triggers began.

Empaths and highly sensitive people have a lively nervous system, where all engines are go all the time. Within this nervous system are a collection of programs that enable empaths to store, modify, and extract information to make sense of life.

While a typical person may have a personal computer to account for their intake of outside information, an empath has a huge system that runs on multiple mainframes. An empath, or at least one like me, picks up every nuance of emotion in the environment, which builds extreme overwhelm if the body and mind are not cared for.

To add to the ecstasy, and accompanying horror, of feeling the emotions and even the physical maladies of others, an inexperienced empath struggles to decipher whether or not the feeling is her own or if it belongs to another. When the trigger is felt, a process of over analysis may occur to make sense of the sudden surge of emotions through the empath's body. In essence, we are feeling and reacting and thinking long after an event is over. I call these triggers, nested triggers. Just like a hand grenade explodes in all directions, a nested trigger is like a ticking time bomb in the empath's heart.

There is more. The problem with an empath's database is that within it lies her own triggers and response system, as well as that of anyone who has infiltrated that system energetically, such as an abuser. However, this may also be someone who walked in the door of a party, a co-worker who moved to the desk next to you, or someone who is embedded in your system whom you may not even talk to anymore. Perhaps this person has even passed away.

In my younger years, I allowed many depleting vultures to rob me of my own energy. Unskilled empaths provide endless energetic supply to others and are virtual sponges to the low-energy emotions of others. Absorbing this weight causes empaths to try to save or fix others. *I'll feel better when you feel better* is the mantra of an unskilled empath. We work to provide security within by making others outside of us happy.

Circuits are tripping, the nervous system is overloaded and in need of consistent daily repair, causing exhaustion for the empath. Shut-off valves should be installed and monitoring systems put in place for empaths to reboot their life-force energy after debilitating interactions. Only expert empaths should be consulted on the issue of repairs.

This overwhelm may lead empaths to addictions in order to numb their feelings. However, at no point is an empath beyond repair, and in most cases, if not all cases, the system actually exceeds the operating level that it once held before traumatic events occurred. An empath may come back from abuse stronger and may even reach an optimal performance of being unbreakable.

The Purpose of Triggers

Triggers are presented to you to help you heal. Remember this as your buttons are pushed. Others are in our lives to reveal to us what most needs to be healed within us. Whether it is a fear of abandonment, mistrust, or trauma wounds that keep you in the thick of bad news relationships, it is your time to heal and embrace a new way of going forward.

Go within. Listen to what comes up in your body when another person triggers you. Do the work now so that you may forgo a lifetime of painful relationship lessons, the likes of which I have had. Go within. Discern whether your partner is teaching you to set a boundary and walk away from him or whether he is guiding you toward closeness and intimacy. You may develop this skill, and you may heal yourself.

Now buckle up for the bumpy ride as I take you deep into the darkness of psychological and emotional abuse and out the other side. I have made it to the other shore. You can too.

I no longer dive into treacherous waters to save others, only to be used for life support and then cast aside. I now live ashore and toss out life preservers to those willing to admit their vulnerable state and open their outstretched arms. Take my hand. I am on your side.

CHAPTER 2

Hooked

Dear Love,

I hope that this letter finds you well, though I know that you strain to recall a time when you last felt happy.

I know that you are hurting. I know that you feel stuck, tired, and heartbroken. The torment in your chest is pulsating out into your limbs, leaving you too weary to reach out for a hug or for help. Your heart is heavy, and your throat is feeble from suppressing your truth. Your brilliant mind is spiraling downward, burdened with the impossible task of figuring out this relationship turmoil on your own. Your friends don't seem to understand what is going on with you. His voice is your only elixir.

I know that every cell in your physical body wants to call him, run to him, and reach out for a temporary moment of solace. Clenching your phone in your hand, you wait for him to pick up. One more long ring, and then you may exhale once more. He is your life support, and like a fish on the end of a line, he has you hooked.

You leapt for an enticing and yummy treat, not foreseeing any dangers, and now you are thrashing around in order to flee this trap. As your mind protests in desperation, the frigid steel embeds within your heart. The sensation is hauntingly familiar, and the barbed tip dips up and down, gliding in as if re-tracing footprints straight to your heart. You've been here before.

Can you feel him reeling you in? The drag masks itself as longing and desire for him, and this feeling, so intense and familiar, has you fooled. True love doesn't ache like this. True love brings you satisfaction and peace. True love is swimming in tandem in cool waters.

I know it feels amazing to be with him, but before too long, he will fail you. You know that you can't go on like this. You want to learn to breathe on your own. You want the torture and the all-consuming thoughts of him to stop. You want to rescue yourself from his corrosive embrace.

Follow me. Your first breath is right around the corner. I will show you the way out of this agonizing ploy. All you have to do is turn the page, and a new life will replace what has come before. Whether you read on or close this book, I understand your inner struggle, and I am here for you always.

Love,
The Best Version of You

I am so proud of you. More than proud, I am certain of you. I know, without doubt, that if you've had the tenacity and the resilience to stay in a relationship that isn't serving you, you have an honest desire for true love. This longing is rushing in as an acute need for the wrong man right now, but this passion will turn out to be your strongest ally and guide.

I know this addictive love trap experience all too well.

Your attachment to your object of desire is disconcerting, and yet you want more. The relationship engenders the feel-good high of a drug and causes overpowering withdrawal symptoms to boot.

Together, we are going to detach from this co-dependent grasp, without feeling unhinged, and guide you to your soul's purpose of genuine self-love.

But first, let's consider your emotions and certain points in your relationship (or relationships, depending on how many times you've taken your bike and your heart around this block).

I know, I rode past the same house time after time expecting the relationship with my childhood crush to have a different outcome. The truth is, you may have been employing a specific tedious and unrewarding pattern of behavior since your first love, and you may not even recognize it.

Let's acknowledge this pattern, this truth about you in relationships. Let's be tender but firm here. Remember, you are enraptured. It is going to take a shift in perspective in order to be objective. Forgo all self-judgment, and know that this is a process and not a quick fix.

Being hooked means that you are attached in a paralyzing way and that your heart patters with rapid drumrolls that may shift to life-threatening halts. You cannot seem to push him out of your mind. May we agree that you are in a difficult position from which to make wise decisions for your long-term future right now? Might we agree that you are drowning in emotions and reacting from impulse rather than responding from an intuitive-centered state? Shall we agree that in more than one area of your life you are a badass, but you've lost your grip on your love life?

If the answers to these questions is yes, the best decision that you may make is right here in your hands. Give this book 100 percent of your attention and devotion.

Thank you for that, by the way. Now, thank yourself as well. In fact, rest your hand on your heart or the place where you feel the most wounded and exclaim, *Thank you! I am here for you*. Proclaim this statement out loud, and feel supported. Show up for yourself right here and right now.

The hero for whom you are waiting is you! That special companion who will love you unconditionally has been here all along.

All the Feels

In September of 2014, when I was in my late-thirties, I too was swept off of my feet by a charming and charismatic man. Let's call him Ryan. I had ended a turbulent twelve-year relationship with a guy named Mike, and I felt exhausted and defeated. I desired true love. Ryan somehow appeared out of the mist, and I took the alluring bait.

He had all of the qualities and traits that I admired in a man. In fact, he had all of the qualities that I seemed to lack, or at least that's what I thought at the time. Outgoing and able to summon a crowd, Ryan could talk to anyone and proved to be quick on his feet. I was shy and awkward. My aversion to chitchat deemed me somewhat indecipherable from my self-critical perspective. His natural talent and intelligence shown through in an exceptional way. While I possessed a strong intuition, I marked this trait as skepticism and not a super power. As I mentioned, I had my defenses up in life.

From my weakened vantage point, Ryan possessed a strong sense of self and poise that paraded along a thin line of arrogance. Somehow this image flattered him. My sense of self was depleted, and any illusion of confidence masked the pain of my past relationship failure. The truth is, I admired these assertive traits in him. If I had had one ounce of his apparent self-esteem, I could have soared.

Pay attention, Love, I'll guide us there. You too will fly!

For better or for worse, Ryan persisted as the crowd-pleaser, and I played the role of people-pleaser. We existed as opposites but each gifted in our own right. His gift lived within the mind, and my gift resided in the heart. I believed him to be the yin to my yang, and yet we entered a ruthless empath and narcissist dance.

A true narcissistic, disordered person needs outside validation from someone consistently willing to provide confirmation of his or her worth. The empath and the narcissist may share the same inner wound of unworthiness, which bonds them together. Remember, it takes two.

In our presentation as a couple, I worked away in the background of social events, meeting the needs of guests, while Ryan stepped in and took full credit or grabbed the limelight with ease. He also boasted about my contributions as an extension of himself. I must confess that I bragged about him too. I believed that healthy couples doted on each other, but our affection had a twist that I didn't see.

The first month of a relationship with a narcissistic man in search of a new girlfriend to meet his needs presents itself as intense courting. The narcissist seeks out an unsuspecting woman when he is lonely, needs an ego boost, or his current wife or girlfriend is not hopping to satisfy his every demand. Meeting the needs of men of this personality type is impossible.

To be fair, most healthy singles are over the moon at the start of a new relationship, and let's face it, even though we don't live in castles, we haven't shaken that fairy tale image of Prince Charming. I fantasized that Ryan could be the panacea for my broken heart and that he would launch me out of break-up fatigue and into the life of my dreams.

I was reluctant and cautious at first, but once Ryan made it into my decrepit heart space, I could not hold myself back. I felt a dreamy, high-on-life feeling when I was around him. We conversed about our feelings, my desires, and our expectations related to intimacy early in the relationship. I thought that Ryan was the one. I felt safe, and I trusted him. I never suspected that he would use those dreams to manipulate me in the future.

Sound familiar? Did you communicate your deepest secrets about your life with your newfound crush? Did he mirror tales of heartbreak similar to yours in order to get closer to you? Did he claim to want what you wanted in love? A manipulative individual will always be on the same page with you when working his way into your heart. *Do you want babies? Me too! Not interested in being a parent? I feel the same way! Let's travel together instead.*

Stories of past misfortune and unsuccessful relationships seem to align in miraculous ways. It's as if the two of you have lived parallel lives. Defenses drop, and the bonding begins. Bodies and energies mingle and intertwine. No need to escape. No reason to try. This feels like forever. This feels like soul-bending, mind-blowing L-O-V-E!

Careful, please don't sign that contract. I know, I know, it's too late. Your heart has made a decision that your soul can't support. Here we go. You are all in, and this feeling, so destructive, has blinded you.

When you know, you know. Correct? Take it slow. Why? He's perfect. You are perfect together. Your friends are so happy for you. Your knight in shining armor has arrived. You may now skip down the aisle with Mr. Right.

He was worth the wait. At last, I have been saved from all of my unfulfilled love stories and my past patterns. This new love will disencumber me from all of that.

I wish that this was true. I am so sorry. Read on.

Swoop!

Let's go to those moments, the first few days of this relationship, and use our 20/20 hindsight vision. It is easy to deduce that your destructive relationship has passed for you or at least that you are aware of the existence of one. I know this because this book would not be in your hand if you hadn't acknowledged some hurts. His hand would be in your hand, and he would be planning a future and relishing the present with you. I know that that is harsh, but you must wake up. Let's glance into the past to where your ruinous entanglement began. Where were you in your life when this handsome savior swept in?

Had you bailed out of a dead end relationship like I had? Did you feel low and vulnerable or the opposite? Perhaps you reveled in being single and felt thrilled with a sense of freedom. Had you sworn off of men and then basked in your guarded independence? Was your last relationship a train wreck with someone who first appeared to be stable, grounded, and heroic? Did you feel at the top of your game and had no time for an intimate partnership? Were you in an unsatisfying relationship, and the new man lured you out of it with prospects of a better future?

I know that you answered yes to some of these questions, and your *yes* made you ripe for the picking. This is when he pounces in with his love-bombing tactics, triggers, or explosive emotions that make a new relationship sound like a pirate war at sea.

Feel free to view it that way. Love-bombing is the act of turning up the charm in order to extract attention, love, and devotion from you, only to disparage you down the road. This is a technique that my fragile heart fell for over and over. Ryan and other ex-boyfriends went from boasting about me to throwing me under the bus overnight.

I grew wise enough to be caught off guard and hesitant, but let's face it, I ignored this inner knowing and fell for him. Narcissistic, ego-driven men love the hunt, and the more worth it you are, the greater the gain to their ego and their own sense of worthiness. This trait is not isolated to males, a toxic woman or non-binary individual may hold these same traits.

This is all the more baffling and unfortunate because a stable man is a hunter as well. He will want to win over a woman and value her, knowing that she was not easy to catch. An honest man will also want you to respect yourself above all else and will hold you in that place of respect even on the days when you are struggling. This is the significant difference between a healthy man and a narcissistic man.

Regardless, the juicy details about understanding men are not the focus right now. The focus is you. Let's establish a strong sense of self and reclaim your independence.

Re-wind the tape of your own interactions. Does what I've shared so far resonate with you? How would I know this if I hadn't lived through it too? Do you trust me?

Seeing how he ambushed you is a valuable lesson learned, so please be kind to yourself. This lesson was not taught in our youth, and it is not innate for most of us to have our guard up or to be this suspicious of humankind. It is okay to learn the hard way, as long as you learn from the narcissist's lesson.

In the average relationship, we may mistake the drive to win us over for the honeymoon period. Please know that this is not the case with a narcissistic man. He is on a calculated mission, perhaps a subconscious design well-engrained in his psyche, to entice you into believing that he is your soul mate, your one true love, and God's gift to you...for now.

Yes, he thinks this of himself (at this time), and the truth is, you think that he is that remarkable too.

We will dismantle all of this deception in future chapters. But first let's settle in and shine a light on this love entrapment.

Addicted to Love

After a few weeks of dating Ryan, he had already confessed his love for me. He showered me with words of affirmation. I had already slept with him, and I pledged myself to him with no talk of or mutually-agreed-upon promise of exclusivity. I inferred our role as a couple based on my one-sided covenant.

When I heard his name, my heart sailed into the stratosphere, and my mind visualized romantic notions of our future. I thought for certain that my feelings were the much-talked-about sign of everlasting love. I had met the man of my dreams and felt no need to date anyone else. I believed that I had fallen in love at first sight, but in hindsight, I know that I fell in lust and into a trap that would take years to overcome.

It took tons of brain damage before I could acknowledge that what I experienced was not at all what love is meant to feel like. An anxiety attack felt like this, not true love. A pounding heart signifies that one is suffering from the fight/flight/freeze response. These triggers happened to not be butterflies in my stomach denoting love-sickness nor the itchy reaction to a bite from the love bug. This was bona fide fear.

I did not fall in love with Ryan. I was afraid to lose him and afraid to stay with him. My draw to him resembled an addiction, and I felt triggered by the deceit and unkind words that over time seeped into my romantic idealization of us. His inconsistencies triggered my fears of abandonment.

Let me spell this out. Fear is not love. Love does not equal pain.

It sounds peculiar to have to admit, but I had an underlying belief that love *did* equal pain. If you peek beneath the surface, you may find that you too believe this, or perhaps your history reflects it.

After our relationship imploded in July of 2017, I was triggered into an anxiety attack every time someone mentioned his name or when a smell, an object, a song, or a gesture reminded me of him. I realize now that the numerous times that we broke up never felt like a clear ending. I felt like a boomerang. He threw me out, and then we got back together, more times than I could count. These ricochet breakups strained me to my limits, and the instability was unbearable.

Perceived Triggers

In an attempt to get over him two weeks after the final bust-up, I hosted a dinner party at my house. I had a bit of an open-door policy at the time, related to both my house and my heart. Be sure to wipe your feet at the door.

Well, a woman whom I didn't know attended my party with another guest, a friend of mine. To my dismay, the woman chimed into the group conversation with inquiries about a certain guy she had met, whom she hoped to see at my party. His name was Ryan. Yikes!

It seemed that she had met Ryan at a bar one night, and she angled to learn more about him from my friends. In my own kitchen, I had to await the replies of my guests to her questions about who he was and what he was like. In my deranged state, I wondered how did she not know that Ryan and I had dated. Objectively, this made no sense.

Why the hell is this happening in my own kitchen?

My hands flew to my pallid face as my throat closed up. *Why won't she stop this torture? Because she doesn't know, dummy!* I hosted the dinner party to take my mind *off* of Ryan. I wanted to be in the shelter of friends. I excused myself to the bathroom, though my hawk ears stayed tuned in to the conversation.

Warning: You may discover that your definition of close friends will change throughout this arduous trek. I was not in the presence of true friendship that night. My friend did not stop the woman's prodding, nor did she inform her that Ryan and I were together when he made advances to her at the bar. In another scenario, I attended a friend's wedding and after a few awkward exchanges and Ryan's face turning pale during introductions, I discovered that he had slept with my friend's Maid of Honor while we were together. How could my friend not have told me? Make certain that your friends have your back and are sensitive to your heartache. My inner circle has since changed in a dramatic way.

You will soon learn that you have heightened senses during a perceived threat and that the bathroom is a marvelous gift to sensitive women everywhere. I retreated to this safe haven with this woman's hand grenade lodged in the center of my heart. It exploded as I forced out a breath, pushed back the tears, and soaked up any residual external effects into every cell in my body.

Dare I be brave enough to declaim my feelings of anger and liberate them from my body? Dare I request that she stop and announce to the world that I matter?

Reeling from this woman's lack of awareness about my relationship with Ryan, I strolled out of the bathroom and into the living room and declared in a tactful way that the name of my recent ex, Ryan, was to be banned in my home. I offered a short explanation and relied on mercy but didn't care how the proclamation landed. I was done with this woman and what seemed in my state of paranoia to be an invasive inquisition. Truth be told, this poor woman had bitten Ryan's hook the same as I had. My unfaithful ex had been out fishing during our last two weeks (but really three years) together.

This may have been a mortifying request from a people-pleaser who had distain for confrontation, but my breakup recovery required action. I had to protect myself from the string of women who Ryan led on. My heart could not withstand the blows, and acting with grace felt impossible.

Be prepared to react like this when your soul has reached the limit of abusive behaviors such as lies and cheating. You are going to have to slay dragons on your quest to save yourself. Upsetting an acquaintance is a measly price to pay for your own peace of mind, and any self-respecting woman would agree.

While avoiding daily triggers and dodging bullets, I thought interminably about my misbegotten dreams of Ryan.

Pay attention to this. Obsessive thinking is an attack on all fronts. Are you having conversations in your head while driving to work? Do thoughts of your ex run through your brain in the shower each morning?

I either conjured up a memory and re-lived it over and over or searched to understand his point of view and dissected myself to identify what I did wrong. Reactive thoughts to conversations that we had had earlier in the week that didn't sit right kept me up at night. I thought about him, myself, us, and our relationship non-stop.

Does this sound like you? Are you having a hard time being present with your loved ones? Do you feel like an addict in withdrawal now that the two of you are apart, pacified but feeling his absence?

Not convinced yet that you are out of control? After all, he is the one with the addiction. Whether it be alcohol, cigarettes, drugs, sex, rage, or gambling, it's easy to point out his unsound behaviors. Let's face it, this feels more favorable than analyzing yourself one more time. If he has more substantial problems than you do, somehow you are more okay. Right?

I know, Dear Heart, that that is so wrong. We want better for ourselves regardless of what any man is up to.

You can do this. I know that you are of stout spirit. I am certain that you can take accountability. When you point your index finger at him or at his new woman, three fingers point back at you.

This is teaching you to ponder. It is not healthy to vent when you talk about him. It is the blame trap, and the focus must be re-directed away from him. What you focus on, you receive more of. Are you focused on the hurt?

Be honest with yourself. I believe that you are an honest person. So treat yourself to your own gift of integrity. Which of these situations are you facing? Mind you, recurrent engagement in these ballgames leads to impaired thinking and aggravation. Roger that!

- You've stayed in the relationship long past the useful limits, and this relationship is causing you trouble.

- You desire to stop the intolerable pattern with a disingenuous partner, but attempts to disengage have been unsuccessful.

- Pursuit of the relationship or recovery from it consumes a significant amount of time. (No judgment! I am writing a whole book on the topic. I was possessed too!)

- You have a craving or uncontrollable desire to be with him, near him, or to hear his voice.

- Thinking, actions, and emotions concerning him, the relationship, or recovery disrupt obligations at your workplace, school, or home.

- Participation in the relationship advances despite the social or interpersonal complications that it causes.

- Participation in important social, occupational, or recreational activities drop off or cease. You lose interest in pursuits in which you previously enjoyed.

- Physical or financial risks may exist.

- Engagement persists despite knowing that the relationship is causing or exacerbating physical or psychological problems.

- Fortitude endures. You tell yourself to be strong and fight for the relationship. Pay attention to how you cover for him or make excuses for his behavior or your own.

- You go through withdrawal. This is evident in what you do when he is not around. (Over-thinking, predicting behavior, or using substances as bandages to settle emotions.)

  The severity of the ailment is measured by the number of symptoms present.

  Inhale, exhale, and scream if you must. In my estimation:

- Two to three of the above indicates a mild condition.

- Four to five may be considered a moderate condition.

- Six or more signifies a severe condition.

It is fine, and even recommended, that you sit in silence and let this information sink in. You did not arrive at this place overnight, and reading this one page will not cure you of years of conditioning and self-renunciation, but it will propel you on your way.

It's okay, I am here too.

You are not alone, broken, or dysfunctional. You are going to need to hear this often. I don't mind letting you know whenever you'd like. Consider these words etched in stone for you.

You are not broken, and you are not alone.

Peptide and Emotional Addiction

Let's take the subject off of you and the word addiction and move on to the physical phenomenon of what may be going on here. Another theory that I support is called a *peptide addiction*. Oops, what is the deal with the word addiction?

I refuse to label human conditions as *good or bad*. The word *addict* sits like a boulder in my heart, and that shows me that it is not aligned with human greatness. It demonizes those who are already suffering, and I won't kick anyone while they are down. In my opinion, most addictions occur in intelligent, sensitive beings who are seeking love and attention and coming up short. Respect and benevolence are required as we look at this phenomenon.

Therefore, let's soften our gaze and call it the *peptide connection*, though a more appropriate name would be the Tasmanian Devil's loop. You may feel of unsound mind as you return to your ex time and time again. I assure you that you are not. You may be addicted to the rush of emotions that comes from falling in lust with your dangerous or avoidant man.

Regardless of the label, understanding the peptide connection is necessary to our discussion and recovery.

A peptide bond is the reason for most biological reactions, and there is a peptide for every emotion. Similar to an addiction to alcohol, there may be physical addictions occurring in the case of psychological abuse and emotional addiction related to peptide connections. Like a lock and key, our conditioned peptides seek out their molecular match. If you experienced any type of traumatic event or abuse as a child, you may be primed for destruction as an adult as your peptides seek a match. Hence, we find ourselves reacting in similar patterns, habits, and emotions time after time.

An addict proclaims that he will never pick up a bottle of booze, while one obsessed with love struggles to stop herself from picking up the phone when he calls. Our addictions follow suit, and we wake up with a hangover or wake up next to the man with whom we swore never to sleep with again.

My body made the call on this one, before I had ever heard of peptides. Before I developed the awareness that I may have been narcissistically abused, I suffered the effects of emotional addiction to my boyfriend and drama.

My personal peptide addiction was at work. While a party to these mind games, and mired in the pit of lies and cheating with my partner, Ryan, I began to react out of character for me. I lost control of my emotions and actions.

Holding my phone in my hand while preparing my jet tub for yet another attempt to suppress my nerves with hot water, bubbles, and a glass of wine, I uncovered more shocking evidence of what occurred in my relationship with Ryan.

Let's say that we had an unclear status at this point. Stringing me along with great craft, Ryan had me questioning whether the relationship had ever really existed at any point.

He often held our relationship in a place of uncertainty while he played the field without my knowledge of his actions. Nonetheless, as I blocked Ryan from my Facebook page, I found out that he had more than one or two profiles set up. The one that disturbed me the most featured a picture that I had taken of him while camping with him and another couple. The profile specified that he lived in a different state. My mouth dropped open, and my body kicked into super drive. My reality shifted.

Before I deleted him on Spotify (a song sharing application), I read there that he had disclosed a playlist of songs that he had authored for us to a woman in Europe, with whom he had slept with while on a business trip. I had revealed another woman in his visible trail of betrayal in a harmless forum like Spotify, and I confronted him. To my utter surprise, he asked me how I kept finding out about his lies. My reply, "Did you just ask me how to help you cover your trail better?" Pinch me please, I must be having a horrible dream and I need to wake up now!

I see true narcissism as an illness of the mind, and this man disguised his deceit with others while flaunting it right in front of me. He wanted me to know. He wanted to be seen. He wanted to matter and for me to react. He almost won, but armed with the information of his lies, I would have chained myself to a tree for life before succumbing to his trance once more.

Suffice it to say, I blew a gasket in August of 2017.

The desire to call him and rip into him and his wacky perfidy overwhelmed my physical body, and yet the truth of how that would play out lit up my soul like the north star beckoning, *Don't go down that route! You will crash against the cliffs!*

The rush of fear, anxiety, heartbreak, betrayal, and longing for justice had to be relinquished. In this case, the innocent cellular device in my hand took the hit.

I dropped my phone into the tub full of scalding water.

As I watched it sink to the bottom, I felt total vindication that this free-for-all and the drama would end. I couldn't call him in a rage or view his duplicity across my screen. Not the most well-thought-out plan, I acknowledge, but at the time, it mitigated my wrath to an extent and provided a sense that my love life could change, that I could be free from him.

After draining the tub and staring down at my admirable accomplishment, I snatched up the phone. Oh, my God. My heart dropped into my stomach like the first dip on a speeding roller coaster, the room spun, and I thought that I would vomit. The phone screen lit up like a psychotic doll face chuckling at me.

I then lost it for a second time, and this time failure could not be an option. I had to ward off the peptide addiction as well. I seized that compact device in a fit of silent fury, darted past my brother watching

TV in my living room, and rushed out the door to my detached garage. I knew what I wanted to do, and it had been a long time coming.

I scanned the walls. On two nails rested a wood-handled hammer. Heck, yeah! I did not hesitate. I grabbed the hammer, found a flat surface, and vaporized my cellphone...one glorious whack at a time.

Relief flooded through my system like a flock of gorgeous first-responders saving me from an unexpected attack.

In some irrational sense, I beat the odds. I reclaimed my control. I bellowed a loud *no* to this chronic pattern of abuse, cheating, lies, and manipulation.

I uttered a few other unmentionable words as well.

Cleansing tears broke through the absurdity, then exhaustion hit, and alas, my brother hovered over me piecing together the scene. I explained with all the brevity that I could muster.

He chuckled. "Well, now he's cost you a cellphone as well."

True, but not sympathetic or helpful.

I tucked myself into bed and slept away the weariness of assault, having no contact with my perceived attacker. I heard not so much as a whisper of a lie from him in my ear. My dreams distilled, I slept for two days, cellphone and abuse-free. Maiming my phone felt like the kindest gesture I could have performed for myself.

You must be asking yourself, *Why would a sensible, educated woman act like this?* This is what the peptide addiction resembles in real life. Peptides became the demanding commanders of my ship. Are you begging your cheating ex to stay with you? Are you tolerating unforgivable behavior like I endured?

Billions of cells freewheel around in our bodies, and each tiny cell has hundreds of receptors on the surface of its external membrane. The peptides seek out and attach themselves to these receptors so that they may supply the cell with a particular emotion, a required nutrient, or an incentive to take some sort of action. If you find this type of work fascinating, please refer to *Molecules of Emotion* by Candace Pert and *The Body Keeps Score* by Bessel van der Kolk, M.D. The draw to relationship abuse is physical.

What's interesting is that if a person has a predisposition to experiencing her physical reality through a particular emotional filter, she will tend to have more receptors on her cells for that emotion compared to other emotions.

Hebbian Theory captures this phenomenon as, "Cells that fire together wire together."

I had been wired for and addicted to emotional abuse. I felt primed for psychological abuse and attracted it into my life.

If you are a highly sensitive, empathic type like I am, you may feel over-stimulated in every cell of your body. If you are not that sensitive, you may at least see the tragic response and the problems that a peptide reaction could be causing in your life or in the lives of others. Due to my nature, and my lack of awareness at that time of peptides and attachment, I had more hooks in me than a tackle box. My physical and energetic body became dis-eased with two decades of virulent emotions that I did not know how to clear.

The problem turned serious. I had an addiction to trauma and abusive relationships. Perhaps you do as well.

The Impossible Task

Now that you possess awareness of what is happening in a physical and emotional sense that is outside of your control, let's examine what you have been doing to remedy this crisis. You may be presenting questions to yourself that are haunting you. You may also be trying to understand what has you so muddled, so in love, and yet so lost. Allow me to explain.

Are you obsessed with trying to answer these questions?

- *What is wrong with me?* This is such a common one. People are treating you poorly, and you blame yourself.

- *Why did that happen?* If you knew the reason for this, you could control the outcome in the future by acting differently.

- *Why did he cheat on me? I must have done something wrong.*

- *Why do I keep making these mistakes? I am such an idiot.*

- *Why can't I be happy? It must be depression or anxiety, or maybe I have a mental illness.*

- *Why are relationships so easy for others and so impossible for me? I am doomed.*

Oh dear, the dreaded question *Why?* These incapacitating questions will only send your mind searching for clarity and find you holding on to the relationship. Remember, as a child, you acted out and tested the waters of life. Perhaps you threw a rock at a car window, with no real consideration for cause and effect.

Imagine that you are now an adult standing over yourself yelling, "Why did you do that?"

Remember the feeling as the child who broke a window seeking to produce an answer to the question, *Why did you do that?* It generates a mind-circus, because you don't know the answer. What occurred next? *Go to your room and think about it.* No! Do not go to your room alone and think about it, and do not tease your mind with why your bad relationship has fallen apart.

Be grateful that it has. If you think in that way, you are giving your mind the impossible task of making sense out of a question that your heart alone can answer.

Why questions can't be answered in conditions like this. If you are having a hard time letting this sink in, answer these additional questions. *Have my questions set me free? Is my mind relaxed and ready for the next mission, or is it gyrating like a top while attempting to make sense of manipulative lies?*

I became mired in the *Why*, and nothing changed.

Even after I did free myself from my twelve-year relationship with Mike, I didn't break the pattern and, in fact, it worsened. Regardless of whether my boyfriend of twelve years had been narcissistic, negligent, unavailable, or not my life-partner the relationship problems intensified with Ryan. I fell for the same guy over and over, all with different faces, because I was the same lost soul seeking out a different relationship ending. Believe that this will happen to you as well if you don't break this pattern and permit yourself to ask more empowering questions.

Experiment with these suggestions. Speak these questions out loud. Sit with them. Feel any emotions or sensations that may stir in your body. Write an entire page to answer in full.

- What can I learn from my difficult experiences?

- How did I participate, and what unique actions may I take in the future?

- What must I have believed about myself, and who I was, to stay in a relationship with a cheater, a liar, an addict, or an abuser?

- What are the advantages of being my current age, opposed to being that younger self with no resources or means to walk away?

- How may my age and wisdom grant me permission to respond in a different way to others and to dialogue with myself in an empowering way?

- What characteristics do I possess that allowed me to stay in this relationship?

Fabulous. Now, as an empath, I can feel you across time and space, and I know right now that the new perspective that these questions has jimmied open may bring in mixed emotions. You may have sighed in relief knowing that there are options other than your circular thinking. You may also feel shame for your past decisions, guilt for your problematic choices, exasperated at the passage of time, and any other combination of dishonor toward yourself and others.

I want you to scream it out. Grab a blanket or a pillow, and screech as loud as you can. Holler until the tears spill from your eyes.

You have been operating in madness. Madness has a strong and destructive vibration. If you don't release it, you will attract more of the same. Rattle it out of your body. Stand, crank up the music, dance, and pound the air.

You pay a price for keeping this energy inside of you. This amounts to emotional bankruptcy. Shake off the chains, rip to shreds the ropes that bind you, and squeal until your throat and neck expand and the links break free. Advertise your freedom from abuse, even if it's only to yourself.

You have my permission to lose your shit right now.

Toss this book down, and do it now. Let it all out.

Okay, how do you feel? Ready to proceed? Since your energy shifted, answer once more after having acknowledged, honored, and discharged all of the old, scrunched up energy in your body. Make these questions a resource in tough times. Come back to this page whenever you are triggered.

If you followed my prompt, you may have heard a whisper of altruism cry out to you. As disempowering as your relationship may have been, you didn't give your power away. I don't know why people claim that. Your inner light has never, ever left you. You did, however, suppress it, starve it, and (let's admit it) give up the ship. Like a withering plant, we will nurse you back to life, and you will bloom.

You will regain the self-respect and self-esteem required for reciprocal, romantic relationships. Those of us settling for scraps and unrewarding bonds convince ourselves that we love ourselves and have self-confidence, but if this was true, we would not have been in these unacceptable relationships.

Darling, if you always place his needs first, saying *yes* to him when you don't even know your own *yes*, or you are reacting rather than responding to others and your environment, you are not demonstrating self-love. You are bagging your own needs and perhaps being co-dependent. Are you being that good girl so that you will earn love? I am not in the business of selling you the lie that being good will get you the life that you desire. Authenticity is the path to your transformation.

With that, it is time I offer you some aid.

 SOULutions

I am excited to introduce you to a few SOULutions that resolved conflicts for me in real time in the midst of relationship confusion. I wish that I had had all of this information in one place when I scrambled through the thick of it, so it pumps me up to be able to share these SOULutions with you here.

I need your word about one thing before we proceed. I need you to be willing. Willingness to try anything and to participate is the attitude that you need to succeed. I too had to pledge my willingness. What I was doing did not work. Success feels good. The thick of relationship dis-ease feels heavy. This one undertaking will go such a long way in your recovery. So summon up a touch of willingness, and utilize these SOULutions.

SOULution #1:
Emotional Freedom Technique (EFT)

EFT! OMG! EFT!

The Emotional Freedom Technique is such an incredible tool. I just have to let you in on the mystery of this hidden gem. EFT may fly under the radar because it is free, and free does not get broadcasted. Emotional Freedom! Sounds remarkable, right? Are you game to feel a bit silly for a reprieve?

The Emotional Freedom Technique is a form of acupuncture without the use of needles. This self-administered procedure occurs by tapping the fingertips to stimulate energy points on the body. It feels funny to do at first, but humor me.

This form of counseling intervention draws on various theories of alternative medicine, including neuro-linguistic programming, energy medicine, Thought Field Therapy, and the aforementioned acupuncture. This is a technique that involves gently drumming the fingertips on meridian points to clear negative emotions.

For me, my symptoms appeared as anxiety, racing thoughts, and pressure in my chest. EFT cleared this resistance so that I could make decisions based on my morals and not my reactive feelings.

Here is my best example of EFT saving me in real time. I met a paramedic, named Mitch, on a dating site almost a year after ending the relationship with Ryan in 2017. Our initial desire for each other was off the charts, superhot and heavy. Once again, lust took over.

Enter the adrenaline rush.

An adrenaline rush refers to the hormonal release that triggers the fight/flight/freeze response. This surge occurs in times of danger or excitement. The inconsistency and intensity of my relationship with Mitch elicited both danger and excitement. We both bought a ticket for the tilt-a-whirl, closed our eyes, and held on tight.

Between the lack of communication and commitment and the potency of our attraction, the relationship couldn't sustain itself, and we parted. Mitch and I were dramatic in our interactions, and we over-fantasized the possibility of our union. As a result, we tore ourselves apart from each other. I would suppose that this break left us both spinning, but I can only vouch for myself.

I turned inward again, stumped as to why I attracted and chose such over-the-top and unreliable intimate partners. We remained in contact, which I do not recommend, though I knew that our relationship did not benefit me. My heart dropped into my stomach whenever we spoke.

As with all of my relationships that I held on to for too long, problems intensified.

I fell to my knees when I received an unexpected text from him. Mitch had broken his back in a sky-diving accident and had been airlifted to the hospital. Paralyzed from the waist down, he sent me a picture of his back with a foot-long line of staples holding his skin together. I hyperventilated on the floor until I caught my breath.

I cared for Mitch, so I packed my car with the intention of driving to him post haste. Gasping for air, I sent a text to him inquiring about the hospital's address.

He then broke the news to me. "I'm dating someone. She found me after the accident. She is an angel. She saved my life."

This did not feel like a trigger. This felt like a bazooka exploding in my face.

I shuffled on leaden legs to the park, planted my bare feet in a grassy field, and fastened my eyes somewhere in the distance. Once more, that inspiriting pulse, the same one that I had found from the wooden classroom floor, appeared from the earth elements, engulfing me. I felt the grass breathing, and my own breath regulated with this pulse. I saw vibrations coming off of the bright emerald landscape, and these vibes rippled from me as if I was a pebble tossed into a lake.

I uttered the words, "I'll be okay. I won't try to save him."

I hung a *Closed for Business* sign on my front door and self-medicated with wine, hoping to get over Mitch and recover from the complete helplessness oozing through my veins. In fact, I barricaded myself inside to prevent myself from running to him, despite the unwelcome news about his girlfriend. My body felt trapped in resistance. I bawled for days like a colicky baby.

Somehow, I pulled myself together. Summer had ended, and I had accepted a teaching job at a new school. Change was on the horizon.

A month after Mitch's traumatic news, a ding from my phone interrupted my work day. Mitch texted me that he needed financial rescue. He required money to keep his leased truck after being disabled and to pay his outrageous medical bills. I felt inclined to dive head first into the deep end and save my crush from anymore suffering. Let's acknowledge that I did not inquire about his girlfriend. I did not have the voice to ask difficult questions...yet.

The $2,000 for which he petitioned necessitated some thought on my part. I considered myself bright and capable. *I can do this.* Already distracted from my planning day, I found myself rummaging through my mind seeking ways to deliver Mitch from his financial dilemma like my own house had caught on fire. I decided that I could tack a gift to him on to my credit card debt.

Whoa, whoa, whoa! Wait a minute! *Am I going to go into debt for Mitch, the same guy who replaced me seconds after we broke up?* In the midst of his trauma, visiting him as a caring friend did not appear to be an option. *Where did his woman, his angel, go now?* I needed a reality check. I needed to stop myself from over-giving. I needed to make a conscious decision.

As my body erupted in triggers, I tapped my fingers on the EFT touch points, starting with the crown of my head. I rushed to the sacred room of tiles, otherwise known as the bathroom, and I proceeded through the tapping technique while reciting, *Even though I don't have money to help, even though Mitch is not in love with me, even though I am suffering with intense anxiety, even though he calls me names, puts me down, and claims that I can't understand his struggle, even though I feel guilty...I love and accept myself.*

I revved up the emotion and tapped meridian points. With both hands, I thumped the top of my head and then above each eyebrow. I moved down and patted under my eyes, between my nose and top lip, and then the center of my chin. I strummed my finger tips on my collar bones, then the sides of my torso where my bra rested. Finally, I drummed the outside of my hands below the pinkies where one would land a karate chop.

Not right away, but somewhere in the midst of this healing process, a blanket of peace fell upon me. The nerve-reconciling calm created a movement of response in me rather than a frantic reaction to his unmet need.

This tranquil feeling did not provide a direct route to a self-honoring solution. I reviewed the balances on my credit cards to see how I could make the $2,000.00 gift (which I would not expect to be paid back). It took some time for the healing to set in, and I reached a conclusion, a SOULution.

I texted him:

> I'm sorry that you're going through this. I know that you are resourceful and that you will figure a way out of this. I love you, and I am here for you.

His response?

> I don't need love, I need money.

Today I am indebted to EFT rather than to my credit card. I don't know where I would be if I had kept reacting with such little consciousness. Mitch did not want a monogamous, honest relationship with me. Most likely I would be heartbroken and bankrupt if I had continued to engage with him. Remember the Maya Angelou quote, "When people show you who they are, believe them the first time." Be aware.

This EFT technique is priceless.

I want you to implement this technique. I want you to have emotional freedom. I want you to exit the cycle of abuse.

SOULution #2:
Pulverize The Word *WHY*

Why me? Why can't I? Why did he do that? Why did I do that? Why does this always happen to me? Why is he texting me? Why is he flirting with that woman? Why is he quizzing me about my successful girlfriends? Why is my brain thundering and my heart frantic? Why am I so exhausted? Why didn't he call back or text? Why? Why? Why? Woman, stop!

Remember what I did with that phone in real life? Let's do that with the word *Why*. Produce your visual hammer, and hold a picture of the word *Why* in your head. In fact, make it ginormous, or visualize thousands of *Whys* crawling all over you. The more detailed the better. I can imagine a printer spitting out *Whys* at me. The *Whys* are slithering up my legs. These *Why* questions have infiltrated my bed as they scurry through my mind. Grab that visual hammer, pesticide spray (organic of course), chainsaw, or whatever you desire to smash those *Whys* to smithereens. Feature yourself exterminating the *Whys*. This word is not serving you right now.

Awesome! If any more *Whys* emerge, drop-kick them into the universe. For the time being, you don't need to know *Why*. I understand that you are flummoxed and that your despondent mind is searching for answers so that you may feel safe and secure.

Remember that I will let you know that you are a stable and sound human being whenever you need it. You are not turning into a crazy person, though it may feel that way.

You can see how the word *Why* might drive you mad. This simple exercise resolved another problem of the mind for me. *Why* makes one anxious. When the *Why* surfaces, catch it and crush it.

You may also want to write all of your *Why* questions down and burn them (in a safe place). You may even add, *Dear Brain, You no longer have the task of answering my* Whys. *I now have better questions for you.*

When you are ready, use more enlightened questions. Below are some that I have learned along the way. They foster growth, intuition, and change.

Improved Questions

•   What must I have believed about myself to tolerate this relationship?

•   When I am feeling triggered, I lovingly compel myself to answer, *What is the trigger response telling me right now?* Then I listen.

•   At what age did I first feel this physical stress reaction in my body? What occurred in my life during that time? What is the advantage of being the age that I am now?

•   How would my most confident and serene-self handle this current interaction?

You will notice that these questions allow the hamster to cease and desist from turning in circles and allow the cuddly creature to hop off of the wheel. Infinite streams of distressing answers are not possible with empowering questions as they are with the *Why* questions. As you sink into a deeper heart-centered place, these questions will evoke feeling answers rather than monkey-mind responses.

You can return to this page often. In fact, go ahead and turn down the corner of this page.

SOULution #3:
Stream of Consciousness Journaling

Part of the problem that you may be having is that you continuously follow the endless chatter in your head. I am certain that you are familiar with journaling, but perhaps not like this. What I would like you to do is easy, and you will be rewarded by the volume of writing that flows out of you. A new perspective on life will unfold. Write for ten minutes every single day.

I want you to unload your every racing thought on to the page. This is not to be shared. This is not even for you to review. Please do not go back and analyze or judge yourself. Write what surfaces. Believe me, your greatness lies beneath this layer of filth that has collected around your mind, your heart, and your soul.

Designate a journal for this stream of consciousness writing. Start a timer, and keep the pen moving for the entire ten minutes. You may write for more time but no less. Spend ten minutes recovering control of your mind.

As you will see, thoughts twirl around, which is fine. This journaling is for you to identify and spit out what is rattling around in that brain of yours and pairing you with venomous partners, friends, or co-workers.

Restorative images and words are going to be revealed. Your heart will shine through. Troubling thoughts will bubble up as well, and this is normal. In fact, the more off-putting it feels, the better. Extract the garbage and the defeating thoughts, and slap them on the page. Do not be ashamed of the shocking realizations, scenes of abuse, or your own ignominious behavior from the past.

You are worth this time. Devote yourself to it.

Free your mind.

Write.

CHAPTER 3

Kryptonite

By definition, kryptonite is a green, crystalline material that emits a strange radiation that sickens Superman. His enemies used kryptonite to rob Superman of his super abilities and render him defenseless to their attacks.

Kryptonite reveals the Achilles heel (the flaw, despite other talents) that all humans are born with. As you might predict from my previous anecdotes, kryptonite is that ex, that boyfriend, or that crush who has the ability to weaken your resolve. Once you are close, escape is futile, and the abhorrent storyline plays out.

In my boundary-less state, a glimpse, a smile, or a text brought me to my knees. It doesn't even seem fair. Kryptonite, that alluring man, should not be able to call you out of the blue or bump into you at the grocery store. This happened to me every time I felt confident. A radius limit for kryptonite's reach did not apply. I could be states away, occupied and happy, and then my phone lit up, and the cycle repeated itself.

I lost all resolve and any plan of action to ignore, block, or flee the relationships with Ryan and Mitch, and I succumbed to the greed of this addiction over and over. I cancelled, skipped, or re-scheduled events in my life that I had deemed important. I love sports, and yet many times I drove to Ryan's house because he had had a hard day and wanted to see me, rather than respecting my obligation to playing for my soccer team.

So much for self-integrity. These poor choices chipped away at my self-worth. Chip, chip, chip.

I often sat in bumper-to-bumper, rush hour traffic with other sad-faced souls in order to meet Ryan's needs. This would have been conceivable had I been driving toward the majestic mountains, but instead I headed east toward the barren plains of Kansas. Yuck!

I am certain that the wicked witch from the Wizard of Oz flew by on her broom delivering a warning of eminent danger, and I brushed it off. I ignored all internal warning signs, while afflicted by my kryptonite, Ryan. Cradling my heavy heart, I will continue to take full responsibility for these actions. I could have chosen better for myself. That is all on me.

I longed for my unrestrained behavior of always being there to be reciprocated. The times when I sought comfort from Ryan grew fewer and farther between because I stuffed my problems to the pit of my stomach so as not to be a burden to others.

However, the first time that I had a challenging day, Ryan admitted that he couldn't handle it and that he couldn't console me. The second time, when I explained a tough conversation with my assistant principal to him, he sided with her. He did not support me.

I'm not so self-indulgent that I couldn't listen to other points of view, but his comments took on a form other than a friend playing devil's advocate to broaden my perspective. It became his opportunity to shake my sense of self by using my administrator's possible perspective to protect himself from blame while downsizing me in the conversation. His technique was crafty, intelligent, and for lack of better words, emotionally criminal. These conversational attacks developed into the norm.

I also backed out of plans with friends when his mood turned sour. I didn't want my friends to see him, or us, in this light. Ryan did not have a grip on his emotions, and I didn't want to expose my friends to this kind of behavior. Perhaps I didn't want them to see the truth.

As if this wasn't grimy enough, they then had to hear my stories of befuddlement, and his triangulation tactics thrived in the company of others.

The term *triangulation* steps into play here. Triangulation is the manipulation by one person to control communication and perspectives of two other parties. These interactions leave one party pining for attention from the manipulator and the other party feeling validated and sided with for the moment. Adding my friends or any other people to the mix gave Ryan more of an audience to pull from, more pawns to move around and position for attack.

I am proud to share that in September of 2019 I shut a scenario like this down in a dating encounter with a match mishap named Eric. We had been dating for two months, and I had been pacing the relationship, though my feelings grew and made me lightheaded.

Eric didn't care for the recent behavior of one of my girlfriends. He indulged himself with a diatribe to me about all of her faults, sugar-coated with his concern that she could not be a good friend.

He even pontificated like a legal scholar. "I am surprised that she is your friend. In my opinion, she is no good for you." Needless to say, I never even met one of Eric's friends or family members.

He further invalidated me and my choices.

However, he then turned the tables and glorified her behavior in an effort to turn the attack toward me and point out that she had been more welcoming to him at a recent party that I hosted than I had. He censured her and then twisted it around to her being kinder than I had been to him.

I called him out on the triangulation attempt, disengaged, and informed him that she had zero to do with our discussion. If he had a problem with how I engaged at my party, that had to be between us only. While this small victory seemed awesome to me, I often felt that kryptonite powder lingered in my purse and pockets.

I changed from being a strong communicator to a frail character with no backbone when faced with triangulation, manipulations, or flat-out lies. Each conversation felt like a boxing match with Eric, and the gloves were off. He judged and commented on my every move.

As for Ryan, I announced countless times to friends that our association had ended. I acknowledged to myself that our relationship had fallen apart, that Ryan had been no good for me, and that he was not the man that I had perceived him to be.

I pleaded with Ryan to stop the carousel, as I did not have the resources to resist his charm. I can almost hear his muffled smirk. He knew that I would not let him go. He knew that he had me entranced and that I had little means to escape the three years of extreme highs and lows. From 2014 to 2017, he felt like my kryptonite. Following 2017 and having found a new post-Ryan man, I clung to Mitch in a similar fashion from 2018 to 2019, and the hysterical draw to unhealthy relationships intensified.

Does this feel like you? Is there *one guy* causing you to lose yourself more than you have with any other man? Have you dated a series of men offering the same feeling of instability? Let me guess, you pretend to yourself that he is your soulmate, your true love.

Is chaos the norm for you too?

I will remind you of this. Love does not hurt. I know that you are a *I'll believe it when I see it* kind of girl. With these love-sick blinders on, it is impossible to see what you need to see right now. Real love and kindness begins with you, after you detach from him.

Why You? Why now?

So, why does Superman (in our case, the Super Woman that you are) become ungrounded around kryptonite when typical humans do not? Why had I become smitten by Ryan, but my kind-hearted best friend, Anna, recognized at her first encounter with him his inconsistencies? Disgusted by the way he treated me, she summoned up the nerve to insist that I see his true colors. She called him trash and saw better for me.

Name-calling is not a practice in which either one of us typically indulged, but desperate times called for desperate measures. My loyal friend wanted her words to sink in!

Anna had no fear of kicking Ryan in the shins, in the metaphorical sense. It is even hard to write, but it does convey the extent to which she witnessed me being used and discarded.

Regardless, let's examine why you may be tempted by a man similar to the men I have described. Please think of who this person is for you right now. Remember, I am here to help you.

What makes you vulnerable to this narcissistic, or emotionally abusive, or unavailable man? While your attraction may be subconscious or addictive, the power to choose is within you.

Are you intuitive? Do you see the best in people? Do you look past any shortcomings and revel in the positive traits? Are you financially or emotionally reliant?

If you are with a man who is hurting you, his heart may be deeply injured, and he may be lashing out at you. Do you feel his inner discord and want to alleviate it? After all, mending the heart of a damaged or angry man will make the world a safer place for you. Perhaps you grew up around these type of men and never put your upbringing under a microscopic lens.

How many relationships have you hurtled toward in hopes of saving or changing the man or his circumstances? Did you hope that if you fixed his problems, this would reconcile your own past?

Another reason for being with him may be harder to hear. You are staying in this relationship because you have accolades to earn. Be real. You are attracting these men and choosing them. I am certain that other suitable candidates are interested in you, as other men were attracted to me. I did not give these men my attention. I favored the unavailable, narcissistic types.

It is quite possible that his struggles light you up and make you feel needed. When he holds you at arm's length, does it ignite a challenge in your brain? You may be familiar with this feeling and, therefore, you attract and seek a compatible match of destruction.

Don't be mistaken, he sees your loving traits and wants your attention. He is attracted to you and the light you exude. His affection toward you is inciting your ability to discern the health of the partnership. This makes the relationship even more challenging from which to extricate yourself. Staying in it is costing you more than any gift or monetary item that you have received from him.

Hurting Yourself

Are you ready for some more hard truths?

You are disempowering yourself by expending time and energy on the kryptonite that is your man. Do you enjoy emotional bankruptcy? You do have a choice. Do you think that Superman lounges around in his bulletproof briefs awaiting an invitation from his archenemy to stop over for a kryptonite cocktail? Throw in some peptides and cortisol (the stress hormone that depletes all the feel-good hormones), and Superman will be shackled to a ticking time bomb that will take him and the universe that he adores out. This is you, waiting on your own Lex Luthor to text back.

Of course, Superman is not expecting a call from Lex. This may be the hardest truth that you will have to embrace. You have a choice, and you must take responsibility for your life and your happiness, right now.

So, allow me to emphasize how this is all going to play out. I already know that your logic is intact. Love doesn't equal abuse, and any guy who treats you with disrespect is not for you.

Awesome, now resist him.

I am not serious, of course.

You can't resist him...yet. After the intense love-bombing, followed by the rapprochement and discarding, you must be beyond perplexed. Attempting escape right now will make it worse. This returns us to all of the physical responses related to peptides, but in real life a breakup will feel and appear like you resisting him as long as you can until you give up and settle for the skimpy side dishes that he doles out to you.

You will also feel worse for not being strong enough to resist his advances or pleas to give him another chance. One crack in your true intention to end things, and you will go on a love binge that will leave you in full-out withdrawal, panic, and ill from an emotional hangover for days, weeks, or months. Please, let's not do that.

Oh, sure, the initial interaction with him will kindle so much happiness and hope throughout your body that you will light up like a Christmas tree, but it will fade before your clothes even hit the floor.

Don't worry, I have every intention of setting you up for success. Following are a few other ideas that you will need to digest.

- **Helping him is not nurturing either of you.** No matter how he frames it, no matter how broke, sad, depressed, or broken he may be, he does not need your assistance. He is a man, and he will be okay on his own, without you. If he is not, it is in no way your responsibility to meet any of his needs. Thinking that he needs your help is a co-dependent mindset. A healthy man does not need a woman. A nurturing man wants a woman and values and adores her. Do you hear me? We return fixer-uppers to the shop.

- **You do not need to fix him.** Neither your ex, nor any other suitor, believes that he is broken and in need of your mothering. He is not lying in bed at night thinking about a self-improvement plan and hoping to be rescued by a woman. That is not in a man's character. Even if he sought reprieve, you don't have the means, the tools, or the credentials to counsel him from where you stand.

Throughout the book we will smash the idea of this external focus on saving others. A strong and profound connection could be tied to an unfixable, dysfunctional relationship that you had early in your formative years. I seldom promote giving up, but give this up. Learning to console yourself, and knowing that *he is not your problem to fix*, will give you the control to rescue the person you can. Yourself.

Know Your No

Now, let's also scrutinize your *yes* and your *no*. Do you acquiesce to his suggestions? Do you claim to love his ideas and insist that you are an easygoing, go-with-the-flow kind of gal? Slow down. You know that he isn't good for you, but if he called you to hang out right now, would you say *yes, yes, yes*?

This is my favorite litmus test. Have you ever sat in the car with a boyfriend or your husband, and you both profess that you're hungry? You engage in a debate about where to go for lunch.

By the time the two of you have reached a consensus, you are frustrated, have no appetite, and are on the verge of tears. This is a clear sign that you do not know what you want, not for lunch but in your life. This is a problem. This is your life, and you can't even determine if you want Mexican food or Thai food.

Imagine your ability to make important decisions, like whether to have babies, how to pay the bills, and if you want to marry this person. That decision-making skill is a muscle. It is your voice. Without it, you are just a leaf blowing in the wind.

This is not about tacos and noodles. This is the tip of the iceberg of a mammoth underlying problem. Soak that up, accept it, and feed your soul what you truly desire. At least have a number of restaurants in your contact list in case this quandary ever presents itself. Practice decisiveness. Hesitation and speculation hurts. Abusive people pick up on this, and they pry their way into that empty space for the attack.

SOULutions

I feel like I have stirred the pot of your fears and anxieties. I hope that you have identified your kryptonite. Are you feeling overwhelmed or self-critical? Let me show you the simplest steps by which you may soothe your soul and pull your strength back to you. The steps are minutes in action but huge in growth and expansion.

SOULution #1
No-Contact, Gradual Release, and Limited Contact

Recall our discussion about the peptides racing around in our bodies searching for a designated key hole? In the same way, you are seeking your chosen man as your drug.

Theories abound about how to break an addiction, and I would agree that complete abstinence from your kryptonite is the goal. However, this is where I enter with forbearance. Yes, this relationship is hurting you, and I also know that you are so enmeshed that it may take time to disentangle from the partnership.

I know that you feel that you love him.

Take a minute to discern what you are capable of, what you may do today. This is not a New Year's Eve whimsy. Your life, not your waist line, depends on your decision and your resolve.

No-Contact. Can you go no-contact? This means zero face-to-face contact, no phone calls, no texts, no visiting the local bar or coffee shop, no driving by his house, no *oh, this reminded me of you* picture exchanges, no mentioning him when visiting with friends, and no searching for information about him on social media.

I have done all of that. Have you? I am not a stalker, and I trust that neither are you. I was captive with a kryptonite necklace binding my heart like handcuffs. Can you stop these behaviors cold turkey?

Going no-contact felt impossible for me at first, and it looked like this.

Late one fall evening in 2016, in the midst of a disappearing act on the part of Ryan, I called my parents. My father answered in his carefree way and perhaps kicked himself for his decision when he noted the frantic tone of my voice. He preferred to leave crying, emotional fits to my mother. Who can blame him?

I gave my Pops my Facebook password, and I instructed him to change it so that I couldn't access my account. I needed a break, and I didn't want to be dramatic and shut down my page. I had some voice of reason on my side. After all, closing the account would attract attention and concern from my friends, and I did not want attention. Ridiculous I know, but I would rather shame myself in silence than have egg on my face in front of hundreds of acquaintances and high school buddies. Massively skewed reasoning on my part!

Regardless of media etiquette, I wanted to crawl under a rock and never be seen again. I knew that I had lost control.

Well, a few days later, I requested that my dad send me the new password, and he did this, no questions asked! He did not understand my helpless situation. How could he? He had handed his baby girl her drug of choice after a few days of detox. If he reads this, he will be shocked.

Please understand, it is your job to heal your wounds, to keep yourself safe, and to stand in your power. Friends and family members will not recognize the abuse, sometimes disguised, unless they have lived it, as so many of us have.

Round two of the delirium manifested a few months after one of many breakups with Ryan. I somehow thought that it would be appropriate to message a woman whom he had started dating before we even broke up and let her know that he spent Christmas Day making out with me!

He arrived at my house bearing Christmas gifts, serenading me with song, and feeding me spoonful after spoonful of lies with cherry kisses on top. I felt for his new girl. I didn't see her as a threat. My empathself saw her as being manipulated as well. I felt for both of us.

I advise you not to contact any women who you suspect are being duped by your ex. In my case, the other woman did not want to hear from me, and I sunk further into shame like quicksand sucking me six feet under. I now looked like the rabid other woman.

At this point, I could not solicit my parents for guidance. I could not bear the shame. I felt humiliated for reaching out to his other woman. *How far from love have I landed?* Instead, I assigned my older brother the task of changing my password. This was the same brother who witnessed me destroying my phone.

I expected him to understand the gravity of the situation. He saw how unstable and destructive my relationship with Ryan had become. When I felt more grounded, I requested the password in order to move on with my social life.

I include this story to illustrate that there is no knowing where you stand in your ability to go no-contact. You may go for it. Block the phone numbers of all of the men with whom you have harmful relationships in your life, and delete all e-mail addresses.

Oh, dear, I even inquired of customer service representatives at phone companies on how to not only delete but also how to block a number. I blocked and unblocked, talking myself into the never-ending circle over and over. I searched for reason because my mind could not register that a person could be this dishonest.

So, sad and true to the form of twisted abuse, I called Ryan, even after I had blocked him. In retrospect, I realize that this is a violent disease of the mind, and I am not at all surprised that I begged for a diagnosis for my neuroses.

Yes, I felt that I had lost my mind. But I am here to tell you that I am not daft, and neither are you if you are having a hard time severing an addictive relationship. Toxic factors are at play here, but we will not capitulate or accept defeat to the insidiousness of the addictive cycle. You will push through, and you will survive and eradicate this pattern from your life. You are more powerful than this attachment.

If the thought of breaking free from your husband, ex, or crush is leaving a lump in your throat, anxiety in your chest, and churning in your stomach, these symptoms indicate to us how sickening your relationship has become and which of the three options listed in SOU-Lution #1 you may handle.

Gradual Release. A gradual release with support is the best approach if you are highly co-dependent. We want long-term change, not temporary fixes and endless engagement in abuse. If the thought of going no-contact has you obsessed over losing him, gradual release will be your warm-up. You will need support, though, because you are playing with fire.

Part of the desire to engage over and over is a result of the love-bombing phase at the beginning of the relationship. A narcissistic man establishes a foundation of ecstatic memories that he hopes you rely on to carry him through as he devalues you. The shiny and alluring phase of love-bombing bonds you to him as he later holds you in his back pocket while pursuing other options. If the early memories of love at first sight are haunting you, throw these relics out now. Put down this book and delete the reminders that keep you hooked.

We are going to climb into a mental time machine, haul you out of these past memories, and bring you to the present. Please, save the messages to your computer and delete the text messages that he sent you from your phone. You know the ones, the texts that you keep reading over and over because he loved you in both words and actions, the deceiving ones that contain bits of both truth and lies that are keeping you under the influence and percolating. Save them somewhere out of sight and then delete them all from your phone.

If you are now or suspect that you may ever need to appear in a court case with your ex, take pictures of the texts, save them somewhere safe, or send them to your lawyer. They do not need to be in your face.

Now, this is not my first rodeo, and I know that delete buttons send messages to another realm. Even your phone needs to know that you mean it. Access your deleted-items folder on your phone, and eliminate the trashed messages as well. Take out the garbage, and dispose of all of the evidence of the past forever.

Your love, your true love, when you meet him, will support you every day. You won't have to question his commitment or his love. His presence will be your evidence. You won't have to preserve remnants that your love once existed, because it is alive in front of you.

Let go, and take your life back. I call this Gradual Release because you will need to keep going until you are strong enough to let go forever. You may slip. Rise and persevere. You may take a sip of whiskey and shoot him a text. You may retrieve his number and dial him up after a glass or two of wine.

The pull to reach out may be intense. Forgive yourself. Move on. Please, do not beat yourself up if you call or text him. No one is keeping score here, and know that your ultimate goal in gradual release is to gain the strength to go no-contact.

To this day, I save, move, and delete all of my text messages from my phone. I do not find it constructive to hold on to the past, and I am certain that it is not healthy for any person with an abusive past to do so. Focus on feelings. If it feels bad, it is.

Limited Contact. Alas, I know that some of you may have children with your harmful ex. You must find a way to set boundaries, and I implore you to seek legal advice and possible mediators for your interactions. You may also use an app for that! Explore the world of virtual communication, and access the application that best suits your situation. Having a third party privy to your communication with your ex will hold both you and him accountable. Do not be fooled that you can handle this on your own. Seek and receive outside help. Do it today. Your world will free up so that you may focus on your healing, and your ex's shenanigans will soon be on display.

Just as it would be difficult for an addict to have booze in the house or hang out with drinking buddies, you will want to do whatever it takes to spend as little time as possible in the presence of your ex. The goal is to disengage and move forward in your own life.

A few pointers here if you need to go limited contact:

- Avoid contact when your emotions are running high. You will be susceptible to participating in arguments or mental battles.

- Keep conversations short and direct.

- The shortest distance between two points is a straight line. If he takes the conversation on a detour, direct it back to the original intention and goal.

SOULution #2:
Reward Yourself

Yay! I'm sending you an imaginary high five for the steps that you took in establishing no-contact. I recommend that you find at least one person to whom you will be accountable, even if this person is a paid professional. Discuss your no-contact plan, and gather support. I recommend that this accountability partner not be a friend. Seek out a neutral party. I am also happy to be this person for you.

Also, let's celebrate! It is so difficult to change a pattern. This is equivalent to your puppy peeing outside and not in your house for the first time. It's such a momentous occasion for your happiness and all others involved.

You have treated yourself like rubbish for so long, and it has become familiar. You deserve to treat yourself right. If you are concerned that you can't afford a treat or that you already schedule a pedicure every month, I am going to push my hands through this book and give your shoulders a nice wake-up shake. High-end fashion and expensive spa days are not what I mean. I already know that you are remarkable. A narcissist would never settle for an unkempt woman.

Allow me.

I want you to reward your soul, and I want you to schedule a block of time for yourself. Mark off four hours on your calendar. Hire a sitter, whatever it takes for you to be free.

Alone time may scare you. Please, exploit whatever pre-reward actions steps are necessary to make this day all about you. Ask a friend to take your phone so that you are not tempted to monitor it every five minutes. Purchase some candles, bubble bath, aromatic oils, paint, journals, and/or your favorite dessert. You are going to meet your soul's desires without any outside influence.

This prep time may take you a minute. A few pages ago, you didn't even know if you wanted enchiladas or green curry chicken. Assign prep time to journal what you feel you need right now. Dream! You may have whatever you want. Don't be surprised when the answer is a free and priceless nap!

This is when I hand complete control over to you. I trust you. You are strong. You know what soul care you need. I do not have to diagnose or prescribe. Make your own list. You are unique. What did you feel deprived of as a child that you most wanted? Give that to yourself. Put yourself first. Your dreams have been shoved to the back of the closet. Dig them out. You, more than a friend, a parent, or a lover, know what these soul rewards are.

Here is a peek at what I did for myself, meant for inspiration for you:

- **Wandering in nature.** I glided through the park with no agenda...and no shoes on. My feet kissed the ground, and I threw a rock down the gravel pathway. I felt the leaves and raised my gaze toward the vivid azure sky through the branches hanging overhead. I sipped hot coffee and recognized the heat of the mug warming my hands. I smiled at strangers passing by as if I held a mystical secret. I do, and so do you.

- **Fly fishing.** Standing in a rushing river, I focused on the still and subtle life of a majestic fish just feet away. Fly fishing became my meditation. My troubles dissolved around me, and my mind and my heart felt free. On my first attempt, I lost my footing on the rocky bottom of the river, and water flooded into my waders. While shocking and cold, this uninvited bath cleansed my body, my heart, and my soul. Since this adventure came after isolation from narcissistic abuse, I laughed for the first time in a long time. When I heard myself laughing, I cried. The sound of my own laughter felt profound, like a perfected, piercing, long note of a violin. Can you feel it? When was the last time you laughed? My smile and heart broke open that day.

- **Sunrises and sunsets.** To build trust, I searched for a reliable source to heal and redeem myself. Every morning the sun ascends, and every evening it descends. The lessons in attachment, integrity, and trust are immense. I woke early to see the sun peek through the horizon. The sun felt like proof that reliable sources existed, and then it set sail over the mountains at twilight. The rising and setting sun is a gift and a reminder of trust that I rely on to this day.

- **Candlelight.** I turned out all the lights and filled my night with the flames of fragrant candles. A subtle, peaceful guest of acceptance joined my evening. I slowed down. I cooked dinner and savored every bite. For once, I tasted the flavors of life.

These rewards are moving, inexpensive, and self-focused. You do not need to contemplate any external prize, a radical hair color, fancy nails, or an expensive purse. These items are uplifting for a moment, but we are renewing you from the inside out. A confident, radiant woman may throw on a sack and light up a room. Your light has always been there. It doesn't go out, and this glow can't be taken away. Yes, it may feel dim. Turn it up!

SOULution #3:
Media Divorce

If a Netflix binge appeared on your reward list, I am so sorry, but dig deeper. For many reasons, parking yourself in front of the screen is a poor idea. You may not see it now, but media is loaded with triggers.

Commercials designed to pull on those heart strings, that advertise cures for a broken heart, that promote glamorized sexual encounters and affairs flourish on the airwaves. It's called drama for a reason. It's called romantic comedy because it's funny. We all have our go-to romantic movie, one that leaves us sobbing when true love finds a way. Somehow this does not depict soul-soothing self-love to me.

Avoid exposure to misguided lead characters turning around their relationship patterns in an hour and falling into the arms of their dream partner. Choose not to expose yourself to this modern fairy tale fallacy. Decide not to be led astray by the lies that you must kiss many frogs in order to find your prince. Navigate toward a path of healing instead.

The neural highways for these false beliefs about Mr. Right arriving to save you are strong. Cut the cord on those beliefs for now. If you don't believe me, I understand. We often need to learn the hard way. Try it if you'd like. Embark upon a night of heartache on the couch. I chose this avenue when I needed to cry. As long as you are aware during the binge session that the unrealistic storyline is hindering your success at love, you will see what I mean, and being on the same page here will benefit you.

Experiment if you'd like, and then let's take a media break from the television, the radio, your phone, your computer, and your tablet. Press the pause button on your favorite movies, the news, and your music. Can you make it for one evening and then a full day? See what happens. You might resist and feel a need to flood your mind with these distractions. Awesome, that feeling means that change is coming upon you.

I wish that I could offer you an enchanting escape from the cacophony. I can't, and I don't want to. It is part of the process. In fact, let your genius mind know this. *Feeling uncomfortable is part of the process, and I am in the process of change.* Be with the feelings that come up during your media fast.

In addition, you may want to look at these mindless activities and recognize that they are nothing but crutches to hold you up as you dismantle your co-dependent relationship with your ex. I drank wine, read self-improvement books, and indulged in spending hours on social media to muffle the sounds of my failure and to ease the anxiety coursing through my veins as I wondered if he would send a text.

Form new relationships using these phrases at the beginning of a sentence: *I am in the process of changing my relationship with myself. I am in the process of changing my relationship with men.* My mind grabbed hold of these mental commands and worked on solutions to break my pattern of relating.

These avowals open the cognitive doors of change. Change is what we want. Change is unpleasant. In fact, change may feel terrifying. Your ego loves the familiar place of pain in which you have been residing for years. Your ego would like you to stay there. In fact, this battle within is *cognitive dissonance. Cognitive dissonance* is when a person holds contradictory beliefs, values, or ideas. I think you will find that your mind and your actions follow the worst of these beliefs.

For example, I knew that spending hours on social media was not a life goal. I knew that comparing my status to others did not benefit my love life. My authentic self knew that comparison robs us of joy, authenticity, and independence. However, my subconscious received a different message. *Social media allows me to connect with friends and family. It is important to stay plugged in.*

The *I am in the process of...* mantras aligned my goals with actions, and I refrained from surfing the internet alone because my mind had evidence of change through my words and actions. I let go of this habit. The subconscious mind wants to hear your true beliefs as well as see some follow-up. Every time I chose a healthy alternative, every time I declined isolated screen time and walked in the park instead, my stupendous mind paid attention. After persistent repetition, my mind stopped sending out inconsistent messages, thereby establishing harmony.

It will take effort and fortitude to move you out of these malignant relationships and heal the wounds of disappointment. I wish to caution you, though. Your internal foundation may crumble, as mine did, while we re-build you from the inside out. Put down the devices and ask yourself, *What would I do with my life if it was not on display and no one was looking?*

Take control. Kryptonite, be gone with you!

CHAPTER 4

Hot Mess

I s your mind spiraling, unsettled, or out of sorts? Does it take insurmountable energy to hold yourself together? If yes, perfect. You are building awareness. I am concerned, however, if you feel as if all is copacetic. I am worried if you feel that you are healthy and secure and that all of your exes are the problem.

It takes two to tango. Don't take on a role in this dynamic that denies your power of choice. Are you sabotaging your healing process through blame and utter denial of your actions? This is a woman who is a Hot Mess.

You have a steady job. You are successful. You have a lot of friends, and you relate to others with ease. Your Instagram account is evidence of how much fun you are having. We covered how untrue that is! You pay the bills, arrive on time, and juggle all of your responsibilities. You may not even be aware that you are in an abusive relationship, as you ignore the emotional beatings and put-downs and pretend that life is fine. But you save face at all costs.

For some reason, your friends seek your advice. You dispense terrific advice, but do you follow it yourself? You are a fighter. You don't give up, and you won't give in, and you are a Hot Mess!

At times, we must give in. We must exercise the ability to forgo control. If you cling to control with sightless arrogance, this road will become longer.

Do you feel like a pawn in this game called life? Do you feel like you are being dragged through the mud, unaware that you may let go of the rope that is towing you? Are you the life of the party, and then do you wake up the next morning revolted by the face staring at you in the mirror? Are you plotting ways to reunite with your ex? Are you scouring the earth for ways to handle his absence? Have you invested in an elaborate plan to stop this foolishness and then failed to follow through with it?

I know that you are all over the Internet, snooping to stay a step ahead of an imminent attack. Do you ask his friends what he is up to? Your mind is now wired for self-protection, fear, and hyper-vigilance. This is no way to live and is textbook madness.

A Hot Mess is full-on berserk in action. It is a well-put-together woman on the verge of bedlam. It is a chick in torrid pursuit of control, answers, and understanding. Have you been there? Have you seen your girlfriends go there?

We laugh our way through these demoralizing rendezvous and coach our fellow love-seekers out of the trenches over a cocktail. However, if you have been isolating yourself and pretending that you are as cool as a cucumber, or if you have been soliciting advice from others who do not suffer from the same infirmity from which you suffer, you are in for a skirmish with life.

If, by chance, your current or ex-partner is certifiably dangerous, you must know about the three anti-social personality traits. According to our good friend Wikipedia, *Narcissism is characterized by grandiosity, pride, egotism, and lack of empathy. Machiavellianism is characterized by manipulation and exploitation of others, and absence of morality, unemotional callousness, and a higher level of self-interest. Psychopathy is characterized by continuous anti-social behavior, impulsivity, selfishness, callous and unemotional traits, and remorselessness.*

If you are acquainted with the sophisticated emotional and psychological manipulation of any individual with one or more of the dark triad mentioned, and you have remained mentally intact for some time now, prepare for all-out inner pandemonium.

You are locked in your own personal prison cell, pacing in circles, babbling to yourself, and running your own tainted decisions by the one person from whom you should not be taking advice right now. You! This confirms your lack of control, confidence in your strong false beliefs, and the construction of a wide hole from which you are going to have to climb out without a ladder.

Is That Me?

So, what is the avatar for a Hot Mess? How do I paint a picture for you of a girl who is lost, addled, and tattered, while still holding herself together?

Many times, too many to count, I noticed that I could not hold my gaze in the mirror. The image facing me did not correlate with the being within. When I did pause for a moment in the mirror, I examined my hair. *Is every strand in place?* I stared down a wrinkle in horror, while peeking at my slim tummy and tight butt. *I've still got it!*

My soul cried out to me while I applied makeup and curled my hair. I may have kept the exterior intact, but I hit rock bottom after hitting rock bottom countless times within.

Oh, yes, Pretty Thang, this is what a Hot Mess does. *Is my eye liner perfect? How about my lipstick? Does my ensemble fit me well?* Young and aloof, I admired myself through rose-colored glasses. I allowed my perception of myself to be tinted, blurred, and distant. I did not know that I had fallen out of touch with myself. Without wit, I kept myself far from the looking glass in order to evade facing the open wounds of the present and scars of the past.

If I had contemplated my countenance with intention, I would have seen my younger self crying out, and I would have crumbled to the reality of my present life. Then, I would have had to admit to being a Hot Mess. This all flew under my radar, mind you. A Hot Mess is not aware. Her eyes may glow, though depth is missing. It's an eyes-wide-shut situation. Her actions don't match what is in her heart. She wants marriage and babies, but she is a far match to it. Pay attention if you cringe at the person looking back at you in the mirror. Is this you?

For a Hot Mess, triggers are inevitable. I could be conversing with a friend, and out of the blue, I could be bushwhacked by a text from a past lust. This might have been a cryptic text along the lines of, *I am at our favorite place. Thinking of you.* This kind of script from an abusive ex is a lure to the best of nowhere.

If I had been wise and ignoring messages already, the texts might have had less gunpowder packed in. Two weeks after the final breakup, I received a text from Ryan. *I'm out with friends, and a woman here smells like you. It made me think of us together.* Unabashed, Ryan drew in some innocent woman wearing the same body oil that I had worn in the hope that I would feel jealous enough to correspond with him.

In hindsight, breadcrumbs thrown out to me with the expectation that I would engage had me grasping at him as a lifeline. True to form, I turned his texted words around in my mind all night visualizing him with this new woman or wondering if he made up her existence as a ploy and blaming myself for the end of the relationship. Regardless, my mind went into circular thinking, and my body tossed throughout the night.

Other examples of true enigmatic text messages that I received from exes during my late thirties include: *I have been working on myself and want to try again. I want to say that I'm sorry for how I treated you. I know that it's too late and that you probably hate me, but I realize now what I had when you and I were together.*

The last example here, from Ryan, pulled me in with ardent hopes that Ryan had changed and that perhaps we could forge a successful, satisfying relationship. This type of hope is kryptonite in its purest form.

The fact remained that Ryan's apologies and sudden awareness baited me. He texted me when other women dumped him, not because of a true desire to reunite with me. I came to my senses. He showed no contrition for the way he had treated me. Authentic regret is changed behavior. Within hours of an apology, Ryan returned to the same old tormenting conduct. This had been his standard operating procedure over the course of the three years between 2014 and 2017.

Flying Monkeys

Strategic manipulators rely on innocent people to do their dirty work. These flying monkeys carry out the abuser's agenda, similar to how the soaring anthropoids in the Wizard of Oz fulfilled the evil deeds of the Wicked Witch of the West. Typical people do not suspect this tactic because they cannot conceive of participating in a deceptive campaign. This controlled move allows for no direct path to the abuser and makes it easier for him to deny accusations. It also may lead you and others being abused to fear anyone in relation to him.

I avoided any person within three degrees of separation from Ryan. After invites to outings where Ryan somehow positioned our mutual friends all together, or direct calls from him inquiring if I had any reason why he couldn't join the group, I felt that I had no choice but to retreat into solitude.

Ryan also frequented the same bars as I did and left inevitable trails of his presence on which I would pick up. A server might mention his name, or a woman would bring him up in conversation. When I could no longer maintain my delusional image of Ryan, I disengaged and fled to the safety of my home. A guy too prideful to be the front man in his own game is a tremendous danger.

Another example occurred when Ryan's friend sent me a text a month after we parted. *I am here with Ryan. We miss hanging out with you. Hope you are well.* His friend didn't know that Ryan had been lying and cheating and that I wanted nothing to do with him. This devious ability to coax my heart with a bit of attention, while excluding me from their activities, was disturbing. However, his oblivious friend did indeed miss me and saw no harm in texting me.

Flying monkeys are pawns in this multi-layered attack. High-level, manipulative abusers use well-crafted techniques to confound your understanding of events and actions. The messages are not invitations to join him on his life's journey, your abuser wants to be reassured that you are on the end of his line.

Self-aware people don't behave this way. It is hard to believe this after living with this poison for so long, but trust me, your future man will not miss you for ego-gain, he will be with you. You will never wonder where he is or if you are or are not in a relationship with him.

After receiving texts like the one from Ryan mentioned above, the whole scene changed. The peptide addiction cycle sparked a chain of explosives in my nervous system, derailing me from the present. Ambush texts don't take over your life, they become your life, and a horror movie unfolds that seems to never end, with anxiety and fear as the lead characters.

A glazed expression pasted itself to my face, my chest caved in, and my hands sweated following the dinging alert of Ryan's text. When in the company of friends, words zipped past my ears, but I couldn't hear them after hearing the phone. My mind became consumed. I reverted inside to tend to the inner war of gaslighting messages.

My amygdala converted my nervous system into a team of first responder junkies. Leaping out of their seats with an adrenaline rush of excitement as the sirens rang and ignited their hero instincts to a call for action, they slid down poles, rattling my limbs. Terrified and thrilled about the thought of hunting down this fire and snuffing it out, my invisible rescuers ran themselves ragged through my system, only to fall exhausted (mission incomplete). I looked like a vibrant woman and felt like an aching geriatric.

It could be hours or even days before my rescue crew iced the burning fire in my heart. That's it! A restroom retreat would not be long enough to gain composure. Time for an Irish Good-Bye. An Irish Good-Bye is an impolite and necessary defense that allows one to sneak away from the party, the bar, or the gathering without farewells in order to save face.

I avoided confrontation and any situation in which I would have to admit that I did not have control over my own life. Ryan had me feeling like an emotional hostage in love with her capturer. Stockholm Syndrome was in full effect. Stockholm Syndrome is a psychological response wherein a victim of abuse bonds with the abuser. A state of fawning occurs where one uses people-pleasing skills to diffuse conflict. Does this ring true with you?

My friends never questioned my erratic behavior when I fled without warning. In retrospect, they were not close, caring friends, or perhaps they battled their own issues. If they discussed concern for my well-being, it was not with me. Taking full responsibility, my misery matched these unhealthy and unsupportive ties. I accepted friendships that aligned with this chaotic, out-of-touch inner energy that I possessed.

Without much effort, I attracted other wounded souls. We partied together, as misery loves company, and my tribe and I were a match made in hell. We were the life of the party. Whether a celebration or a pity party, we rocked it out to disguise and drown out the truth of unfulfilled dreams. Conversations turned into nothing but a battle of dramas. We swam in our own aloofness, denial, and poor advice.

You may feel somewhat vindicated in your irrational thoughts. *Awesome, she is a colossal hot mess too!* As you nourish each other with your recycled traumas, healing eludes all of you.

If you could rise above this and peer down at yourself, you would have a hard time believing this disabling scene. You would see how you contradict yourself and play into your own confirmation bias. You would be appalled by your blatant disrespect for yourself, how you are treating your own body, and the choices that you have made in the company you keep. With all of the love in the world, I hope that these fellow Hot Messes have moved through and out of this scene, as I have. At the time, however, a *save yourselves!* mentality propelled my emergency exit.

I can hear myself complaining, searching for solid ground, clawing on the door of reality, unable to pry it open. In fact, I did attempt to escape. My awareness tapped at the window and peeked around inside, showing me the mess in which I resided despite my tidy and well-kept living space. I paid attention, I saw it, and so will you. Go easy here. I know that facing the reality of your emotional, psychological, verbal, and physical abuse, whether present or from the past, may be difficult. You are stronger than you think.

Time Out! Where Are You?

In writing this book for you, I need to take a time out. The following is an excerpt from my writing journey as I moved from surviving to thriving. When you meet this kind of resistance in your own healing, keep going.

December 26, 2019

> *This right here. I don't feel like writing this. My body is annoyed and unsettled. I keep adjusting my legs in my chair and wiggling around. What is stirring? What is irritating me? Maybe I overindulged in the holiday cookies that I had for breakfast. A dumb move with qualms on top. I know that sugar makes my stomach churn.*

But, it's not that. This song is bothering me, and I love this song. A warning untoward is gripping me.

It's this writing. It is this book. I don't want to do it. I want to be normal or average or whatever the word is for not abused! I don't want to be trapped in recovery of narcissistic abuse, and there are some days that I fail to prove to myself that I am not. I feel sick, and in writing this, I do not feel free. I feel cursed and as though I will never heal from a victim-mindset. I feel damaged and assaulted, and I bet you do too.

I confessed to a friend that I wished that this stupid book was finished, and she gulped in astonishment. *Don't say that! Your book will be great.* The listener to my rant objected, scolding me for my expression and informing me that my words shape my reality. *This book is bad* also slipped from my mouth to a kind-hearted listener. I scurried to stuff the disparaging words back down my throat, but it was too late. He missed what I wished to express and built up my writing abilities, insisting that I not put that pessimistic energy into my book. I felt ashamed for uttering the truth about how I felt.

I wish that I had been allowed to vocalize my emotions. I did feel that this book had been wrought with my personal tribulations (my exact sentiment at the time) because abuse was not a topic that I enjoyed wallowing in while writing. I did wish that this book could be finished because I wanted the experiences that I detail in *Trigger Happy* to be far, far behind me. I also wanted those around me to understand how insidious the psychological abuse became.

As you might well understand, this is more than a book, and once I made it out of that limiting belief, now I am able to help you.

More emotions emerged from this uneasy place within.

Why can't I find love? Why does it require so much intentional effort for me and not for others? Why am I spending another holiday alone after shelling out thousands of dollars for intense inner therapy to help me find my soulmate?

I feel that I have to explain to any man who may want to be intimate that I think that I am defective, that I may have attachment problems, and that I have been manipulated, cheated on, and abused. *Am I so difficult to love?*

Did you notice how I fell into that aforementioned dreaded cycle of *Why?* I felt like damaged goods, unworthy of love, like I had been branded as faulty, and that I am not good enough for marriage and family because a self-centered mate chose to cheat, lie, and abuse. Those had been his choices. Why must I miss out on true love?

Trauma changes us. This is no joke. I wanted to turn away from writing this book for myself and for you. I felt like a phony and like I haven't really healed and have no right to attempt to show you the way out because I still feel scared and triggered too. I wanted to delete this section so that you couldn't see it, but this is real. This is what I want you to see.

I thought that I would never recover from narcissistic abuse, and I want you to know that I felt this way. I am not standing on a platform yelling down to you, *Look at me. I am healed.* There will be times when you feel like giving up too. Know that it is okay to feel this as you are exiting the Hot Mess stage.

In order to reclaim your authentic truth, you will have to abide your irritating feelings until they play out. Sit with your body as it stirs, and love yourself through what appears as uncontrollable sensations in your body. Don't reach for a crutch. Ride it out. I have done it in this second with you, and you can do it as well.

Warning!

A sudden recovery from narcissistic abuse is haphazard. The trauma did not develop overnight. Leaving the relationship is the essential first step, and it has often taken people years to withdraw. The *Why* questions are implanted in our schema, the pattern of thoughts and behaviors that organize information and morph into our belief system. Perhaps these beliefs are sometimes difficult to find and may have been running the show for decades.

At a habitual level, reactive patterns toward abuse are being reinforced. Similar to following the same ski track, over time the impressions become permanent, and taking alternative routes require greater effort. In fact, if I would have stopped writing this book when I became so weary of the whole thing, I would have been allowing one of my patterns to take over. I did not. I stayed with it and with you to forge a new path. Instill within yourself this connection to self and to others to hold you up.

Don't abandon yourself in your recovery. If you desert yourself here, you will flee an advantageous ally when challenges appear. That is not what you want. Your relationship with yourself is vital. Your relationship with yourself is training ground for the love you seek.

Now back to the mirror and our precious Hot Mess...

One pitfall that a Hot Mess may encounter is an inability to stay focused on healing. We live in a society of distraction. Even the most heartfelt aspirations to overcoming abuse and implementing change may fall to shreds in split seconds when face-to-face with societal temptation.

Whether this means hopping on a dating app to seek attention (Train Wreck move), partying the pain away (A Hot Mess Rally), or fixated on making money (I Don't Need a Man Positioning), our pleasure center may grab the wheel, and instant gratification replaces a genuine cure. The cycle of survival extends to years.

It is important that you seek support in taking responsibility, or you should expect to become derailed time after time. Imagine what this does to your self-esteem. Imagine the heartache that you will suffer when you realize that you can't keep an agreement with yourself.

A Hot Mess tries to go it alone. Abuse takes on a life of it's own long after the abuser has fled the scene and you need support. Ending the relationship is most often not enough. Decide in this moment to whom you will turn for help. With whom are you willing to be vulnerable and confess that you need a hand? In rising out of my own turmoil, I made the commitment to be that hand for you. I implore you though, to take the route that is right for you. I stand in partnership for your liberation from abuse.

A second grueling factor that adds tenfold to the problem when you're a Hot Mess is the onset of paranoia. As you bring awareness to your love life, you may sense a dramatic feeling of being overwhelmed. *Oh, my God, what else did I neglect to acknowledge while avoiding the mirror?*

For example, I defended my use of the Irish Good-Bye as a way of not interrupting the enjoyment and partying of others. The reality is that I had been rude and that I ran from the truth.

With this fresh awareness follows fits of self-judgment. This becomes a frenetic time. It's as if the ego shrieked, *Okay, we are going that way. Let's go!* This leads to the swinging of the pendulum to the other side, from oblivious to enlightened. It also is a strict and degrading way of thinking in black and white.

You may pounce right to the Internet to check up on him to find out what you misunderstood before. You might trace past e-mails and texts to hone into where and when he cheated. You may see yourself as a super sleuth, doing detective work as to when, where, and how he met her and why you didn't see it coming.

After executing an investigation into my past, I discovered that cheating on me had been the norm. Mike had been with another woman when I accepted an overnight babysitting position. Ryan flirted, kissed, and perhaps pursued more with strangers on business trips, all the while answering my texts until he disappeared for the night with another woman.

Shocked by the betrayal and by my own trust in these men, I lost confidence. I gave my heart away expecting that it would be protected and honored, and these men had a different perspective on love and relationships than I did. This was my mistake. Owning it now gives me power to choose a different future. You are the only one in charge of protecting your heart.

Be easy on yourself as you recognize your own missteps. Do not judge and blame yourself. Do take responsibility and accountability for your actions. I don't know why we flood ourselves with blame, but the ego highlights our shortcomings as a signal notifying us that we could have avoided this quagmire if we had done x, y, or z.

The ego keeps us safe with this behavior as if we're being attacked by a lion. But it equals crazy-making in modern instances of adultery.

Paranoia and judgment equate to a Hot Mess of catastrophic proportions. Brace yourself, there is more.

A third predicament occurs when emotional abuse is present. One tactic of narcissistic abusers has been coined *Hoovering*. Named after the Hoover vacuum, the abuser sucks his unsuspecting woman into a relationship with him by using manipulative tactics that cause his target to respond, react, and to hand her power over to him.

This happens at your most vulnerable times and plays off of your instability, contributing to the mayhem. He may appeal to your caregiver instincts by needing your loving support. He may blab to you about his troubles or let you know of a sick parent or a pet, tugging on your heart strings and pulling you closer. Yet, he makes no mention of your needs for a relationship.

I saw this as cultivating rapport, but I never once revealed any of my problems to Mitch, for example, because there had not been room for it. He relayed stories of his travails and his dilemmas as I remained silent while overcoming skin cancer and searching for an answer to severe nerve pain that I developed in my arms and back. Never once did I divulge to him how I suffered. I made his issues top priority and utilized the martyr tactic to which I had been exposed by my Catholic upbringing.

The sole purpose for which I am writing this chapter for you is not to call you a Hot Mess, but rather so that you will know that you must get real about yourself and your own relationship patterns. It is easy to ignore emotional and verbal abuse when you are swimming in it. It is a survival mechanism to dress up and carry on with your day as if there is no other choice. I want better for you. I want you out of abuse and living a life that you will love.

I did the excruciating investigation, the trial and error, and the manic research in the hope of freeing myself. Those hopes solidified into wisdom and tools for you and me both.

Read this book to the end, and love that you are doing it for yourself. Even if it is the first commitment that you keep to yourself, you will recover your dignity. I hope to make this easy on you and allow my words to flow with you along the way.

SOULutions

I am choosing to deliver this content in a way that you may hear it right now. I hope that my attention to detail and understanding of what you are going through is evident. You may encounter blocks and barriers in your recovery that you may overlook. These low dips that fly under the radar may take you out of the healing game, keep you rooted to a cycle of abuse, and falling prey to the same old patterns. Don't despair. I have been there as well, and let's take you past the barricades.

Below are three SOULutions intended to guide you through the Hot Mess stage. Use the same intensity that you bring to relationships to care for your own soul now. Your own spirit will lead you out.

SOULution #1:
Earmuffs

Despite attracting others in the same low, miserable spirit space in which you find yourself, you are also going to attract those who wish to give you advice. Chances are that the people offering you guidance are in the same boat as you are. Taking advice from friends in the same sinking ship is counterproductive.

You may also be bombarded with words of wisdom from people so outside of where you are that you can't even hear these precious nuggets. In fact, these words may feel piercing or condescending. These folks cannot relate and shouldn't be expected to.

For all of these reasons, I am offering you an easy, convenient tool called Earmuffs.

As you may have guessed, you cover your ears with imaginary Earmuffs and then nod when people offer you their unsolicited advice about your life, your traumas, and your feelings. I am not exempt from using Earmuffs myself.

I suggested that my friends protect their own ears with me. No friend, family member, or coach knows better what you need than you do yourself. The reason why I am able to prescribe this SOULution for you at this time is because you chose this book and this information for yourself. A part of you is called to these influential words.

Allow me to elaborate. Please don't take unsolicited advice right now, even from sane people. This may make you feel even more like you're going nuts. Receiving unwelcome advice from the well-established, coupled people in your life is like cauterizing your open wounds with a red-hot poker.

This is not the goal, yet. Don't aim to be like these couples for now. You may even admit to them, *Yes, I am a bit of a hot mess. I appreciate our friendship and your advice, but I need to listen to the one person who I have not been hearing. Myself.* You will, in time, seek out solace and wisdom from others, when you are ready to hear it and you are all on the same level.

As for the viperous people swirling around you, shut them out as well. I opened my house to an acquaintance after she lost her job. I felt shocked by the way she ended up treating me. Close friends cautioned me that she would confabulate about me with others behind my back. I thought that she needed to be loved, so I didn't let these words bother me.

After Ryan visited one night, he even exclaimed, "That girl is not your friend!"

When I heard her gossiping about me on the phone in my own home, I realized that things had gone too far. Granted, I had been a Hot Mess, so in a way I invited this drama into my life. I heard her suggest to her comrade that I take all the guys, that it's not fair, and that I had been unfaithful to my boyfriend. When you are a Hot Mess, you might be careless enough to justify this type of soliloquy.

However, her accusations were not based in fact and felt to me like delusions based on a competition that I had not entered into with her. I had not cheated on my narcissistic boyfriend, nor had I even slept with him yet. Not only did she engage in her own verbal onslaught behind my back, she became the sole ring leader of a smear campaign against me. A smear campaign is a plan executed to tarnish a person's reputation and discredit their worth.

I know of her efforts because friends relayed her comments to me at the time, and my friend, Levin, even told me that she had sidled up to him at a bar three years after we stopped speaking to each other and had vilified me. He halted her attack, *Ellen is my friend, and I don't agree with you.* He shut her down. When Levin informed me of this, my face paled, and the trigger cocked back. To this day, I am perplexed and terrified by her behavior, and I would avoid this person at all costs.

She didn't count on the fact that real friends knew the truth about me, my values, and my life. How would I have survived this without them? They believed in me when I felt at risk of losing myself.

The point of sharing this smear campaign against me is to point out to you that I believed this person to be my friend. I went to her for advice. I am grateful now that I did not place my self-worth in her opinion. I did the healing after over-trusting her and others. If you have people in your life like this, please use the earmuff strategy.

People believing rumors are not helpful to you now. You don't need justice from these people, especially if they are not inquiring about your well-being.

If you're in the middle of your own betrayal or smear campaign, disengage from the abuser, and seek shelter in the arms of friends who care for you.

You may question how a friend or a peer you once trusted or cared for could turn his or her back on you. I puzzled over how my peer could hurt enough to spend her time talking about me. I welcomed her into my home because I had the resources to do so. I offered food to her in order to help her get back on her feet because I believed that my friends would do the same for me if the situation was reversed.

Throw your Earmuffs on, wrap a scarf around your mouth, and ride away.

I now recognize when a person is talking out of both sides of his or her mouth, and I run in the other direction. If you choose to hang around and make sense out of the nonsense of a smear campaign, you will fall into a hole of your own making. For now, slide some cozy ear-muffs over your ears and listen only to your own heart's desires.

SOULution #2:
Shut It Down!

Okay, Sweetheart, that ornery self-talk that is draining your inner being needs to be silenced. Yes, that voice in your head convincing you that it is your fault and that if you changed who you are your love life would improve needs to go. The voice that is stopping you from choosing better and has you believing that you are unworthy of love is lying to you.

After ceasing to listen to the fallacies of others, it's time to shut down your own inner scoundrel's voice. Sounds awesome, right? Flip the switch off, and gain inner peace. I want you to enlist the fierceness in you. I want you to be serious about this. After you shut it down, I know that that inner voice will flick back on like a psychotic horror movie. I do realize what I am requesting of you. I have done it.

Today, at this point in time, you are going to stake claim to your life, and you are going to shut down all unfriendly self-talk. An awareness of this inner chattering is occurring right now. You will hear the voice that has been claiming that these problems are all your fault. You are developing an awareness that you did not have before and transforming as a result.

I believe that you have been so outward-focused that you hear your abuser's voice and the opinions of others more than you hear yourself. You have to hear the inner critic to shut it down. This is the first step in a series of progressions that will occur in your magnificent brain.

Let me break this down. I want you to listen. Turn off the car radio, take a stroll without music, and listen. Be an observer in your life, and listen to the words sprinting, swirling, dancing, and jolting around in your mind. Pay attention to the words that land like bricks and the thousands of put-downs scurrying around in there. If you lived there, you would be nauseated by this scrambled negativity.

Fair warning, that cute and endearing inner critic that likes to keep you where you are, it will also lob spectacular compliments your way. A decoy to distract you from the truth, the internal dictator shifts blame away from itself. *I don't push you down, we got this. You are confident. It's those other people with the problems, not you.*

Sit with this. Nod, and wait until the truth surfaces. When you spend time alone, without distractions, you will hear the truth and the words that have been playing in the background of your life. Your alone time will unveil the puppet master yanking the strings of your choices. Surrounding yourself with silence will diminish the consistent noise that is at play.

You will climb out of this, and you can meet this challenge by taking full responsibility for your life. If I had not conquered my negative inner dialogue, I might still be trying to convince others that the lies spread about me were wrong. I would have desperately needed them to know the truth. Can you imagine that dead end road?

As horrible as it sounds, Who in your life would like to see you fail? Shut down your inner critic and you will recognize whom in your life needs to go as well.

SOULution #3:
Crushin' It

For a short period of time, you may feel like you are at war. Anger, resentment, fear, and confusion may surface. This is not a time to be graceful, this is a time to be serious. Focus on you.

When I recommended that you crush the *Whys*, did you do it? Maybe you did this in solitude, but are you also calling up that girlfriend and running *Whys* by her, hoping for answers? Let's crush the *Whys* in that scenario too, and let's grind those quarrelsome thoughts about yourself into atomic particles.

This is all overwhelming when you are in it. Others threw advice at me when I felt like a Hot Mess, and this led to my irritation. I felt incompetent, alone, and lost. I couldn't live up to childhood expectations, and I felt pissed off at what I saw as the fallacy of love. I was angry that those around me acted like I was in a hard spot when they were unwilling to admit that they too had been stuck.

Take my hand, and I will lead you through this jungle inside your brain. I want you to know that you are not alone. Human beings have negative thoughts ricocheting around their heads and taking them out of the game. This includes the successful married couple whom you want to emulate, your sister, your boss, your friends, and your enemies. It is how we handle these thoughts that determines how well we fare.

Following are some simple steps that you may take to crush your disagreeable thoughts:

Step 1: Notice your self-talk. The reason I suspect that you have the diligence to conquer these rodents in your mind is because you may be engaged in blocking, drowning out, and avoiding this uncharitable self-talk. This takes massive effort and is the reason why you are exhausted.

We are going to take that same vitality and turn it head-on toward combating this derogatory chatter. In this step, I want you to listen. Write down these thoughts like you are on a mission to capture them and store them on a page.

Step 2: Be your own best friend. Read your inopportune thoughts as if the person you love most in the world spoke them to you over coffee. Perhaps your niece, your best friend, or your sister called you and shared this brutal inner dialogue about herself. Think about how you would react when she blames herself. *It's all my fault. I can't do anything right. I should have... I could have...*

Challenge these false truths, stand up to them, and shut them down as you would defend the honor of your loved one. Inquire as to each adverse belief. *Is this statement the truth about me? Where did I first hear these unpleasant words?* It is possible that the voice of a parent, a teacher, or a coach is gallivanting around in your mind like a gremlin on the loose.

Can you feel the false belief dissipate from this angle?

Step 3: Replacement therapy. What do you do with shoes that are too tight or items of clothing that don't fit in all the right places? Simple. You return them and replace them with a more suitable choice. Slap a return-to-sender label on those distasteful thoughts, and order up phrases that you have been longing to hear. Below are a few examples of statements that I have returned for an upgrade:

- You think too much. **Upgrade:** I have an outstanding and active brain that needs my attention.

- You are too sensitive. **Transformation:** I am sensitive, strong, and capable.

- It's all my fault that the relationship is over. **Re-frame:** I take full responsibility for my part in this relationship and accept only what is in my control.

If I hold the reins to alter the trajectory of the situation, then it is my responsibility to own the situation. If I can't adjust the sails, I acknowledge that it is outside of my control and cast my line into the wind. The relationship tension may belong to the other person, or it may be beyond the control of both of us. Accept this, and claim what is yours and yours alone to own. Return destructive criticism back to the sender. The heavy load will decrease.

Bit by bit, you will regain your sanity by availing yourself of these SOULutions. It is vital to your recovery that you schedule these action steps every day. This type of soul care needs to be a part of your daily routine in order to gain momentum. Without the repetition, your ego will slide right in and nudge you over to repeat your old patterns.

The resulting frustration is mind-numbing and disheartening. I don't want you to hurt. Follow these steps, no matter how elementary they seem. Find the strength in the simplicity. Complex analyzing will hold you captive and beholden to your Hot Mess self.

Your house is crawling with Automatic Negative Thoughts (ANTS). Take the time to crush these ANTS, extinguish these creepy intruders, and censor the outside noise. I know, facing these thoughts feels intimidating, but I am certain that you are bigger than any of your fears.

CHAPTER 5

Freeze

The fight/flight/freeze response is the automatic natural reaction to danger. What once was considered a survival response to imminent danger from a life threatening attack from a flesh-eating animal has now evolved into a maladaptive reaction to modern perceived threats and stressors (like a guest posing a few questions about your ex at a dinner party). It is clear that this may cause uninvited anguish in our lives.

In short, one will either stay and fight, flee to the hills and hide, or freeze and become paralyzed to ward off danger. A chain of hormonal and physiological reactions assists the target in fighting off an attack, fleeing her predator, or freezing in the moment. Thank goodness for this. This is how we have survived here on earth. However, our concrete jungles are now crawling with non-life-threatening stressors, such as relationship and career pressures as well as traffic jams and frustrating inconveniences to our routine way of life.

I cannot speak from the perspective of a fighter, and fleeing terrified me because my legs would not move. I have been freezing in the face of danger since I was 4 years old.

At the impressionable age of 11, I had an encounter with a grade school friend that was worth suppressing, according to my highly sensitive mind. Memory suppression is a complicated and controversial phenomenon.

I believed that a therapist would suggest that I had suppressed a dramatic and scarring trauma because I was caught up in repugnant relationship patterns as an adult, and then I would re-live a ghastly event on the therapist's couch. In my mind, I thought the awareness of the catastrophic problem would interrupt the lives of my entire family and leave me cast out for life for revealing a hidden tragedy.

It seemed that the bias around suppressed memories is that a family member, a teacher, a coach, or someone close had to be revealed and blamed. The thought of going to a therapist brought to my heart fear of being made helpless and a significant fear of retaliation from the threatening person. The whole scene meant that I must be damaged goods and unworthy of love.

However, suppression didn't last as my awareness grew. As I chipped away at the brick wall encapsulating my heart and soul, excavating the events behind my false beliefs and reoccurring patterns, I found answers. The once-suppressed thoughts brought ease and understanding rather than alarm and despair. My feelings related to the past felt manageable because I am an adult now, and knowing the root of my destructive relationship patterns and my defense mechanisms was monumental in my recovery.

As this suppressed memory from age 11 surfaced, I knew that it had happened because I recalled detail after detail. Neither a false memory nor shocking, I simply reviewed the scenes and did not re-live the attack to my boundaries, which I will soon describe in detail. Suppressed memories will emerge when you are hardy enough and ready to heal. Believe. Know that you are strong enough to handle it.

I was ready, and the memory popped up inside my thoughts where I could see it. Before, it had passed by my consciousness every now and then like a cloud sailing by with no real feeling attached or emotion involved. The memory played on loop in the background of my mind. It felt so familiar that I didn't notice it. One gloomy fall morning in 2018, however, I investigated this memory.

Yikes! That is not a healthy childhood experience!

My therapist at the time pointed out that I had been physically and verbally assaulted more than one time throughout my life. We discussed this in a matter-of-fact way, like two television broadcasters announcing today's weather report. I did not feel hysterical, and I did not flip out on the therapist's couch. Traumatic events had been my norm. I had survived the events already and had either dealt with them or numbed them out. I simply saw what needed to be seen here in the present in order to heal the past and move forward.

I found odd consolation in receiving validation that I had been violated and that I had cause to have been defensive and anxious for most of my life. Many infractions surfaced, some more dominant than others.

A childhood classmate crossed the line of my physical boundaries. I had been lied to and cheated on by a plenitude of partners in college and then verbally gaslit to hide their deceit. I had close friends sleep with my boyfriends behind my back, and my problems continued to evolve to a point of physical abuse. The reason why I couldn't see or understand the assaults on my soul was because I was in survival mode, and these events were typical and normalized. From an early age, I believed that this world was a shit show and that I had to endure it.

My instinct was to freeze and ignore abuse as fast as possible. I have resorted to bottling up my fear, brushing off the ass-grab by a man with ill intent or deflecting the glare of a sick adult male undressing teenage bodies with his eyes. I never mentioned verbal abuse or boundary invasions as a line of personal preservation. It was easier on me to pretend it didn't happen.

Presented below are a few of the childhood stories of when I froze and why I think that the survival method of freezing, especially as a highly sensitive person, causes such long-lasting impairment for individuals.

As a child I felt rejected by my sibling. Whether this is fact or not, I felt it at the time. I had no choice but to join my other siblings in their rough and tumble outdoor activities. If I didn't play sports with them, if I couldn't hold my own, if my school friends were busy, I had no one with whom to play, and I felt alone.

My best friend in kindergarten happened to be a boy. Kyle lived on my block. He didn't play sports as the other boys did. Instead, he spent hours indoors honing his craft of origami and playing a tuba, which he could barely hold up to play the notes. His unique way of seeing the world and his peculiar hobbies fascinated me, though I had been forced to walk the tightrope of fitting in as I balanced between the group of athletic boys and my quirky 5-year-old soul friend.

When I reached seventh grade, other girls pressured me to be interested in boys in an intimate way. I could not switch gears. How could I kiss the boy who had been my best friend since kindergarten? The thought overwhelmed me.

Plus, Kyle and I had played *I'll show you if you show me* in his basement in the midst of a game of hide-and-seek while in kindergarten. Kyle must have been feeling the peer pressure as well, because in seventh grade he divulged to the other guys that he had seen me *down there*. Mortified, I ducked out of sight any time I saw his crew together.

The boys teased me as if it had happened in that moment rather than at the innocent age of 5. My feeling of shame felt so great that I did not tell a soul about this until after college.

I also stopped attending Kyle's birthday parties and explained to my parents and his that I had been the only girl in attendance for seven years. I felt as if I had done something morally wrong, and my attempts to reason with the middle school boys only added fuel to the teasing.

As troublesome as this was, an unexpected and manipulative blackmail attack left an open wound in my psyche during this same school year.

Joanie, a seventh grade friend from a neighboring public school who happened to be sexually active, hinted to me that I must be homosexual, since I didn't have a boyfriend yet. *Oh, here we go.* I assured her that this was not the case, but somehow I developed an inability to plead my case under these false accusations. I have come to know that defensiveness is one of the weakest of all energies, and manipulators thrive off of it when you take this stance. I did not understand why she targeted me at the time.

I thought that I made a good argument. My seventh grade class at the Catholic school had four boys and thirteen girls in it. Slim pickings, even if I had wanted a boyfriend.

Joanie shot my rebuttal down. In Joanie's eyes, the facts remained. An athletic, flat-chested, tough girl like myself with no attachment to a boy at the ripe old age of 11 years equaled lesbian to her, and she felt set on proving it so that she could spill her discovery to others in the class.

I recall standing in her bedroom doorway when she decided that she wanted us to see if I liked girls by physically touching me to discover how I felt about it. This concept had not crossed my mind for even a single moment of my life to that point. I had zero interest in engaging in her plan.

In an instant, my nervous system skyrocketed. At the immature age of 11, I verbally defended my sexuality, and I appeared to be the underdog in the debate. She then struck biases as evidence. Joanie claimed that I was good at sports and that I had never kissed a boy. Both true, and yet her convictions discombobulated me and did not point at a sexual preference for girls in my mind or my body.

Yes, I kicked ass on a soccer field and a basketball court, and kudos to any of you girls and women who can too. Athletic performance does not define your sexual preferences.

As the debate subsided, Joanie threatened to inform all of the kids in the class that she thought I must be homosexual. She hinted that she would not reveal her misinformed label of me if I participated in her touching experiment to see if I liked girls. I protested, and the issue dropped for that moment. I stuffed my fear of her manipulation into the pit of my stomach. I prayed that she would soon forget about this topic.

During another visit to her home, however, we were playing pretend house in her basement when she flabbergasted me. I was feigning sleep as a character in our role play of house when she lay down on top of me and pressed her body into mine. She rubbed her well-developed breasts on my chest as she pinned me down.

I froze.

Paralyzed, I had no idea how to handle this advance. I disappeared into my mind, and to this day, I feel like I blacked out because I don't remember much, until her mom interrupted her actions by opening the basement door and inquiring about what we were doing. Thank you Joanie's mom!

Following this event, I lived in constant fear that she would spread the rumor that I was a lesbian. In addition, I worried about Kyle's news flash that I had revealed myself to him in kindergarten. Ill-equipped for this kind of combat and lacking self-confidence to go head-to-head with him on the social battlefield, this state of fear and anxiety became my normal.

I believed that I would meet my husband in college and that I would be a virgin skipping down the aisle. With this far-off fantasy intact, I saw no need for physical distractions and sexual experimenting. The consternation, the fear, and the threatening manipulation of these incidents sent my body and my mind into a dark tunnel of turmoil.

I didn't want to go to school. I pleaded to stay home, and the emotions that I pushed down produced a consistent tummy ache. I also had strep throat so many times that I am now allergic to the medication used to heal it. Physical ailments resulted in the true loss of my voice.

I believe that I manifested physical pain from these ignored emotional problems. If this is the truth, it is not surprising that my throat (needed to express my objection) swelled and blistered all throughout grade school and into high school. My throat felt like I had swallowed glass, and I lost both my physical voice and my authentic voice. The impact of these childhood events planted a seed of low self-worth within my being. Unbeknownst to me, this seed was nourished by every attack on my boundaries thereafter, and my poor self-worth flowered within.

Assaults

Assault refers to the act of inflicting unwanted physical harm or contact on a person. Threatening or attempting to hurt another person is also a crime. For the sake of our discussion, assaults may be physical, verbal, or emotional as well as energetic.

The string of assaults that I suffered started with verbal manipulation and then turned physical. The slow initiation of these assaults could not be recognized as so egregious that I ran or fought for my life. A man did not bust down my bedroom door and assault me. Covert in nature, these sneak attacks resulted after giving my trust to a person whom I thought I knew.

I am confounded by socially accepted terms for covert attacks that disenfranchise the victim because of the relationship to the aggressor. Date rape, for example, is still rape, and yet the woman often freezes instead of fights, as the evening shifts to a place that the woman never expected. Placing herself with the assailant lands her in a position of choice, and she may be blamed for asking for it. How many of us have become paralyzed when innocent interest in a guy turns to physical boundary intrusions?

One may then question her feelings, wondering if she did cause the problem by her willingness to go on the date or to have the man in her company. Twisted within, we, therefore, bury the shame of not defending ourselves by fighting or fleeing and live with the inner shame of the assault.

I have done this, and I want you to know that I understand if you have as well. It is still an assault, and you have the right to heal this wound to the fullest extent possible.

As with my seventh grade boundary-blur in the basement of a childhood peer, I had no idea what to do within the confines of covert attacks. I didn't want my friends or family or teachers to know. Enter shame. I decided that adults do not listen. Enter not being heard. I decided that my secret was not safe to disseminate. Enter *You are alone in an unsafe world.*

I must admit that the intrusion into my physical space felt difficult, and freezing up brought shame, but I managed to protect my mind and my heart by detaching. The verbal accusations pitched a tent and set up home in my subconscious. I had been called a lesbian by one girl and a prude by guys with whom I moved too slow physically.

When Joanie could not convince others that I must be a lesbian, she spat ugly words at me. "I hope that you never have kids. You'll probably end up fat someday. So there!"

Children may be cruel, whether because of nurture or nature, we may never know.

As an adult, I may now review these boundary invasions in an empowering way. To what level have your own boundaries been crossed? My seventh grade friend had been another hurt child seeking to make sense of her own suffering. My kindergarten friend succumbed to peer pressure that he felt early on as he discovered how to fit in. Most important, we were all children. You may understand and forgive mistreatment while not condoning it or allowing any further blurring of boundaries in your life.

As a vulnerable, impressionable child, the threats, words, and accusations stayed in my subconscious, and patterns of *not enough* thinking flourished, a perfect cocktail that led me to be buried in self-loathing and misled about my worthiness. You see, I am 44 years old in April of 2021. I have never been married, and as my seventh grade classmate wished would happen, I have never had a baby (yet).

Now what would make a loving, monogamous woman not see marriage and family for herself?

Fear.

Fear of emotional and psychological abuse will rob you of your life, long after the abuser is gone. If you suppressed physical and psychological attacks and froze, the impact needs healing even if it is decades later. My shares are of the simplest and most innocent, and yet the negative core beliefs were adopted.

I can't recover the days that I spent plotting a way to stay safe to thwart Joanie's attempt at manipulation, to make sure that the class did not find out about the rumor that she planned to spread. An internal battle may ensue when you attempt to stay on your abuser's good side in order to avoid more harm. I am using the childhood example here, but apply this lesson to your own life. I know that there are more atrocious assaults that occur. I do not wish to expose you to those stories. My goal is to awaken what needs to be healed within you.

I compartmentalized the encroachments to my physical boundaries and the verbal assaults in hopes that they would fade away. I also thought that I would die if people found out. As you can see, it is not just the event, it is how you interpret the event that matters most.

I can't change what happened in the past, and that is all right with me. I am not out to accuse anyone of assault. I can, however, take back today. This is why revealing suppressed memories is so rewarding. Your power is in you. This inner wisdom is easy to find if you follow the trigger to its source and heal what lies beneath. The answers are not hidden, and you will find them when you are ready. Prepare yourself.

Fight and Flight

I believe that challenging life lessons emerge in order to test our resolve and commitment to our values, to help us heal the past, to manage life in a different way, and to simply figure this nonsense out. As a result, I needed to find another way to face adversity besides freezing. Without sending any type of request to the universe, I had been granted myriad opportunities to respond in different ways.

At the age of 22, I had graduated college in Memphis and was dating a guy who lived in Nashville. I believe that I met Scott at my work and then again at the jam band concert to which my friend took me. No matter.

All I know is that I thought he was pretty damn amazing. Scott was tall, dark, and handsome. His hazel eyes made me weak in the knees. The fact that he seemed to like me too surprised me. It makes me laugh now, remembering my naiveté and acknowledging that I crushed hard on Scott. Wearing a veil over my face, I fell right in, head over heels.

Though sexy and smart, Scott also acted invincible and decided in haste to get in the middle of a party scene at the concert. To him, there would be no harm done, though it was clear to all that the guests were partaking in something more than booze. Well, to make a long story short, his choice to engage with the group caught up with him. He was sent to prison. Yes, prison.

Six months after we began dating, Scott was snatched out of my life. As the band played the first set of the concert that we attended in Asheville, North Carolina, Scott's life of freedom was interrupted, and he was thrashed down with his face on the concrete by four police officers twenty feet away from me.

I froze at first, seeing Scott's disoriented, beautiful eyes. I watched in horror as the scene unfolded. As the police officers propped him up on his feet, hands cuffed behind his back, Scott's amygdala hopped directly to flight mode. He bolted toward the exit and out to the street, running toward freedom with his hands secure behind his back. Three cops chased him down and slammed him to the ground once more. All of them disappeared into a police vehicle.

I felt lucky that I had thought to ask Scott for my car keys, since Scott had driven my car to the concert. He had no idea what awaited him, and the account here is based on my recollection and piecing together other elements of the story later on. Without even a good-bye, our relationship changed in a snap, and another traumatic event filed away in my psyche.

Shocked, I felt like an electric ball of energetic mess. Not a hot mess or an ugly mess, this was an in-your-face disaster of a mess. My only saving grace was my intuition, which is what had allowed me to retrieve my car keys before he ran away.

I wish that I had known how to let go of unavailable men. Though my body fled the scene, my heart joined Scott in prison. We stayed in contact, and our bond grew deeper with this trauma. I opened each letter that he sent to me and answered each prison-pricey phone call, and we built a surreal relationship via our mutual hopes and dreams. A great deal of my attachment stemmed from an overwhelming need to know that he was alive.

As reality sunk in, however, I decided that the infatuation of a future with Scott had gone too far. It had to be time to date again. Now 23 years old and in love with a man in prison, I needed a smack with a two-by-four.

The pipedream of meeting my husband in college, per my 11-year-old fantasy, was now nothing but a distant memory. So I dated.

This, my friend, was yet another poor choice. Dating when you are a Hot Mess is challenging. Dating when you are attached to an unavailable man should be forbidden. It is like falling off of a glacier into icy water and grabbing every guy you can so you don't have to drown alone.

Dating while you are attached to an ex is the exact opposite of taking full responsibility for your dating life.

If you are dating while recovering or still attached to the past, this is an excellent time to check yourself at the door.

Unguided, I plunged feet first into the dating scene. I met another attractive, smart guy, a skater and writer. Enticing, right? We met, and yet I was not prepared to dive head first into a relationship. We grew closer, but I didn't want to be his girlfriend because Scott's dramatic absence still lingered. Now I became the unavailable one.

It turns out that my skater crush, Mark, and I operated from the same place. He suffered from bipolar disorder and took medication to regulate his mood. I, too, was a frantic emotional mess of depression and anxiety due to circumstances both present and just past. We soothed one another, as like attracts like. We could relate to one another's heavy emotions.

In contrast to Mark, I recognized an inner knowing that lives within me. As an empath, I can feel the deep pain of others, but I cannot deny the plain truth about me. I do not suffer from chronic depression. I feel chronic joy. It feels innate and lives in me. Despite all of the trauma that I have endured, this light has never left me, and I bet that it is within you too.

Well, the six-month-long depression bond with Mark came to an abrupt end on the night of August 20, 2000. Having gone out with friends, I saw him at the bar down the street from his home in a small suburban area of St. Louis. We had both been drinking and decided to head to his place with intentions of furthering our closeness.

Upon arrival at his apartment, the scene took a turn for the worse. You know the labels on prescription drugs that state that one should not take the medication with alcohol? Mark ignored this warning. Unbeknownst to me at the time, he had already transformed into a combustible blend of his prescription drug and a few shots of whiskey.

After questioning me about Scott, who happened to be approaching the end of his prison term (a subject about which I had been open with Mark), he flipped into a fit of rage.

"No guy in prison deserves you." He threw this protest at me with considerable venom.

Mark snatched my phone because he wanted to give the inmate a piece of his mind and to defend my honor. His drunken mind didn't realize that one can't simply call a prison and request a chat with an inmate.

Regardless, before I could blink, Mark's disgust escalated, and he pushed me onto his bed. He squeezed my neck with his left hand. My body went limp, and I made no attempt to scream for help. My voice had been silenced too many times before then, and I knew that freezing and staying quiet would allow me to remove my sweet self from this situation.

Mark clenched his right hand into a fist. He punched me in the side of the head as if he was in a bar brawl, though I hadn't raised a hand or my voice. He punched me six or seven times before letting up.

Now what do you suppose entered my mind? Get me out of here? Au contraire. *Here is my chance to fight instead of freeze.* An obvious attack had occurred, as opposed to the covert manipulative assaults from my past. I could fight him off, and I could justify it as self defense. I wouldn't have to defend myself or explain and be blamed.

For one split second, I felt the strength in me to fight, to stick up for myself. I felt that I had some power. I thrust my arms, which had covered my face in protection and shock, into the air and made a valiant attempt to push the possessed Mark off of me. Yes! Finally, I fought back.

Whoops, well, that lasted for all of two seconds. Mark clasped both of my wrists with one hand. I pushed up once with all my might and realized how ineffectual that would be. When Mark felt my resistance, he crushed my neck even harder. I felt the weight of his muscular arms and his rage. This could not be the time or the person to fight.

In my hyper-vigilance, I caught a glimpse of the kitchen knife set on the counter behind him. The knives seemed to light up, and I felt frightened beyond belief. The kitchen was just feet away from his bed in his cramped studio apartment. Mark noticed me glance past his shoulder toward the knives, and he caught me mulling an escape. At that, my fear transformed into complete calm.

My arms and my legs hung from my torso like limp noodles as if playing dead. Mark stepped back as I withdrew my threat to defend myself.

I dared to speak. "Can we talk about this?"

I had either come into this world as a peacemaker, or I had learned how to be one. At this time, I took the well-known position of making problems evaporate for everyone involved.

I have this uncanny ability, to this day, to suck all aggressive tension out of a room and transform it into neutral energy. I suck it into my body like a vacuum that cleans the air.

Mark relaxed and moderated his behavior. He controlled himself with my changed presence.

At that moment, I noticed that my shoe had come off in the scuffle. I scanned the floor for it while holding the calmness in the room. However, I had my eye on the door and didn't care if I found my shoe. This tactic distracted him to the point that he helped me with the hunt.

Meanwhile, phoning from the bar, my friends had left me a voicemail stating that they were on their way to pick me up at Mark's apartment. I did not know this, but I did know that I could hurry to the bar if I could escape Mark's grasp.

I spotted my shoe, and I sat down on the bed to slide it on. Mark moved toward me with caution, and I panicked. I bolted to the door. I threw it open and ran down the stairs and out of the apartment building, shoe in hand, leaving my phone behind.

Once outside, I stopped running. Recognize my shame here! I didn't want to draw attention to myself, and I feared that other residents would see me disheveled and fleeing. Yes, you heard me. I didn't want to be confronted or for any passerby to witness what had happened to me. I didn't want help, and I protected Mark from repercussions even though he had strangled and punched me.

I had scurried ten feet outside when the door of the apartment building flew open. Mark shot out of the door! *Holy shit!* Time to flee. *I played out both instinctual reactions in one night.*

I dashed away, but it was a strange sprint. As if I had jumped the gun in a race and wondered if my coach would call me to return to the blocks on the starting line, I ran, but in disbelief. *Should I stop? Am I being chased?*

I turned to see Mark thrusting my phone into the air and yelling that he would call Scott to punish me for my abrupt departure. Just then, I saw my friend's car, and the driver beckoned me to hop in.

I ran straight to the car and lurched into the back seat.

"Go, go, go!" I entreated my friend.

He sensed my distress.

He pulled away from the apartment building and then stopped the car. "Wait, what happened? Are you okay?"

"I'm okay. Please, let's just go." I wheezed in terror.

With reluctance, my friend took his foot off of the brake as Mark reached the car and whacked his hands against the door. At this point, my friend caught on.

Unlike me, he went straight to fight mode. "Did he hit you?"

I kept silent. I did not want a hero right now or to put my friends in danger. I wanted this to end.

That's when I begged. "Please, please, please take me home."

That repetitive pleading survival tactic flooded in. I implored him not to return to give Mark a much-deserved ass kicking. I convinced him of all of the trouble that it would cause. In fact, I submitted that it would cause me even more disgrace and that I could not endure it.

I would rather take the hits on my own than have my friend hurt or in trouble for defending me. I was focused on the well-being of others, to my own detriment. I was over-protective of other people. I did not even want Mark to get into trouble for hitting me. I had seen the inside of a prison after a visit to Scott, and no one needed to go to jail on account of me tonight. I couldn't live with the thought, and so I promoted peace in the middle of the riot.

I softened and eased the tension for my driver friend and my co-worker in the passenger seat as we headed down the highway to my home. They wouldn't have to worry about any of this. I took the burden off of them and pretended that all was fine now. I scorned myself in this process.

As you can see in my stories, and perhaps you have experienced in your own life, the fight/flight/freeze survival instincts stay with us long after the threat has passed. Our bodies remember the rush of adrenaline that we hold inside, and the traumatic memories solidify in our minds, causing depression, anxiety, and post-traumatic stress disorder.

There is no avoiding the wrath of fight/flight/freeze responses.

To fight, one releases anger and aggression right away. However, a price must be paid for causing another person harm or from the feeling of losing control and choosing to strike. The fighter's mind may later run through the scenario, searching for another way to handle the problem.

When the injured party flees, the feeling of living in fear of an unresolved issue is haunting. There may be a sense that in escaping, one does not stand up for one's self. This would mean, then, so the distorted thinking goes, that one welcomes future attacks and that one may then feel like a coward.

When I froze, all of the emotions of the assault and the physical chemicals that flooded in felt captured within my body and my being. The shame of not speaking up clogged my throat with self-doubt, and my attacks remained frozen in time. I carried this weight with me like a cinderblock of fear in my chest.

Impact

The reason I feel that we are so impacted by these three survival responses is due to how they are stored in the mind, and the body after an assault. The stress response becomes a part of who we are. We identify ourselves as fighters, escape artists, or we are frozen in silence in our daily interactions and can't make decisions. We tend to over-generalize and label ourselves by the way we reacted during an inciting incident. We may label ourselves as having anger issues for defending ourselves, being a wuss for fleeing, or feeling that we deserved the abuse since we froze and didn't leave the attacker.

The emotional impact of the trauma, combined with the negative self-talk, sears the event into our mind as fact about our identity. We believe and, therefore, act out the same fight/flight/freeze response over and over as if it is impossible to change. We wear it like a cloak of armor. I believed that I would always freeze and hand over my power as much as I see in the mirror that my eyes are blue.

It is important to recognize here that this false notion following abuse is not a fact about who I am, and your response does not have to be the truth about you. I will not always freeze when faced with physical, mental, or energetic attacks. I am living proof that this is not true. I will not always react like a frightened, feeble child. We are spiritual beings living out human experiences and we, all of us, have the instinct to fight, flee, and freeze.

What I see that keeps us anchored to one reaction is both shame and false confidence. Our shame allows us to believe that if it happened in the past, it will forever define us. Our shame also may have caused us to adapt an aggressive fighter response later in life because we froze as a child. Therefore, we conceive counter responses to make up for the past.

This is wrong. Our past does not have to dictate our future, unless we allow it to. Let's step into that ring of power and responsibility that I aim to deliver to you.

One's over-confidence, perhaps as a fighter, may lead to adverse outcomes. But, in fact, there may be a time in your life when it is time to drop the defensive boxing gloves and take a stand for your authentic need for love and acceptance without the fight. Having to prove strength leaves you bonded in a cycle of your own making.

We must stop feeding ourselves these lies. We are limitless in our ability to change. All sufferers of abuse have access to all three survival instincts. Yes, our amygdala is a proud and unyielding force, but so are you. It's time that your amygdala met its match. It is time to take control and eighty-six the shame and fear and stop the pattern of abuse.

Releasing Trauma

In an excellent book related to the study of trauma, called *Waking the Tiger*, Peter Levine explains in detail the animal instinct to release energy through fight, flight, and freeze.

Levine emphasizes the fact that animals move in and out of the threat responses like cycles. Alert one moment and grazing in a meadow the next, animals move through the survival responses with little effort. Our human rational brain (our neo-cortex), however, distinguishes us from other animals and interferes with our restorative process of cycling out of this tension as other animals do. Levine states, *Trauma occurs as a result of the initiation of an instinctual cycle that is not allowed to finish.*

I was fascinated by this research, which explained in such terrific terms why my nervous system was always on and in high alert even when out of the grip of danger. It explained why I felt glued in place in life, in relationships, in work, and in daily functioning.

Without any awareness, I did find ways to yield some of this stored trauma in my body. I took up kickboxing after watching Scott get arrested. I played soccer, and I signed up to play Roller Derby as soon as I saw my first bout. These activities constituted a ceding of pent up tension on a physical level. However, on an emotional and psychological level I remained constricted.

From an emotional standpoint, I found myself emancipating pent-up trauma feelings while wailing in the car by myself after the slightest trigger. I also had many a moment on the kitchen floor, curled up in the fetal position, bawling like an infant.

I am certain that these outbursts allowed me to extend the dating patterns that plagued my life, but they didn't set me free. These emotional breakdowns when the dam broke were no more than a consequence of my actions and a temporary assuagement of my inner turmoil. True healing eluded me.

Transforming my love life took willingness, humbleness, and a side order of guts. I needed to be indomitable, as do you.

I learned to react in more thoughtful ways to my triggers. In a getting-to-know-one-another texting exchange, a man whom we will call Bob referred to my Roller Derby stint and my knack for home improvement as an indicator that I might be a lesbian.

Mind you, this awful tease has caution written all over it. My nervousness about online dating and the fact that my independence has been deemed intimidating by some men, I refrained from throwing stones at Bob. His comment, though innocent, felt like a direct hit. I whirled into the child-like state of defense mode. I found myself defending my sexuality, as I had as a child to Joanie.

I felt myself spiraling into an inner free-for-all. I had developed feelings for Bob, and now this! *Will I ever stop being haunted by this bullshit?*

Whoa! Self-soothing, grounding myself, and riding the wave (not making waves) had become a daily habit by now, and I knew what I had to do. (As you gain control in these areas, you will be able to do this as well.) Chagrinned by my protesting behavior, I responded via text. *I don't know why I am defending myself here.* Then I took a positive tack. *I would make an excellent home improvement partner.* Retreating from an old reactive conversation had me feeling like I had performed a triple backflip out of the situation and landed my dismount! Is there a trophy for mature responses?

After the finale, I left my phone in the kitchen, and I slunk to the privacy of my bedroom. I knew that this trigger carried a message of importance and that it needed my attention. Triggers reveal what most needs to be healed. Please do not place blame or attention on the Bob in your life, the person who throws a punchline your way. Bring your attention to yourself.

I placed my hand upon my heart. *What wants to be revealed here?* Then I dropped my exhausted body down onto my bed.

As I listened, the 11-year-old child seeking protection from being touched by her classmate appeared within, both in images in my mind and through sensations in my body. I could feel the freeze response wanting to be discarded. I could feel me wanting to sock that 11-year-old classmate who called me a lesbian to my face and be done with this freeze response forever.

Of course, I have already established that I am not a fighter. As a visual in that regard came and went, I felt called to action.

I sat up and yelled, "Get off of me!"

Yes, in real life as a 39-year-old adult, I re-enacted the vivid memory of my childhood friend pressing her body on top of me and rubbing her chest on mine against my will.

In this moment of being triggered and in the safety of my own home, I re-wrote the event. I stood up for myself in this new script. I claimed my boundaries and shouted at the girl to get off of me.

I also engaged my mom in this imaginary exchange. I pictured myself going home and enlightening my mom as to what had happened. I envisioned her listening to me and acting on my behalf. I gave my 11-year-old self a voice that she had been too frightened to use. In the current scenario, my mom protected me and granted me permission to never have to go to this classmate's house from then on. This constituted a moratorium for me.

Your mind has the power to heal these old wounds. Two and a half decades later, and in minutes, I jettisoned this old storyline about being helpless and unheard. I felt the ever-present fear cycle out of my body. I felt grounded and in control.

Most significant, I felt that I could engage with Bob from a place of stability instead of a place of imbalance and defense. I texted Bob one last time letting him know that I preferred to communicate by phone calls. I explained how texting felt to me and how it did not result in a closer friendship on my end. Bob agreed with and respected this new-found boundary that I chose for myself. I did not have to articulate my childhood trauma or hold a grudge against him for an insensitive comment related to an incident that he could not have known about.

SOULutions

If you find yourself at a loss when wanting to release emotions cemented within yourself, it may be because you have not discovered the underlying trauma yet. When you are triggered, challenge yourself. *At what age did I first feel this emotion?* Go into your body and scan yourself for sensations, uneasiness, or constriction.

If you cannot locate the emotion, tighten up your body for a minute. Clench your fists tight, seal your eyes closed, and squeeze all of your muscles. Then release. A calmness will emerge in most areas except for the part holding the past.

My past felt like an elephant sitting on my chest or like an invisible force had a death grip on my shoulders, holding me down, holding me back. For quite some time my triggers rested in my chest, around the heart chakra.

Some people feel their throats constrict. Others have back problems, stomach aches, or migraines. Where do your traumas reside in physical form? Has your bottled up anger, resentment, and hurt created disease within your body?

Once more, make a request of yourself. *What is this ache or disease trying to say to me?* Then listen, and respond with love. Let's place all of our healing efforts in the location of that greatest injury.

Use the following SOULutions to move toward the root of your problems and closer to your true self:

SOULution #1:
Speak Your Truth

I made one error that I will implore you not to duplicate. I kept my traumas and emotional abuse from others. We all have a reason why we may do this. Perhaps it is shame or fear that you will not be accepted. Maybe you think that your whole universe will collapse if even one friend or family member knows. I even thought that others would not believe me.

I also imagined re-igniting the cycle of having to defend myself and having to prove the trials through which I had lived. All of this reasoning is false and fear-based.

Sometimes the right way is the simplest way. You owe it to yourself to speak and own your truth regardless of how others may receive your message.

Take my hand. As adults, we no longer need to care about who believes us. We are going to step out of that paralyzed, childlike state. We are going to speak our truth out of self-respect.

Others, outside of you, may shine a light on your suffering, yet no one, not your therapist, not your parents, not your friends, not even me, may save you from the memories and stories that you feed yourself. You are the one responsible for changing your circumstances.

I am not blaming you. Think of the power you gain by knowing that you are responsible for your life. Think of the motivation you now have to change your life. You now know that it is all up to you.

How to Speak Your Truth

- **Listen First.** Your patterns may make an appearance. Listen. You may be triggered, but listen. Watch yourself in social situations, around that one guy who bugs you or that one friend who crawls under your skin, and listen.

    The first step to being able to speak your truth is to identify when you are out of alignment with your morals and values. Practice patience with this step. It may be difficult to perceive this awareness. Be the observer in the scenario that I detail below (one of my own), and notice if you feel set off by this sequence of texts.

Eric messages me in the middle of my party:

> I'm tired from being out with the guys all day. I'm going to be late for your party. I might not make it at all.

Me:

> Oh, that's okay. Did you have fun with your friends today? You must be so tired. I understand.

Eric:

> Yeah, I'm beat. In fact, I'll see you at the end of the week.

Me:

> Sure, have a good night.

I then set the phone aside and felt crushed. Eric had known about this party for a month. I had been preparing for it all week, and all of my friends were dying to meet Eric. He chose to go out all day knowing that he would be tired. How could he bail on me at the eleventh hour?

Instead of providing a truthful response of how I felt, I fawned over Eric and disguised my disappointment.

Then, guilt for being angry at him rushed in, and shame for losing face with my friends knocked on my door rather than my new beau, Eric. I downplayed my feelings and forfeited my worthiness of love and the right that I have to respect. I dismissed the texts, pushed down the rejection, and pretended that it was not a big deal. I played it cool.

Oh, Sister, playing it cool, minimizing your desires, and not making waves are all forms of self-abandonment as well as a trauma response of people-pleasing. During this first step, notice when you find yourself doing this.

- **Be brave.** After you identify opportunities to speak up, and as you speak your truth, you may be scared to make those waves. You are going to do it, anyway. Practice with friends and family whom you trust.

I once spoke my truth, holding on to my quivering chin. My heart raced, and my voice trembled. I voiced my feelings, anyway. At times, tears slid down my cheeks, and I continued to convey the words in my heart. Speaking my truth had been so outside of my familiar territory that I sobbed as I enunciated the words. However, my duty to myself held steadfast. My entire being shook, as I let my listeners, partners, friends, and family know that I mattered.

Fear. I had so much fear of being disliked. I believed that a disagreement meant that the person I loved was angry with me and that they might stay incensed for eternity. Then it occurred to me that I took away my basic human rights by allowing a partner, a friend, or a family member to dictate to me what felt best for me. I gave control of my life to others who did not even care about how I felt. I trusted unsuitable mates with my heart and soul. Rookie move!

This is what it may sound like when you use that voice for the first time. Let's go back to Eric ditching my party at the last minute, after choosing his friends that day. Shall we flip the script and respond like the rebel you are?

Your text is bold and assertive:

> I'm disappointed that you're choosing to miss the party. I thought you knew that it is important to me. I won't wait for your arrival.

Depending on your personal circumstances, you may add more of your own voice to this message. The point is to state how you feel. Do not throw any demands on the guy. You can't control him, and you don't want to.

Eric knew that he had let me down. He also knew that I felt hurt and didn't share this with him. He seemed to love having this power of attorney over my heart.

Remember, express your feelings. He can't argue with your feelings. If he does retaliate with some defensive comment, own your hurt and state, *This is how I feel,* and (this is important here) then hang up the phone or end the exchange of texts. Go to your party. Have fun!

This is going to be hard given your peptide addiction, the possibility that you may drink, and the possibility that you may think of him all night long. If you're worried about calling him mid tequila shot, please pace your drinking, and phone a friend instead!

Do whatever it takes to keep your boundary with a man like this and to stay true to yourself.

SOULution #2:
Stay Tuned

In order to commit to your truth, you have to be tuned in to what your truth is. If you have spent most of your life appeasing others, forsaking yourself, and calming the waters, chances are that you may not know your truth.

Also, if you believe your truth is that you want others to be happy, I understand, and I am telling you that this is a false belief most likely as a result of pleasing caregivers to stay safe as a child. Others do not become happy through your enabling, appeasing, and pretending.

So, in order to tune in to what you want most, do this two-step (country style if you'd like):

First Step: Make a decision. Give yourself time to make a decision without the influence of other people or the pressure of time. Here are some statements that you may use when you are invited to an event or on a date:

> *May I let you know tomorrow afternoon?* Then do let the person know at that time. This is not a way to back out of the decision or to lead others on.

> *I need some time to think about that. When do I need to let you know?* If the person insists on an immediate answer, decline with kindness. *Oh, that's unfortunate that you need an answer right away. I am not ready to make a decision, so I will pass.*

Second step: Reflect. As you pay attention to the decisions that you make during the week, journal about how you feel. Review what felt true about yourself at the time you made the decision. You may discover times when you felt rushed or influenced by your peers. You may also acknowledge that you made that poor decision while tired, or drinking, or upset. Notice the results of forced or thoughtless decisions. When I duck past the gym, I am short on patience and make careless mistakes at work.

Also, reflect on the decisions that you made that you loved. Though it felt like an impulsive and wild idea at the time, I leapt at the chance to go on a last-minute white water rafting trip, and I loved it. Or, whenever I wake up early and catch the sunrise, I feel full all day! Reflect on your decisions, and you will move closer to the true you.

SOULution #3:
Safe Haven

The third SOULution is to identify your safe haven. Remember my escape route of excusing myself to the bathroom in order to cycle through my triggers? Your nervous system isn't familiar with your healing journey, and your body will continue to explode within when you least expect it.

Save yourself the drama show and the hyperventilating in front of friends. It is time to move past that stage. We have already established that the bathroom is your shelter in the storm. Now, don't linger in there too long. People may wonder, but flee to the powder room when you need a safe place to which to retreat. Collect yourself until you feel centered within your body, and then return to the present event.

Remember, you have tools now. If you are triggered in the presence of others, retire to the restroom and perform EFT. Splash some cold water on your face and your wrists. Shake out the putrid emotions. I urge you to let it out rather than to let it go. Letting go doesn't make sense to the activated nervous system. Letting it out does!

If you have your purse with you, keep a journal at the ready. Scribble whatever is on your mind. Do not censor your thoughts or judge yourself, expel it all. Feel free to tear it up and throw it away right there and then. This isn't about allowing others to see your thoughts, this is about moving that physical energy out of your body so that you may respond without misgivings when your past is suddenly thrown into your present.

Ask yourself, "Where is the fire you are running from?" You may laugh when you acknowledge that there is no real imposing danger.

The ultimate goal is to assert yourself so that you are able to speak your truth. Your truth is not a train wreck filled with sporadic, illogical thoughts. Your true self is heart-centered, compassionate, and knowing. We want to live from this juicy center!

CHAPTER 6

Undone

There is beauty in the breakdown. I found this premise questionable, at the least. From where I stood, if you saw light in what I suffered through, you must either be a sick human being, a robot, or an asshole. The breakdown story does not feel like a glorious breakthrough or a comeback victory. In fact, it feels depressing.

If you are handling his affairs and mind games at all well, it's possible that you have not hit this stage quite yet.

I would like to offer you a warning to brace yourself, but I am not that catastrophic, nor do I wish to predict your ruin. I am here to bring awareness and to shed light on the reality of emotional abuse.

Since you are reading this, I hope that my story will resonate with you such that you answer the call and make the changes necessary to avoid a breakdown. You are, however, human, and with that brings a sense of stubbornness. Like me, you may wish to find out the hard way.

Regardless of your choices today, you will hear this message either now or after the fact. An immediate or a retroactive effect is occurring. Though wiser, more mature, and experienced women warned me, their words did soak in with time. With their last breath of advice, they knew that I would hear their words in my own time. The same is true here.

"I am so tired," I murmured.

"I am tired for you." My friend commiserated during a visit.

Neither she, nor I, could believe that I was enduring the same relationship cycle as a year ago, two years ago, even five years ago. *What the hell is the problem?* I continued to fall in lust with the same guy with a different face and name, and my window for having a family was closing in.

After meeting Ryan, my friends and I felt elated that my ship had at last come in. I glowed in photographs. I peered at Ryan with eyes of endearment. Even I was taken aback when I saw my radiant smile after giving up on love. *Could this be real love?*

Oh, yeah, after pressing post and my puppy-dog-eyed face whirled into fantasy cyberspace, Ryan criticized me for breathing wrong (not really, but he pointed out all of what he perceived to be my imperfections). Most accusations began with *You always...* or *You never....* This type of black and white thinking left no room for error. My smile revealed a hope for my future, not the truth of my circumstances. I believed that I was in love and could share my bright social media rapture with the imagined crowd on the other side of the computer screen. Alas, this was a mirage, and I felt like a fool.

A lofty high exists before coming undone. Coming undone is the breakdown that unravels as you see the truth about your unhealthy relationship. Perhaps you summoned the nerve to make your last ditch effort at love, and it fell apart. Your extra effort is why it feels so grave when it ends.

I thought that I had lost it before Ryan. I had gone through heart-wrenching breakups. I had held on too long. I had struggled to rise out of bed. I had wept. My besties and my mom had consoled me, and I had always patched up my broken heart and managed to pick myself up. Dazzlingly resilient, I thought that heartbreak proved effort and that this must be the path to love. A relationship worth having requires sacrifice, right? This had indeed been my false perception.

Proud and determined, I would not give up on love despite the broken heart and the late-night sobbing fits. I longed for true love. When you withstand breakups and breakdowns, when you have been cheated on time after time, and when you have held relationships together with every drop of your energetic glue, the glimmering hope within fades.

The desire and the certainty that I once revered were now coupled with desolation. This illustrated a loss of faith and a harsh realization that I felt my belief that I would find my soulmate disappearing from my being. The sequence of breakups and fruitless patterns were no longer stories of hardships on the path to true love, they now proved that I had failed. I did not have the fortitude to go on. I no longer believed that true love was possible for me or that there is someone for everyone. My resources had run dry.

All of the effort, the sleepless nights, the believing, the hoping, the bending over backwards, the dismissing of your needs for his, all of this is woven together in the name of love, and it disappears right in front of your eyes. Defeat sets in.

I wish that I could tell you that I behaved with grace during the time that I acknowledged that I sucked at love. I did not. I came undone.

Prosecco became my ally in times of when I could not cope. I drank a bottle of Prosecco every night to numb my perceived reality of being deemed a prisoner of unrequited love and now solitude. I attracted men, but not love. I met men who drank with me and took me out and showed interest in me with agendas that I never questioned. None of them ever screamed *Long-Term Commitment*.

From my perspective, I had zero positive attributes to give to a relationship after having failed countless times. I questioned my capabilities as a partner, a woman, a lover, and a wife. My track record demonstrated a zero success rate. I felt broken. I felt like defective merchandise.

This stage of disappointment and self-loathing is different than the Hot Mess zone. A Hot Mess is unaware. When you are undone, your awareness is acute. You see yourself drinking or eating too much. You watch as you interact with men who are not right for you and who relate their problems to you more than they plan a future with you.

Life slows down. I went through the motions. I saw my love life for the shambles that it had become. It is challenging to see the benefits in the breakdown here because I watched as my perception of my storyline fell apart, and I could not stop it. Little did I know that grieving this old self and life needed to occur.

I beg you. Don't attempt to stop this disintegration. Allow yourself to tear. Surrender to the phantom, and let it engulf you. Accede to falling apart. Let the truths and the lies unfold and land in heaps at your feet. Break. Fall into the arms of a friend, loving arms that may strain to hold you up. Crack open, and let the tears flow. Allow yourself to split. Come undone in the safety of your own home, on a beach, in your car, anywhere that it might be necessary.

You'll find places that you have never noticed before waiting to catch you when you crumble to pieces. It doesn't matter where it happens. Drop the sword and your shield. It doesn't matter who sees you. You are revealing your true self to others, and chances are that they will stand by you. Melt, wherever and however you need to. Allow yourself to unravel and divide into segments. It will be clear upon which parts you need to build your new foundation. Don't interrupt the process of letting your old self go.

Coming undone is my way of explaining those vexatious two words, *let go*.

I don't know who simplified the majestic feat of distilling a lifetime of efforts into the words *let go*, but my body and my soul disdained the phrase. It felt inconceivable to me to not recognize that I held an inordinate fondness for my past. I felt tied to it by emotions, physical sensations, memories, and all of my senses. More than this, my efforts, my words, and my actions lived entwined in the past. I felt woven into every strand of past bonds with heart strings, not one, but thousands.

Let go. Even if I wanted to, the sheer force of what I had created (the love addictions and the trauma bonds) would not fall away. *Let go.* *I did!* I cried. I screamed in terror. *I did let go of him and the cycle, and it didn't fall away.* The embedded relationship cycle and abuse didn't let go of me.

I understand this. You dedicated all of that time and effort into making the relationship succeed. Due to an addiction to love, it will not let go, it must be pealed down, layer by layer.

Human beings are finicky creatures. We do not like to undo what we have constructed, especially if it is a mess on which we have expended our time and effort. We'd rather back away or slip out the side door. We do not have the option of doing this or closing our eyes and hoping that it all goes away.

See the beauty in coming undone? It's rare. Adults do not renounce their standards often. We are not accustomed to deep-sixing our old habits. We would rather chat about our problems over a glass of wine on a Friday night than take a real shot at clearing away the debris.

In the most elegant and vulnerable way, it is time to break down and fall to pieces. This stage of surrender is when giving up turns into a welcoming activity with lots and lots of naps! It is a time to admit defeat. Fear will keep you holding on to dead end relationships, afraid of the consequences of letting go. It is a time of rest so that you may move forward. It is a time to expand your expectations for yourself and harness the energy that you will call upon to move in the direction of your dreams, once and for all.

Let's take a peek at what has been keeping us in the water and cut loose some of these seeming life preservers. During this time, we will wield some much needed get-it-done methods, followed by a time of inaction. This is an incubation period. The damage has been done, we will soon have to take inventory of what to salvage and what to discard.

 SOULutions

SOULution #1:
Values Versus Emotions

To assert that coming undone is stressful is an understatement. After spending a month traveling with my unrequited love, Ryan, I lost my ability to cope. My mind could not withstand the psychological battlefield on which I lived with him. After we returned from our travels and after learning about another affair, the dam broke. Tears would not stop streaming out of my eyes as I read the children's book *The Giving Tree* to my kindergarten class. When the class left the room for lunch, I phoned my principal and requested that she join me in my classroom so that I could ask for a leave of absence.

"I can't stop crying. I can't be here. I can't teach the kids like this." I uttered as few words as possible to convey my agitation.

She did not know that my mind raced with thoughts of Ryan with another woman after he had been sleeping with me all summer. My life shifted right before my eyes from bliss to battle, and I felt a frantic resolve to figure this problem out.

Scared and on the verge of going nuts, I didn't know how much I wanted to disclose to my boss. With little information, my principal retreated to her office and then returned and handed me Family Medical Leave Act papers and urged me to sign them right then and there. Her actions added more fear to the fire. Feeling pressured and unsure, I chose not to sign but agreed to take the papers with me to my therapist. My hesitation stemmed from the fact that I thought that something was wrong with me and that by signing these papers there would be a record of this.

Please don't make any decisions when you are already vulnerable and irrational. Do not permit yourself to be forced into an on-the-spot decision if you fall apart in this way. Only make decisions with two feet planted firmly on the ground and your head in a tranquil place.

In haste, I escorted myself to a cognitive behavioral therapist, who produced proven results, according to my Google search.

I slumped into his office in a huff. "Everything I am doing is not working!"

I then introduced myself, sat on his couch, and informed him that I intended to do whatever he instructed me to do. After all, three days had passed, and I had not stop crying. Even while having a garden variety conversation, my eyes dripped with tears. I felt ridiculous, and I affirmed to him that I understood the gravity of my problem.

I complained, pointing to my face. "Do you see this! It won't stop!"

Dr. Goldmann interrupted my rant and insisted that both the crying and the anxiety would stop. I had never believed, read, heard, or seen any mention of overcoming anxiety before this moment. I had, however, researched all of the tricks to soothe anxiety and live with stress, and I knew the names of most of the medications prescribed to treat anxiety. Never had I heard this most healing word, *overcome*.

Concerning medications, my primary care physician had prescribed an anti-depressant for me in the midst of my exiting my twelve-year relationship with the aforementioned Mike. As I sat across the table from Mike at a restaurant, I pulled the bottle of pills from my purse and placed it down on the table between us.

At the end of my rope, I gazed into his eyes. "Is it me, or is it us?"

He snatched up the bottle and read the label. "Anti-depressants? Ellen, don't take those. You don't need them."

His response solved the puzzle for me, yet the co-dependent nature of needing his approval concerned me. Once more, I felt relief, but that pattern of seeking validation outside myself re-surfaced.

This is a wound that requires urgent care. You can overcome your anxiety, depression, and co-dependent patterns when you have the right information and tools in your hand.

Dr. Goldmann agreed with Mike and congratulated me on not taking the pills, and he set me in the direction out of crazy town.

I had taken the rest of the week off of teaching. On Monday I had cashed it in, and on Tuesday Dr. Goldmann claimed that I would return to work before the end of the week.

Not only no, but hell no! No way can I return so soon. I am having a nervous breakdown. Did you forget?

Wait just a moment. I re-framed the problem. *I consented to following his instructions.* I gave up the reins to an authority worth trusting, not another man in search of control.

I moved out of my own way, and together we made a list of my values. Dr. Goldmann instructed me to henceforth act in accordance with my list of values, not my emotions. My emotions had been running the show and, in fact, had taken over my life a long time ago.

In order to change, my mind needed proof that I could change my ways in the form of actions. Staying home would show my brain that my emotions kept me safe. Returning to school would break the cycle of messages that my amygdala produced. Dr. Goldmann helped me conclude that I valued being a loyal teacher and that I valued showing up for my students over allowing my emotional state to entice me into avoidant behaviors and depression.

On Thursday, I attended an afternoon staff meeting. As the bell rang out on Friday morning, I greeted my students at the classroom door for a full day of teaching. I *overcame.*

Returning to teach through the blanket of fear and anxiety felt like one of the greatest accomplishments for me in recovering. My nervous system did not want to be there. I wanted to call Ryan and scream at him for the number of problems his actions had caused for me. The truth is, though, that I wanted Ryan to save me. I wanted him to admit to the cheating and patch it up and make it better. I wanted him to heal the wounded child that he had exposed in me and bandage up the new misery that he had inflicted.

During those first few days of anxiety recovery boot camp, my thoughts raced. Not at times, but all day every day. As I read a book aloud to children, my mind drifted a million miles away. When the class left the room, I tamed my mind by writing out my thoughts and then throwing the pages away. The tears fell as I stayed in the classroom alone. I wanted to give up. I wanted to walk out and disappear. I wanted this, and yet I stayed.

Fake it until you make it? I coined the term the *Do-Do Method* for the strategy that I devised to break through this trying time. Do what you have to do, even though you feel like crap. I am sure that a clinical name exists for this, but the Do-Do Method summed it up for me, and I continue to utilize this technique to this day. However, now I apply the method to my life with ease, not by force. At the time, following through with the game plan to focus on my life as if Ryan's behaviors had never impacted me felt damn near impossible.

The Do-Do Method is a response to your amygdala that you do not need the frantic message or irrational thought being sent your way and that no real threat exists. I know, betrayal feels like your house is on fire and that you must snuff it out, but in reality, please know that you are safe from true harm. We need your mind to get on board with this. (Of course, if you are in real physical danger, you must seek professional help.)

Assuming that you are safe right now, drop this book, and jot down what you hold dear in your family life, at work, as a friend, and for yourself. What kind of person do you want to be? What morals do you stand behind in relationships? What drives you in the area of your contribution at your workplace?

Then act on what you have written. When your emotions kick in and you want to pull the blankets over your head, don't! You are feeding the enemy if you act on these helpless emotions. In time, you will regain stamina and control and feel empowered by your engagement in the Do-Do Method.

SOULution #2:
Identify Your Crutches

We all have crutches. In this case, our crutches are the people, the behaviors, or the activities that we use to avoid our problems or to take the pressure off of us. Yes, some activities may be beneficial to our bodies and minds. Another trip to the gym outweighs five glasses of wine and a pack of smokes in terms of positive options.

Not all crutches are as obvious as this. The most apparent crutch may uncover a more substantial crutch behind the scenes.

Let's acknowledge your crutches and eradicate them from your life so that you may coast out of here on your own two feet.

The first place to start is to acknowledge to yourself the names of the people to whom you turn to in a crisis. These people are your crutches, and we all need them from time to time. For me, I phoned my mom. She knew the pattern, and she stepped into her role to lecture, prescribe, and save me from my decisions. My mom propped me up on one side, allowing me to stay in my co-dependent cycle.

I also reached out to my best friend, who had watched my patterns play out for ten years. Anna had faced her own relationship challenges and had learned her lessons. She offered me honesty and some useful tools. Together, these two women held me up. I imagine them lugging me out of the wreckage, holding me up on each side as my feet dragged like a dead weight and tears turned dust to mud on my cheeks. To whom do you turn when you have a problem?

Now, why would we want to erase these helpful people from your life? We don't need to do this forever, yet it is time to stand on your own, and now is the time to see if you can.

This step takes courage and trust in your people. You must trust in a way that you have never trusted them before. If these friends have been with you through the messes in which you keep finding yourself, they are going to support you and celebrate this newfound independent you.

Let the friends and family members that you use as your crutches know that they are not going to hear from you for a while. Confess to them that you have to change your relationship patterns and that part of doing that is to end the cycle of imparting the dramatic stories. The stories that you have been presenting to your crutches are shaping your reality. It is possible that you are also re-traumatizing yourself in the process. These stories need to stop, and you are not strong enough to not talk about them with your crutches.

My mom and Anna supported me through this process the best that they could. Know in advance that your crutches are human as well. They have been playing the role of a saver, world's greatest mom, or a loyal friend, and their role is now being threatened. Their role is changing, and their egos will have to adjust.

They may feel rejected or like you no longer need them. The right people will stay in your life through these changes and will love seeing you grow. Both of my crutches questioned my decision and wondered if I would be okay. I gave them adequate reason to worry based on the past. Both of my crutches called me within a few days to see how I felt. Knowing that I had such dear loved ones in my life even now engenders tears.

I indeed felt okay, and my awareness and inner fortitude grew. Like the moment in which you take a cast off and move your limb with caution in hopes that it is stable, I had to make my own way! I forged ahead into the unknown.

I focused on these relationships as crutches because this was one of the more significant crutches for me. My co-dependent ties had been a crutch that I didn't want to cede. However, please take inventory of the most offensive crutches: drinking too much, partying, interacting with the guy you don't want to be with, seeking attention for validation, having sex for acceptance, and flirting on dating sites when you know that you are emotionally unavailable. Other crutches may include binge eating, zoning out in front of the television, shopping, overworking, smoking, and yes, over-helping.

Take it easy on yourself, but stay real. You have to make a change, and the choice is yours. Also, be dauntless and vulnerable. Reveal the truth to yourself and others. Admit that what you are doing isn't generating the results that you wish for and that you are changing your approach. Solicit support and accountability. Don't moderate, it depletes your mental resources. Drop the crutches all the way, and watch them shatter on the ground. You may no longer pick them up. You don't need them as you now walk on your own. That strategy of relying on crutches is now eliminated from your toolbox and no longer an option. That survival mechanism is of no use to you now.

SOULution #3:
Take No Action

Aside from dropping the crutches during this time, you may feel deep regret for making any changes to the relationships in your life. Your mind will want to return to how life used to be even if this did not benefit you. You will have thoughts of returning to old ways of being or reaching out to your ex to inform him that everything has changed, because your mind loves the familiar and wants you back with your ex even if he was abusive or wrong for you.

Moving into the unknown may have you feeling ill equipped to handle the wonderful experiences available to you. You may even have loved ones sabotage your desire to change or berate you for wanting better for yourself. All of this cognitive dissonance of wondering whether to stay in the same place or move forward wreaks havoc on the nervous system.

When your nervous system is on heightened alert, anxious, and stirring, it is nearly impossible to sit and do nothing. It feels like your house is on fire with your child inside napping and that you have been directed to sit still in a lawn chair and relax.

I know you feel like you need to call him, or fix it, or express yourself, or douse the fire. I know that every cell in your body is bursting like a volcano ready to erupt, and yet I am telling you to *relax, and don't do anything*.

This is the difficult part. Don't call him. Do not rush to your car and embark upon a road trip to escape. Refuse to phone your old crutches (remember this is no longer a strategy). Don't sign up for yet another self-help class. In fact, do nothing.

I am certain that you feel like you could combust right now. Inaction seems impossible when your heart has been taken for a ride through the dirt. I would never exhort you to relax in this circumstance. We are going to do what your amygdala wants you to do. We are going to take no action!

We are going to trick your sensational brain into believing that it is acting on your behalf. Words have the power to heal and to harm, and the words that you proclaim to yourself are the most significant. Your own words may shut down your system and soothe your body or ignite it into a frenzy. Just like you are in the process of changing your relationship in critical areas in your love life, you are going to take no action in the face of relationship despair moving forward. You will find that most, if not all, problems, misunderstandings, and accusations may withstand the test of time. Commanding your mind to not take action positions you in a place of personal power.

Here is the trick. Your nervous system and your brain need you to believe that you are in action. We are conditioned to do, do, do. We want your mind to believe that you are running into the house and saving your baby, and yet you are going to remain still right where you are.

Your baby will be safe, and you will remain unscarred from any further trauma. In turn, you won't enter into any adverse conversations with your ex-abuser. In taking no action, you will win those battles that you once fought tooth and manicured nail to the end. You will also override the instinct to flee. There is no need to run. You are here. You are safe and may take no action with ease.

This time of inaction, this time of rest, is a critical time in your recovery. Coming undone is a superb sign! A virtual bubble of light is being formed around you to protect you from all that once existed in your love life. You must fall apart in order to proceed toward the true desires of your heart and your personal life story.

I wish that I could sit with you right now, be with you in the stillness and silence and guide you through the self-soothing process. As your heart breaks open and bitter pieces fall by the wayside, please know that you are safe. You are secure in what seems like a vulnerable position. Your sanity, your virtue, and your light live in this space.

Take long naps, and don't repent. Notice how safe you are in your home. Acknowledge that nothing is burning. Any torture is nothing but a thought from the past or fear of the future. Attend to life's requirements in the day time, and at night soothe your own soul. Congratulations on being strong enough to admit defeat and rebuild your life.

PART II

How to Get Out of It

CHAPTER 7

Breaking the Spell

You can't believe that your guy has arrived after all of the heartbreak and waiting. Think of all of the toads that you have kissed before now!

"You deserve this," your friend remarks.

Mr. New Guy is talented and smart and handsome.

Mr. New Guy is your knight in shining armor. It's meant to be! He trumpets that you will be together forever. He stares into your eyes and professes that he has never met a woman like you. Mr. New Guy loves you. He oozes with feeling and claims that he has never felt this way about a woman before.

You rave about him to your friend. "We are going to move in together, you know? He's so great that even his ex rues the day that she broke up with him. We took the most sublime vacation together, and Mr. New Guy paid for the all-inclusive resort and the flights. No man has ever made me feel this way. The sex is remarkable."

Two months later...

"Look at this text. What do you think this means? I am so mystified. My head is spinning. Mr. New Guy's actions don't match his words." You scratch your head.

"You deserve better." Your friend makes a staunch assertion.

"Do you think that Mr. New Guy is dating other women? Do you think that he's the one and that he's afraid to commit? He hasn't replied to my text. It's been three days. I must have upset him. Do you think that I should stop by his house and apologize? Why did he shower me with affection if he didn't mean it?" Your words unfurl until you're massaging your forehead.

Two months later, and the scenario has not only not varied, it's gotten worse.

"Well, Mr. Not-So-New-Guy runs hot and cold. Isn't that typical of men? I am so difficult. I will never understand the male gender. Why can't I chill out? He is busy with his important job. Why do I push him? I read a blog about men and women having different needs for communication. I am worried about him. Do you think he's okay? He told me that he loves me." You yammer on.

Welcome to cuckoo-ville, population one. You.

The second that you laid eyes on your guy across the room, you fell into a trance. With that first laugh that he sparked in you, your brain lost all executive functioning. The first kiss, then the second, then the one that would never end...forget retreating, the venom is now seeping through your veins, and the paralysis has set in.

Alas, you are convinced that Mr. New Guy is the love of your life, the *one*. Your souls and your bodies embrace, intertwine, and merge. Two become one, and the spell is complete. You have signed on the golden dotted line with your energetic spirit. He has drawn you in. You are bewitched. You, my Dear Soul, have been taken. Your heart has been hijacked.

After the spell has been cast and you have sealed the deal, the mirage in your life is now physically, emotionally, psychologically, and energetically bonded with you. Circular thoughts of your love and the relationship are evident.

You have fallen so deep that rational and logical thinking are nowhere to be found. The trance will have you cancelling your own plans to make time for him. You may even abort your plans in anticipation that he will need you, and you want to be available. After all, that last guy you dated accused you of not being there for him, and you want to fix that for Mr. New Guy. You are going to be so available because you are serious about love this time. Right? You don't want to mess this up like you have messed up all of your other relationships. An old friend called self-blame enters the room.

You will, at some point, realize that you are operating with all of the wrong information. All of the books that you have read, the articles that you have skimmed through, and the advice that you have taken does not apply here. The reason why you feel so different is that you are different.

Your pattern of attracting and choosing abusive, unavailable, or objectionable men isn't mainstream. All women attract these personality types, a rare breed choose to stay with them. It is choosing to entertain these men that concerns me.

You don't read a cookbook to learn how to flee the relationship to which you are addicted. Drop all of the other books. Proceed knowing that you are in the right place and that this is the right time for you to be receiving this information.

When I suggest that you are operating with the wrong information, I am suggesting that you may not be wearing rose-colored glasses anymore. The trouble is, you are now wearing blinders. You are in it so deep that you never step out of it, even when you think that you are finding clarity.

As every fairy tale depicts, you are under the protagonist's spell. You are yielding to who you think is prince charming. You conform to his needs and wishes and do not want to rock the boat in any way, shape, or form. Your fear of losing your unavailable guy is high even though the relationship itself has provided you with reason for lofty confidence. The hopeless rationalization is that Mr. New Guy is attractive, and you don't want to be alone.

I imagine that this is hard to hear. It may even feel like I am projecting my struggle on to you. I have been considering that possibility myself. Then I hear a whisper of truth from within. I have to share my story with you. If you are under a spell like I was, I am here to show you how I broke that spell.

Let's shed some light on the subject. Many signs indicate that you have been taken in. First, you have ignored or excused red flags. A red flag is a warning signal that the stability of the relationship, as well as the people involved, may be lacking.

At one point in my dating life, I was so mixed up that I voiced this feeling when a man questioned me about my ability to be exclusive. This was a red flag for me as I spoke about my desire for a life partner, and my actions backed up my desire. I had been faithful to my core. His smoke-and-mirrors tactics and blame-shifting were a clear indicator that I had been barking up the wrong tree for happily ever after, and yet I found myself apologizing and convincing him that his accusations were untrue.

I anticipate that you have your own red flags and that you have in the past or are now ignoring his.

The way that this appears is that you are consistent and generous with giving him the benefit of the doubt. You excuse his absence. You excuse him not keeping his word. Your friends even point out that you are covering for him. In conclusion, your brain is now wired to find a rational reason for buying into pardoning his behavior and keeping you ensnared in the relationship. When the last straw hits the camel's back and you call him out on his behavior, admit that you wait for his apology in order to continue the rocky relationship. A symptom of being entranced is that you don't want to lose him.

My warning here is that this pattern gains momentum. The inexcusable behaviors worsen as the rationalizing increases. Before you know it, you are in a volatile and manipulative relationship based on false promises, deceptive acts, and lies.

You didn't see it approaching, and this is your monster problem. It seeps in like the venom from that first kiss. I often reference the story of the boiling frog, a fable describing how a frog thrown into boiling water will jump out to save its life, but a frog relaxing in warm water will boil to death if the heat is gradually turned up. As in the story of the frog, we did not see the relationship heating up around us until it became too late.

The second fatal mistake is making your charismatic, controlling man your god. That sounds rather dramatic, but hang with me. Do you idolize your narcissistic man? Is he so perfect that it feels like a dream come true? Does he keep you dangling with his every word, and do you run all of your ideas by him first? In a stable relationship, you will feel that your man is awesome, but you will feel confident enough to make your own decisions with or without his approval.

You will also be able to express what you don't enjoy about him without fearing that he will step out on you. A man of sound mind and demeanor can handle imperfection.

Now that your kryptonite has you adoring him, available at all times, and following him around like a cat in heat, he now feels god-like. This is the boost he needed. This is one of the threads that will be holding tight when you do decide to let go.

You are filling up his reservoir. He is as magnificent and wonderful as you have fantasized him to be. As sordid as this may be, your god-like attention toward him may have him realizing that he is better than you. He may point out how you could change to match his superior level, the one that you admire so much in him. Be careful, you will believe that this is true!

It is this sick type of mind-twist that you have perpetuated by allowing a person outside of yourself to be so much more important than you are. This is not self-love, and it is not placing value on yourself. This is a deprecating process that will leave you spun out, grasping for proof of your own self-worth, and reliant on this man for validation. You are under his spell.

SOULutions

As with every internal wound that we excavate from your heart, I will not leave you here to suffer. I will not accept that you are locked away in a tower while I go about my day free from the trance in which I once lived. There is a way to break the spell. A voice that speaks and a heart that listens beyond the hypnotic trance of this relationship is available to you. You have a voice whispering to you, a voice that he cannot control, deny, or shut off. You have a heart that listens. He may make a ton of noise to drown out the truth, but know that your heart knows the truth by the way that it feels.

When children are playing on the playground while their mothers sit on a bench and chat, the instant that her own child cries out, a mother knows. She identifies that this call is for her, and it rings through her body and her heart.

Your voice and your truth may be heard in this way through the din. Your intuition beckons you in a whisper and in a language unique to you. This is why I know that you have the strength to follow through with the SOULutions in this book.

To break the spell, you must stop drinking the poison. Stop inhaling the fumes that are making you sick. Stop swallowing more hooks that are keeping you caught, and stop perpetuating your own abuse. You are participating in a lethal game, and your power lies in hopping off of the game board, not developing your next genius move.

The extreme co-dependent attachment has been termed the anxious-avoidant trap or the narcissist-empath bond, but does it matter what we call it? What matters is that it hurts. If you are in a relationship with a maladaptive person, a lover who has you feeling as if you are under a spell, you may make the choice to disengage.

This may occur in a variety of ways. Following are a few of the ways in which I have ended the wrong relationship.

SOULution #1:
Stop Participating with Players and Users

Inform your partner, the critical friend, or the family member who is pulling your strings like the grand master in a marionette show that you are done or that you are taking time for yourself. Then follow this decision with affirmative action. How many unfulfilling and unreciprocated relationships are playing out in your life right now? Free yourself. You don't respond to this person when they reach out. Your decision is final. When every cell in your body is aligned with your decision, the process is easy.

If you are not ready to stop, the process will be arduous, and you may re-engage and wind up in a stalemate. Here is where I would recruit the question *Why?* Why are you with a cheater who is making you feel ill?

Boldly answer for yourself, "What's in it for me? Why am I playing this game with my ex, the one who is diminishing me?"

Disengaging is the most beneficial decision that you may make. Your heart will perform cartwheels, and a golden crown will glide down from the heavens and rest on your head. If you can be the observer in your life and watch yourself and your kryptonite going head to head on the game board, I hope that you find sensible reasons to quit. My utmost respect goes out to you, as this is a task for the brave of heart.

Stopping the participation and no longer engaging in the banter with a narcissist is no joke. It takes a great deal of mental, physical, and emotional energy, but it will earn you a profitable reward in the long run. You will heal faster and have more awareness. I caution you, though. Don't take your ball and go home until you are ready for the verbal backlash that may unfold from your narcissistic mate.

Without support, you will feel like you have backtracked far into the abyss. Coach yourself through this process. Your attempts to back flip off of the game board may provoke guilt trips and sabotage from others, but it may also launch you onto the next path where you belong.

If you are not ready for a complete end to life-sucking players, having one foot in and one foot out may look super ugly. Read on.

You may pull out of the relationship by cutting ties to activities and emotions that you once ran to as if your life depended on it. Are you hoping to see him on a certain route or at a particular place? Did you take up a hobby to match his interest in it? Drop these activities now, and replace them with other pastimes that you love.

You may block his number. Although blocking his number seems like a flawless plan, it is a quick, ego-centered hit. *Look how strong I am. I blocked him. See, I am so over him.* Your ego believes that it has made a power move. You believe that you have solved the problem, and your mind will move on to other important goals. Like a false start in a race, blocking his number is a temporary and quick-fix jolt. This thinking persists as you are sent back to the start line. This action did not crystallize as a truth in you.

You unblock his number and wait to see if he contacts you, or you call him with the excuse that your phone has been acting up and maybe you missed his call. You don't receive the response that you hoped for, which is no surprise to an outside audience. Embarrassed about calling him, you then block him and the dreaded cycle unfolds. Block on, block off, block on, block off.

Let my anxiety-ridden heartache and compulsion help you here. Delete his number. When he texts, don't respond. If he calls, hang up the phone. If you don't, you will search for love in his text…and in all of the other wrong places. You will search like a hound dog that won't be fed until he finds the clue, a morsel to prove that your ex loves you.

Delete, delete, delete. You are cutting this tie, and it is falling to the ground. Blocking means that you are holding your arms up, pushing him away. Blocking is exhausting, soon your arms will weaken and drop, and you will let him in.

While detaching, you will also let go of some of the memories in your environment that remind you of your kryptonite. After my twelve-year relationship ended, I realized that items in my house had been chosen for Mike and not for me. I thought that he would like them. I dumped books, socks, pictures, and other odds and ends into a box that I took out to the garage.

When you excavate the dead debris of relationships past, I recommend keeping the space empty for a while. This clearing act will bring an awareness to how you felt with evidence of the relationship around. It will also allow the process to unfold.

I know that you will miss him. I know how hard this is going to be for you. I lived it also. You will take his picture down and then hang it up again with hope. You will throw his favorite sweatshirt out and then change your mind and fold it up to donate it, perhaps after sleeping with it as your pillow for one last night to catch the tears. Allow yourself these intimate moments of healing. Healing is a process.

You held a strong attachment. I believe that this attachment exists far beyond the seeing eye. It is physical, mental, emotional, and spiritual. This attachment is implanted in places that you may not even feel yet.

Once you stop playing the game with users and cheaters, inch by inch, step by step, you will detach from less-than relationships and blossom.

SOULution #2:
Detox

Detoxifying is the process of removing unwanted substances from your life. As with detaching, you want to make the decision to quit this relationship and then eliminate the toxin. A relationship detox happens over time and takes cognitive effort. After disengaging, you will need to fill that space with rewarding experiences. You want to pull out of the relationship and replace that time and mental drain with sustainable acts of kindness for yourself.

Since we are not talking about detoxing from alcohol, although you may have that going on too, we want ways to use your anxiety-fueled momentum to move you forward in your relationship life. I don't want him to suck you back in. The same as if you were addicted to alcohol or drugs, you may become triggered by the sight of your ex. Any place, any scent, any person, or any object may remind you of him.

At first, you may not be able to predict your relationship detox triggers. Below are some of mine that may bring awareness to your own.

The phone is the first place to act. Summon the renegade in you, and delete the pictures of him or the two of you together. If you cannot do this, which I know you can, delete them from your phone, and transfer these captured memories to your computer. Hide them away so that they are not at your elbow.

I also had to change a ring tone and a text tone, and I suggest that you do the same. This matters if you assigned a specific ring tone to your ex. Imagine moving on, being engaged in a conversation with a friend, and your favorite love song suddenly sings out on your phone. *Oh, he's calling!* The heart palpitations, sweating hands, and a total forfeiture of focus return to embroil you. You don't want to answer his call.

You also don't want to assign this ring tone or this text tone to anyone else. Forget that it was ever on your phone. You now seem to be hard-wired to react to that ring tone, and it is not worth it. You are moving on, remember?

Other triggers might be places. If your heart sinks when you pass his street or the tree in the park where you first met to walk your dogs together, please take a timeout from these routes. If you don't, you will be doing yourself one of two disservices. You will obsess over that place and cry every time you see it, or you will pass by these places hoping that you will run into him. Neither has a first-rate outcome. You will suffer more needless heartache, and you will set back your recovery.

Addicts do not sober up while meeting friends at the local pub. Leave these places behind. Find unfamiliar parks, different coffee shops, and unique activities. Your heart will thank you, and you may relish the adventure!

SOULution #3:
Lowering the Pedestal and Trading Horses

The third SOULution, in theory, is to knock your glorified ex off of his pedestal or his high horse after you have built him up to be god-like in your eyes. Since I am proposing peace and no physical contact, I don't want you to push him in real life or acquaint him with your internal plan. I know for a fact that you are not that cold-blooded and that you would end up feeling wicked for retaliating. If you informed him of your plan, you would apologize for having such denigrating thoughts about him, and the whole endeavor would be a lost cause.

So, to ensure that your ego doesn't overreact, let's talk about lowering his pedestal a few notches, and then I will discuss trading horses.

You have built Mr. New Guy or the ex about whom you have been fantasizing and this relationship up to be on par with the divine. You have also shifted a surmountable amount of perceived power and influence over to him. This exercise will change that.

Grab a piece of paper and a writing instrument. Write at the top of your paper, *What I don't like about him.* Simmer down, not a living soul is going to see this. I acknowledge the fear that you will have to move through to complete this task. But I want you to be honest.

This is important. You have built him up to be your life support and to be supernatural. We have to make him a human being in your mind. I know that this is hard to see, but he is human. He is not your savior or your hero. Human beings are flawed. Seek out his flaws because not seeing them is killing you.

As always, I will go first. This is sad. This is Mitch. Remember, Mitch flew far above me in my eyes. He could do no wrong. Devising this list opposed all of my lustful feelings for him. However, my veneration of him and my love for him had me worshipping him and disowning myself. I had to break the spell. I bawled the whole time I wrote. That is, until I laughed.

Hmmm. *What do I not like about Mitch, this man to whom I am addicted?* I reasoned that I wouldn't find a single trait that I didn't like about him, but then the truth poured from my pen like a geyser (steam and stinky sulphur included).

- He blasts a condescending remark right after a compliment.

- He snores like a pig. (Ugh! When you are in love, you look past such insignificant human defects. This may be the meanest one I wrote, but I wrote it! I feel ashamed to admit it, but I had to get it down. I wanted to be grossed out because I was infatuated with Mitch, and he seemed to enjoy playing me.)

- He electrifies me with me stories about himself. He glorifies his virtuous self and downplays others.

- He has a subtle way of implying that I need to shut up when I am talking or recounting a personal story. He doesn't want to hear it, and he doesn't care.

- I haven't met any of his friends. Huge red flag!

- He was offended when I asked him to get an STD screening before we slept together. He convinced me that this boundary was unreasonable, and I should trust his word.

This exercise is not designed to emasculate men. The purpose is to allow you to move closer to the truth. Realizing the truth about your kryptonite, the relationship, and yourself is the recipe to breaking the spell. Visualize your relationship with objective eyes. Sometimes the notion of the relationship itself needs a reality check. Feature him high up on that pedestal and you far below him. As you write, imagine the pedestal being lowered.

Keep writing, keep revealing the ways in which he is human. Think of how he has acted toward you or the jab that he took at that waiter in the diner. Dig. Remember. Tune in to your heart. The whole time that you were ignoring his shortcomings, your heart listened. Give your heart permission to speak. *What caused the hurt?* Write until the pedestal is lower and you are at least facing him, eye to eye.

I encourage you to proceed. If you are feeling bodacious, envision your boyfriend up on a high horse. Position yourself on a mini pony below him, while shame and mortification sets in. I love mini ponies, so no offense to our beloved friends here. Conjure up how clumsy you feel, balancing to hold on and not going fast. Sitting on a mini pony is not a fit for you.

Raise your eyes up, and see your boyfriend with his back straight and proud, his eyes staring into the distance like a king. Feel your shame, and notice how much better off he is in your eyes. Build this picture up. This is you taking full responsibility for your own life.

I know that over-honoring your ex was not intentional, but you have made this man out to be better than you are. You gave him your *yes* when your heart pleaded with you to scream *no*. You welcomed and allowed behavior unsuitable for friends let alone for intimate partners. Feel that discrepancy.

Now, step down from your mini pony, and with one flick of your hand, beckon him to dismount from his stallion. In your visualization, you have full control, confidence, and grace. He appears shocked, as you have never stood up to him before now. Yet, he finds his horse prancing uneasily due to your resolve and stature, and he becomes fearful. The horse bucks, wanting this ass off of him. Your once prestigious knight clambers down from the restless horse and trades horses with you.

As he drops to the ground, thankful to be safe, feel free to use him as a step stool to mount the horse upon which he sat. After all, he has been using you for long enough. Now, straighten yourself up, and mimic his posture from a minute ago.

In fact, you may do this in your seat right now. Lift your gaze, and feel what he must feel like with all of the unconditional love that you accord him. Give that to yourself. All of the confidence and attention is aimed at you now. Own that feeling for yourself.

Have you ever allowed yourself to sit upon the highest horse? Have you ever treated yourself with the kindness and the respect that you give to others? Sit and feel this feeling of royalty. You do not have to depict yourself as a queen, though you are one. You do not have to be better than he is. There is no comparison. Know you deserve better treatment and it will only occur when you believe this to be true.

Right here and right now declare to yourself, to yourself alone, that you are worthy.

CHAPTER 8

The Game You Can't Win

He may have cheated. He may have lied, manipulated, and twisted the truth. He may have hurt you and broken your heart. What he did was not okay, just, or right. He was wrong and perhaps insidious, selfish, and unkind, and he took advantage of your vulnerabilities and openness. No matter how hurt and angry you are at him, please know that the blame game is a game that you can't win.

Blaming the cheater, the addict, your mother or your father, or your past in any way is a ploy. This form of retaliation, played as *I am venting*, will keep you straitjacketed in a pattern of emotional and physical abuse. It will also re-traumatize your nervous system, keeping you cemented in the past. You risk sounding like a prima donna by blaming your ex for your life-long relationship woes, and we are going to strive to be better than that.

Two unsuspecting ambushes play out when you blame your ex. One, your integrity is strained. Regardless of your righteous conviction and being a victim of abuse, you are now blaming your ex. Friends and bystanders are listening and watching. They have the ability and the awareness to see the truth of the situation, but from their one-sided point of view. Unless one has been abused in this unconscionable way, taking your side requires others to take a leap of faith in you. I am blessed to have friends like this. I am here for you, and others understand too. But reciting your relationship debacles over and over, with the wrong person, could lead to more brutal feelings for you when he or she does not see the abuse the same way you do.

Stifle your need to convince your listeners of the abuse. You know the truth. Stand in it, and there will be no need to point a finger. Let go of people who don't believe you. Though you may feel like a 5-year-old pleading for your parents not to separate, you are an adult now, and this is a fight not worth your energetic juice.

Of course, crystalize your truth, and don't side with your abuser or feel sorry for him. Protect yourself and your integrity from further abuse by catching yourself when you fall into the blame game.

The second and more important reason is that the blame game keeps you cornered in a victim mindset. A victim mindset is stagnant. When you devolve into a victim mindset, when you relax in to it, your mind sets up a *Home Sweet Home* sign, and you tuck yourself in to stay. A victim mindset is *other* focused. It assigns your abuser the position of being in charge of your present life conditions, and therefore, the trajectory of the rest of your life.

The voice of a victimized woman may sound like this:

- I am not with my soulmate because...

- I am at this job that I can't stand because my boss...

- I can't go to school to continue my education because he...

- I am not married yet because...

- I am not a mom yet because...

- Others don't understand me. I am different because...

- I always wanted to, but I can't because he...

We have legitimate and valid excuses for the tragedies in our lives and for our forlorn emotions. What is your story of blame? Assess the story in which you are entrapped, and see how it is stopping you from fashioning the life of your dreams. How much are you blaming your ex or others from your past? How much are you blaming your family for the strains and burdens of whatever ails you? Do you see how this is holding you back?

The Obsession Loop

When you can't stop talking about him, when you assert that you are through and yet he arises in conversation over and over, you are in the victim mindset loop. Imagine a jail in every sense of the word. Feature a rat maze out of which you cannot find your way, ever! Yet, your mind attends to solving the problem. In fact, your mind extracts your get-up-and-go from your body to solve this riddle. The result is fatigue, stress, anxiety, depression, and a mind running amuck.

Gabbing about your ex may impact your other relationships as well. Your reliable friends have had enough already! Your friends may extend the cycle and misinform you or guide you into more and more of the same.

Within this loop, a dominant preoccupation is also at play. You, My Love, have not ended the relationship with this man. Your endless discussions and lack of closure keep you confined in a relationship with him even if you are not even talking to him. Even if you don't see him, your ex is taking up your time and bankrupting your spirit. He is living rent free in your mind. He is the disease keeping you from your main squeeze!

This illusion of your own creation is keeping you tethered to this man. Sit with this. While the concept may be horrifying, notice the light here. If you have heretofore been responsible for keeping this boat afloat, you have the control to stop it! Give yourself this permission.

We are not going to succumb to Internet claims that you may text him into your life with some seductive four-word phrase that bodes well for entrapping a man. I know, I have fallen prey to all of the scams ever invented to entice your man back into your life. Please learn from my expensive, foolhardy endeavors. Save your money and your time. These sites should be illegal as they prey on the broken hearted.

Using manipulation to coerce a man to love you is dire and inauthentic. This is the opposite of love. If you want this type of love, close this book, and drop it off at your neighborhood coffee shop or one of those cute library boxes. We are on a mission for true, juicy, one-of-a-kind love. Tricks have no home here. Treats for yourself, however, are welcome.

Perfect! Please consider this a delicate admonition. You may give up at any time. The fact that you won't, that you can't, is a reminder of your commitment to yourself.

I am proud of you. Now, let's launch you out of this blame game. You are benched by the officials, so take a seat, grab your water bottle, and catch your breath.

 SOULutions

SOULution #1:
Get Off of the Game Board

Sitting in the office of my Gestalt therapist, I rattled off the most recent scenario of a gaslighting con by Mitch. By now, all of my exes were armed with the same ammunition, and my pattern had been made clear. Dominant, ego-driven men with patterns of manipulation, addictions, abuse, and cheating were my jam. While cognizant of the name of this game, I had every intention of plotting with my therapist about the most appropriate way to respond to his gaslighting. I wanted to figure out my next game move. I needed to know how to respond to win this game with him.

"How would a typical person respond to this text? Can you explain to me what Mitch means when he throws this word salad at me?" I inquired.

I felt open to the possibility that maybe I didn't understand men and that my male therapist would enlighten me.

My therapist leaned back in his chair. "Ellen, how are you benefiting from these encounters and tit-for-tat conversations?"

"Uhhh..." My eyes shifted to the floor, and an energetic and physical transformation occurred in my body.

Oh, shit, how am I benefitting from these ludicrous relationships and childish arguments?

He informed me that every interaction between two people is an exchange in which both parties gain from each other. Whether it be accolades, recognition, or goals for the future, all relationships provide a tangible payoff to both parties...be it beneficial or disadvantageous.

I yelped, "Nothing! Oh, God, at least not anything of value."

As if a game board had appeared on the floor in front of us, I could see Mitch making his move, with me plotting my reaction and my defense. I made no offensive plays with Mitch. I lacked control of my life at this point.

I stood in triumph. "I have to get off of this game board!"

Soul-claps rose from my chest, and the inner crowd burst into cheers! Yes, tumble off of the game board...and stay off. The way to win the gaslighting game is to stop playing. This means that you have no more moves. Don't respond, interact, or inquire of friends. Don't discuss him at all. Pick up the pieces. Fold up the board. Throw the whole kit and caboodle into the box. The game is over.

SOULution #2:
Shift Your Focus

Well done. Now, what are you going to do with all of that time and energy that you used to dedicate to playing this game? So many times this question manifests as anxiety. I understand that this may be terrifying! Your brain is no longer reacting to gaslighting, searching for your next move, and discussing your game plan with friends.

Let's contemplate a different modus operandi. Here you are on the bench, filled with anticipation and drive! What do you want to do when the time arrives to suit up and start dating once more? That's right, what do YOU want to do?

After I awoke to the gaslighting game, my therapist and I parted ways. He encouraged me to split from the bench, also known as the therapy couch, and be the player in my life. In different words, he coached me to stop riding the pine and get in the game.

Hungry to live without the constant presence of the one-track mind related to all of relationships gone wrong, I agreed with him. I had so much desire to explore the world without a relationship dragging me into reactive moves and constant battle. I felt free. I wanted to stop thinking about how to be in a relationship. I needed to stop questioning what felt wrong with me and pondering how I could attract a healthy man. With the phantom of soulmate love in the rear view mirror, my life opened up to the possibility of me!

All of life is now opening up for you too. What do you want to do with your new reality? Assess what you are passionate about. Is there a course or a class that you have been dying to take? Is there a book that you want to read or a Meetup group that interests you? Re-direct this fiery passion that you have been using to engage with the wrong man, and move it toward your own interests and purpose.

Caution: This is not the time to leap into the dating scene. This is the time to re-build you.

SOULution #3:
Re-Direct Your Energy, Not Your Blame!

You may be tempted to or find yourself taking the blame off of your ex and turning it inward to yourself. *What was I thinking? Why did I stay with him? This is all my fault. I wasted so much time.* If you hear yourself doing this, catch yourself, and be gentle with yourself.

Talk to yourself in a loving way like you would advise a friend. Yes, you may feel that all of those thoughts are true, but the truth always is that you did the best you could as the person you were at the time. Give yourself a break. Blaming yourself is a dead end cycle and a form of self-abuse. At some point we will arrive at a place where your inner dialogue is so kind that you will accept zero verbal abuse from others.

This is your time to practice random acts of kindness toward yourself! When the blame monster rears its ugly head, stand straight and tall and protest, *Don't talk to my friend that way!* The way you treat yourself is the same as how you will allow others to treat you.

Think about that. It is critical to change this inner dialogue. A hostile inner dialogue makes you susceptible to more abuse.

Act now. Write out a list of one hundred attributes that you love about yourself. Yes, one hundred! I know that you may think that this is self-centered. Don't worry, not a single person is watching. Jot down these one hundred characteristics. Dig in, feel what arises in your heart, and allow it to reach your pen.

Humble, quiet, and being the good girl characterized my younger trained self. Vanity had been seen as a sin. Writing down that I love my hair and my eyes and my lips brought up childhood memories of being made fun of for having full lips on a child's face. It also evoked sexual remarks made to me in the past that brought shame to my strong, appealing body, as if it needed to be hidden. Push through incidents that happened in the past. Cashier the false stories inflicted by other children who struggled to belong.

I scribbled *outgoing*. This felt like a trait that caused a lot of disruption in my life as I grew up. I am a tad hyper with a jolt of excitability, and I love this about myself! My teachers did not appreciate this at all. Disregard what authority figures believed about you or how you perceived them to feel about you.

All of these opinions from the past have remained bound within us as systemic truths. They are not truths. Change the story, change your life.

Be mindful about what you believe about yourself. If you have received consistent feedback that your legs are ravishing, and you don't agree, please don't list that yet. This is about what you admire about yourself. When you value it, others will follow. This is the practice of validating yourself.

Write down the one hundred essences of you, and, stay with me here, fold the list up, and place it under your pillow.

Each night or each morning, read these one hundred qualities out loud to yourself. You are a gift to this earth, and it is time to honor the person that is you. Some days you may cry. Allow the tears to flow. Some days you may think, *Hell, yeah! I'm awesome!* Some days you may laugh at yourself for writing this list. Keep reading until it is strong, unmovable, and solid within you. Affirm these attributes until you believe them.

When you encounter a man whose feelings, words, and actions do not match this level of love for yourself, you have permission to step away from him. Remember, you aim to win this game!

CHAPTER 9

The Fight for Inner Peace

Peace /pēs/ *noun*

1. a state of tranquility or quiet
2. freedom from disquieting or oppressive thoughts
   or emotions

I couldn't take any more. The war both within and without had become a maelstrom, and it could no longer be ignored. Neither wine nor restless activity would drown out the unrest. Ryan and I were in Cape Cod during the summer of 2017, one of the most beautiful places I had ever been.

My dearest friend, Michelle, and her husband, Jack, own a food truck business there, and they had invited us to their home. Ryan exulted at the opportunity, and I felt elated that the man whom I was dating would go with me on a trip to see my friends. I often travelled alone.

We had spent a few weeks camping with Ryan's son and daughter, ages 9 and 11, with whom I had spent a lot of time during our relationship. I was mentally exhausted from Ryan's gaslighting and all of the mental upheaval that this excursion caused me. I thought that the Cape Cod trip alone with Ryan would be more relaxing than the family dynamics that had played out on our back-country camping trip. Excited to show my love off to my friends, I felt certain that the struggle with men and relationships had ended. Did I mention how smart and talented I thought he was? My famous last words.

I felt like I had brought a possessed person to Cape Cod with me to meet my friends. I am not sure if the extensive time together revealed this hidden part of him or if it was the fact that the façade had faded and he could no longer hold his mask up, but the trip turned into a revolting distortion of reality.

The extent to which I had to go to in order to cover up all kinds of outrageous baloney during the week-long trip from hell was mind-boggling. It seemed that this trip would never end, and it led to my breakdown, recounted in Chapter 6, Undone.

All of the behaviors that were red flags along the way burst into giant flames before my eyes. I was scared to be around Ryan...or whoever inhabited his body at this time, and yet I felt misled into believing that I was the sole cause of any and all problems on this trip. The tension between us was palpable.

Ryan, whom I had placed on a pedestal high above myself, fell apart at the seams. I don't know if it was my persistent questioning and truth-seeking, but he couldn't keep up the Mr. Wonderful act anymore.

He became mouthy and condescending to my friends. Since he had no acquaintances in Cape Cod, he solicited allies at bars and restaurants. For example, when we visited my friends' food truck, which was parked outside a bar, he sat down next to a stranger and discussed our relationship within earshot of my friends and me. His buddy even offered to buy me a drink mid-conversation in the belief that we were all together.

But Ryan sidestepped him. "She can buy her own drink."

Ryan shooed me away with distain.

I wanted to bolt. My whole body was in a panic, and yet I had to save face the best I could. My dream guy acted like a psycho. Speechless and rattled, I pretended that I had not brought Mr. Hyde, of Dr. Jekyll and Mr. Hyde fame, with me to my friends' home. I attempted to diffuse the situation and soothe him in hopes that I could snap him out of this normal but abnormal state of being.

From day one of the trip, Ryan had acted huffy and unsettled. I guessed now that a problem outside of our relationship had been agitated. He tossed and turned in his sleep, complaining about the temperature in and the conditions of my gracious friends' spare bedroom.

I remember stopping Ryan in Michelle's driveway and whispering to him in a last-resort, mom kind of way! You know, where you are speaking slow and low but every fiber of your being is screaming and threatening the person, but you also don't want to be heard. I call it whisper yelling. You simply want the child to stop acting out.

I protested with a quiet shriek. "What are you doing? I can't believe the way you're treating my friends. Pull yourself together!"

He acted oblivious and innocent, and he protested that he wanted to get a hotel room. To escape my discomfiture, I agreed to his suggestion, and we booked a room for the remainder of the trip. Filled with shame, I knew that this would protect my friends from Ryan's unpredictable behavior.

I regret this solution to this day. While my friends did not have to experience his preposterous behavior in their home, I signed up for the mother lode of psychic attacks in a hotel room with no witnesses. Alone time opened up the playing field.

Upon arrival at the hotel, Ryan darted out of the car, leaving me behind to unpack the rental car and find the hotel room.

In a desperate attempt to save the trip and to appear as if we were having fun, Ryan announced the plans that he had crafted. Deep sea fishing had to be our first adventure. *Sure, why not? My love life is a shambles, perhaps I can add motion sickness to the wreckage.* Ryan strutted out onto the dock as confident as could be and made friends with the captain of the boat. I love the ocean and boats but couldn't wait to learn how my sea legs would handle this particular junket.

Well, one of us became seasick, and one of us caught a fifty-pound tuna! Oh, how I wish that I had been the one who got sick!

Ryan's ego could not handle going home empty-handed, and he retreated within like a sore loser. Upon our return from the fishing expedition, my friends celebrated my catch and rubbed it in Ryan's face with playful banter. I pled with them to stop, and I downplayed my fishing prowess as luck.

Luck had not been responsible for my fortune here. This had been some kind of fate, and I was enraged at fate. My monumental catch made Ryan furious at me. He couldn't hide it, although he faked being nice while posing in pictures with the tuna I caught. (I would not have been surprised if he had featured himself on one of his Facebook pages claiming his prize.) As soon as we docked, he stomped off the boat, leaving me alone while the captain's crew sliced and diced the tuna into portable pieces. I hauled five large baggies of tuna to the car by myself.

His actions thereafter were driven by a wounded and dangerous ego. Standing in the hotel room, I resorted to joking with him.

"There isn't room for all three of us in here." I referenced his giant ego, which had been taking up a ton of space.

What a foolish idea! Never poke an angry bear. I, too, had slipped into fight-or-flight mode at this point, and my patience with him was depleted. I was now ready to fend off his verbal attacks. Ryan honored me with a scary look and spoke in a tone that I had not heard before.

"Watch it. I can make you sorry, you know." He threatened me.

He burst out the door and spent the night away from the hotel room in which he had insisted we stay. He fled the hotel to sing at a nearby bar, and I do not know where he slept. I now realize that Ryan needed to feed his narcissistic ego, as I had no more accolades to fill his tank.

I, on the other hand, lay in bed terrified with my eyes wide open and peering at the ceiling. I was on heightened alert, and yet I did not move. I did not fight or flee, rather I attended to my freeze response. I did not go after him nor did I call my friend to come and pick me up.

When he entered the room the next morning, he was surprised to see me waiting for him. He thought that I would have bolted, and I do not understand why I didn't.

The last three days of the trip were traumatizing. We stopped talking, and I needed help. Ryan and I had been to a couple's therapist following one of his cheating episodes seven months before. At that time, I was willing to forgive his infidelity if he found us help.

From the Cape in Massachusetts, I sent an e-mail to this psychologist explaining to him the morass in which we found ourselves. My intuition called out, but I did not listen. I knew that this psychologist wouldn't help me.

When searching for a therapist to reconcile Ryan's cheating and my anxiety about it, I agreed to find a therapist to whom Ryan would listen. I knew that he would need a doctor who would match his intelligence level and a person who he would respect. I thought it a miracle that he would even step foot in the room with a therapist, let alone go with me. Therefore, stupid me, I gave Ryan the freedom to choose the therapist.

We met with four doctors. Ryan downplayed an exceptional man who was an expert in the field. I knew that this expert was capable of revealing the rift between us. I thought that he would hold us both responsible and did not seem to take sides.

The therapist who Ryan chose, however, was a month away from retiring. He mediated Ryan's clever attacks, for which Ryan now had an audience. Somehow going to therapy for Ryan's infidelity turned into me having problems.

To be exact, we discussed the subject of having babies. He did not want any, and I did. The sessions were designed to rid me of that desire so that Ryan could have what he wanted. I almost gave in. I almost caved and moved close to uttering that I didn't want children and that his kids would be enough in my life. I almost did, but I couldn't!

Of the ten therapy sessions, I left each one crying, and he left with the attention off of him and pride in his eyes. He then became the hero as he consoled me while I dealt with all of *my* problems. Ryan was a brilliant manipulator.

Dr. Ready-to-Retire did not even respond to my cry for help. Terror and panic set in. I called my mom. I failed to explain the complexity of the psychotic absurdity in which I found myself, and therefore, she offered sound advice that would work for a common relationship problem. In support, she advocated that I put my best foot forward.

If she had known the truth of Ryan's deceit, she would have demanded that I stick my best foot squarely up his rear end and head home.

In urgent pursuit of aid, I found a website that addressed the topic of anxiety and booked an appointment with the aforementioned Dr. Goldmann. Frightened that I wouldn't make it to the appointment date, I implemented some of the suggestions to relax that I found on this website.

First, I focused on one object in my environment until I felt a sense of being grounded and being present. The strategy took my anxiety from a ten to an eight, and any improvement felt like cause for celebration.

Despite this, I could not stay around Ryan for a minute longer. I avoided him. Communication failed during each pursuit to engage with him and mend our strife. I escaped for a jog on a beach trail and skidded down the path when a tree root seized the toe of my running shoe. Thank you, Mother Earth, for grounding me!

When your nervous system is out of sorts, computers seem to glitch, keys and credit cards go missing, and life malfunctions.

Eating sand pushed me over the edge. When I returned to the hotel with bloody knees and found out that Ryan had also gone for a run and now felt rejuvenated, I was livid. He treated me like I held on to problems and like I simply needed to get over all of his childish behaviors. All the while, he gaslit me and acted seven kinds of irrational.

At this point, full panic mode exploded inside of me. All of the sirens blared. Ryan pouted, sitting across from me as we ate, making no eye contact, and then taking off so that I would have to catch up or wonder where he had gone. These were strange and subtle behaviors that led to me following him around, but he did not go far or leave! He enjoyed this game of cat and mouse. I did not, but I felt as if I was the mouse in a maze scrambling for a way out down every dead end.

With one teeny glimpse of awareness, I stopped chasing my tail and stood frozen in the grocery store aisle. He noticed right away and threw some breadcrumbs my way.

"I hope that we can get through this." He took my hand and offered an ameliorating touch.

This was not true reassurance. It was a hit that kept me hanging on to his drug.

The vacation reached code red when we volunteered at the food truck during a spectacular wedding event in Cape Cod. This should have been a vision of love, but my heart felt tainted with agony. At one point during the day I borrowed Ryan's phone because I forgot my own. When I tapped the screen, up popped an article titled, *The Best Way to Break Up*.

When my face turned white, Ryan snatched the phone out of my hand. He demanded that I not overreact and belittled me into believing that if I responded in any way, I must be the one causing the problem.

In abusive relationships, blame-shifting is the norm. His shortcomings, cheating, and lies had always been my fault. As a loyal, non-cheating, people-pleasing partner, somehow I ruined our relationship. If I expressed my feelings, he told me that I dwelled on the deficiencies in the relationship and that I didn't know how to have fun.

I stuffed down the shame and humiliation and buttoned it in my chest and held my tears in. I then fell into a trance. I faked it and acted as if I was fine. While Ryan stole credit for any compliment given to chef, Jack, I laid low in hopes of not interacting with the group.

As with the fishing scene, unsolicited attention found me. A 5-year old boy at the gathering decided that he needed to compliment the cook of his grilled cheese sandwich. I happened to be that cook. Thrilled, this child thanked me for his grilled cheese sandwich. Like a teacher guiding a student, I demonstrated how to give credit to the real chef and deflected attention away from myself and toward Jack. After all, I had heated up the grill and thrown Jack's pre-made sandwich on the heat. Jack had been the culinary genius behind the sandwich, not me. Though I gave Jack the credit, Ryan derided me in front of an entire crowd.

So many times, I imagined myself stepping out of the food truck and drifting away. The food truck trauma felt like being trapped in my own personal trip to the underworld. I was not present. I wanted to escape with no plan. I wanted to vanish into the ocean, slip away unnoticed. Drowning myself seemed like a viable alternative proposition.

I recalled the overwhelming sense of fright when my teacher called me out in grade school when I wanted to go unseen. I knew that disappearing mid cheese sandwich would draw too much attention to me and that I would break down in front of my friends when questioned about my parting. Maybe these images of leaving protected my soul in some way, for I no longer participated in this psychological thriller. I had vacated this shit show in my mind, while my body moved through the motions. I managed the remainder of the vacation detached and aloof.

Alas, our departure day arrived! Had it been a week? Most vacations go by fast. This one dragged on forever. The flight home was no exception.

Ryan ran right to the bar when we arrived at the airport. He didn't invite me or wait for me. He walked away from me after we checked in as if he didn't know me! I had not caused a problem or said a word, though Ryan glared at me with loathing.

I contemplated changing seats, and yet I could not rustle up the mental wherewithal to have that conversation with the representative at the reservation desk.

Ryan had devalued me as much as he could, and I gave him respect in return. Through my studies on narcissistic abuse, I realize now that Ryan could not handle my unconditional love. Perhaps his own wounding had him believing that he did not deserve love, and therefore, he felt disgusted that I could love him through all of the ugliness.

The scenario also forced me to consider what must have been so wrong with me that I stayed mired in such emotional abuse. I mirrored Ryan's insecurities, and he hated it. He disliked that about himself, which made him loathe me. With no love for me, no empathy, Ryan couldn't hide his revulsion, not even through pity. He, like many others in our society, was void of any emotion except abhorrence.

The attendant made the final boarding call. As I willed my feet to move toward my seat, I was dumbfounded as I comprehended that I would have to spend four hours next to Ryan, a guy who despised me for existing. I could not wrap my head around Mr. Right turning into Mr. Not-In-A-Million-Fucking-Years.

I felt a deflating combination of *There is no way that I can sit next to Mr. Absolutely Not Right on this flight* and *This can't be real.*

Experiencing sophisticated psychological abuse for so long, I had adapted to his maneuvers. My defenses and keen subconscious understanding of this game stepped in. Aside from some logical contemplation to change my seat, I chose not to because I knew that this would trigger his next deceptive move toward me.

Knowing Ryan and personality types like his, I knew that he would use this as evidence that I belonged in the loony bin because I had caused a scene at the airport by changing seats. To this point, all you have is my side as hearsay. I understand this, and that is why I am writing to you. I understand the sophisticated nature of a manipulative mind. I understand the fear of lacking concrete evidence for the emotional and psychological shifts that you may have endured.

I survived emotional, psychological, and physical abuse, and I have no concrete evidence to show you. I am certain that a therapist somewhere possesses my anecdotal records, but a narcissist would laugh at any attempt to blame him with these scraps.

I even destroyed evidence of emotional and psychological abuse to protect myself from the narcissistic backlash of revealing the discrepancies to my abuser and to protect the man I thought I had loved from being found out. I was as much a piece of this disturbing puzzle as was Ryan.

Yes, concerned about what others would think, I didn't want to be blamed. Ryan had a true gift for adjusting his position to place me in the wrong. I twisted and turned to avoid attention or confrontation. We were a dynamic pair for hardship and self-loathing.

Other than the dreaded boarding, I don't remember the flight home. As if I had blacked out without a single drink, the flight felt like a blur. I don't even think I moved. I sat there numb for four hours straight, as an anxiety like no other stirred within me.

At one point on this vacation, Ryan had issued a command to me. "Go find some peace."

Interesting how a man who gaslit, projected, perverted my words, and slept with other women while with me could instruct me to go find peace after twisting the knife in my back. Well, friend, that is what I did. After all of this, inner peace seemed impossible. But I did it, and so will you.

Follow my route this way.

I saw Dr. Goldmann seven times following the Cape Cod breakdown. He utilized cognitive behavioral therapy with me. Yes, that's right, seven sessions, and I felt free. It is now six years later, and I haven't needed to see a therapist on the topic. I paid the substantial price of $160.00 a session, and I had never made a better investment in myself.

Vulnerable, with all of my wounds fresh and wide open, I gave up all control and trusted Dr. Goldmann. I did not have any other choice. His expertise felt like my last resort. If this did not work, I would have diagnosed myself as demented, unhinged, batty, or whatever worse would have been.

I'll give you an excellent view of what the days in my life looked like after breaking free of Ryan. As soon as my eyes opened in the morning, I cringed. Within seconds, the thoughts surged. Sometimes I didn't even notice it right away, but then I stopped myself. *Crap! Have these thoughts always been there? Is this how I have been talking to myself? No wonder I didn't notice the emotional abuse. Perhaps it aligned with my bellicose inner dialogue.*

It turns out that a combination of my nauseating self-talk and years of outside depleting words were careening around in my mind, shaking hands, and making destructive frenemies against me. As soon as my body awoke, I heard a quiet voice. *No, I can't be awake. I don't have the strength for another day.* My dreams allowed me to escape, and I detested waking up.

Aside from my mind spewing negative talk at me and feeling certain of my defectiveness, I fought for inner peace. I lost trust in others, myself, and any higher power. Years of betrayal were an insidious cut. Like a cold, piercing dagger, my ex's deception touched places that one would think that I would know how to protect. My mind, my body, and my soul had been attacked, and I had invited this trickery in with open arms.

Peering in the rear view mirror, I see now how hurt and exhausted I was. I could not open up for a hug from a friend or family members. I feared being rejected or disappointed by others. I spoke with mutual friends whom I met during the relationship and explained that we could no longer be friends. I isolated myself or met with a friend one-on-one at my house and discussed the calamity that was my love life. I shared the self-blame, the shame, and my eagerness to change the pattern of inviting contemptible men into my life.

I knew that the cure lived deep within me, and I went on a mission.

I avoided any place that I might see Ryan. When I did go out, Ryan somehow made an appearance, or he had been there the night before, and people were talking about him. This triggered me and caused me to retreat.

My internal dialogue felt tumultuous. I thought that I would never find peace. The trash talk wouldn't stop, and recovery from narcissistic abuse felt like a boxing match. It felt like taking one step forward and two steps back. It felt like an endless amusement park ride. Frightened, my day-to-day life felt void of peace or faith that I would ever recover.

I knew that I had to make changes that would make a difference. *What would have a significant impact on my inner discord? Brain surgery? Medication? Giving up on relationships forever?* I flirted with the idea of buying a few kittens to hop on the trail toward my single, cat-lady life.

During this time, you may have lots of ideas about how to save yourself and discover inner peace, but most of them are Band-Aids. The profuse soul-bleeding will not respond to self-cures and temporary fixes. We have to stop the hemorrhaging. Once you realize that your wounds of abuse are not closing, you may fall into a pit of despair and conclude that all of your efforts are for naught. It is a scary time, and I am here for you. It does feel like you are going off the deep end. You have been fighting an inner war, and you are not winning.

 SOULutions

SOULution #1:
Building Trust

Every single day we make decisions to trust ourselves and others. When you vault into your car, you trust that other drivers will obey the traffic rules. You trust that you'll receive your morning coffee after placing your order with your favorite barista. You trust that you will make it to work without being accosted by a madman.

We all trust that our co-workers will turn up to manage and do their jobs or at least call in sick. We trust that we will receive our paycheck, that pressing the button on the elevator will take us to our destination, and that there will be food on the grocery store shelves when we shop for dinner. We depend on the community outside ourselves to run in an efficient way. Our day-to-day lives operate on trust.

During this time of betrayal and uncertainty, you may want to find ways to trust. I have always been drawn to the sky, and therefore, I searched there. I could depend on one event happening every single day. In the morning, the sun rose, and in the evening, the sun set. Every day the sun rose and set. I found refuge in this. As mentioned before, I built trust with the universe guided by the sun. I will repeat myself and remind you of these practices throughout the book. Change requires repetition.

My ego, my heart, my soul, and my body needed proof that trust was possible. I woke up early and met the day at sunrise. Even if I didn't leave time to stroll with the morning sun, I drove to the park and watched the sun peek out of the darkness. The sun made and kept a promise, and I received it. A loving bond between the two of us formed.

At night, exhausted and worn out, and perhaps moving toward a glass of wine and isolation, I kept my promise to the sun. I retired for sunset hikes with my dog. I thanked the sun for being there for me.

I didn't realize then that the sun grew into being my teacher. I built my own integrity with the sun's guidance. I learned to trust the universe and a greater power. I discovered that I could trust myself as well. I proved to be dependable. This profound lesson led me home to myself. No pre-requisites required. No training or skills necessary. This lesson changed my inner nature and planted a seed of hope.

Be your own gardener. Plant your own seed of hope, sow it, and bask in an experience that you can trust. Right now, write down what you will do to rebuild and acknowledge trust in your life.

SOULution #2:
Drowning Out the Noise

As I mentioned, as soon as my eyes opened in the morning, the querulous chatter swirled in. In fact, it happened when I slipped into bed as well. I decided to drown out this noise with positive affirmations. I didn't have any of my own. Positive feedback and praise felt foreign to me, so much so that I found it annoying to listen to uplifting words of affirmation.

To stop myself from lying in bed and stewing, I had to wake up and hit the floor with my feet without hesitation. I shot out of bed in order to extract myself from the battlefield of my own thoughts.

You may also be tempted to stay in bed and dwell on your misery. Utilize the Do-Do Method, and haul your ass out of the trenches. When that alarm goes off, spring out of bed like it's Christmas morning! Speaking in terms of energy, it is.

Next, drown out those negative thoughts with positive ones! Listen to recordings of affirmations. I once scoured the internet for free recordings and affirmations, and now I produce my own recordings.

If you are like me, it is possible that you have never been spoken to with high regard. On the rare occasion when others did pay me a compliment, it arose out of an achievement for which I strove. The negative remarks outweighed the positive ones. Once you learn to speak to yourself in a kind way, you will never again tolerate digs or insults.

When you wake up in the morning or when you go to bed at night, play these affirmations. Even if you don't listen, play them. Your subconscious will listen. Your heart will listen. Even if you are judgmental or irritated, listen to these soothing recordings. If your mind tends to wander while in the car, play the recordings in the car, anyway. They'll penetrate sometime soon.

You may wish to be wary of devising your own ideas in this regard. This may be a form of self-sabotage. Perhaps you decide to listen to your favorite love songs instead, and you end up pining for him and crying yourself to sleep. Maybe you take all of the other advice out there and conclude that you have to use a magical phrase or specific text to lure him into your arms. Maybe you believe that the best way to get over him is to get under someone else. Yes, I have heard all of this, and more, from women. Please, please do not do this.

We want to re-wire your brain forever right now. This is for your own well-being. I want you to reach a point where you may rest your head on your pillow and sigh in refreshing relief.

You may hear advice about how to quiet your mind and how to close your eyes and be still. I am sorry, but when you are fleeing narcissistic abuse and your mind is wired to tear you apart, I don't think that you will be able to calm yourself. Your mind may play mean tricks on you, and your old patterns of self-talk may solidify. Also, attempting to be quiet may make you feel like a failure if you find that you can't do it.

I am setting us up to win here. Please reference my website and contact information in the back of this book, so that I can personalize a recording for you to ease your anxious mind. That alone is a positive move that may bring you to more inner peace. I could never find serenity within, so I listened while moving through my day. With no wrong way to find peace for yourself, you'll keep going until you do.

SOULution #3:
The Therapy Dilemma

I have had a substantial number of disappointments with therapists.

My ex, Scott, managed to find me an inexpensive intern while he was in prison. He wanted to help me with my pinioned-up heart. The poor woman psychology student seemed rather unsure about what to do with me. I spent myriad hours and a boatload of money relaying my traumatic history to get her up to speed. No work or intervention occurred.

After I discovered that the inferior relationship patterns replicated and that I could not shake the traumatic thoughts of my ex being escorted to prison, I ventured into finding help for myself once more. My current relationship with Mike wreaked of anxious/avoidant attachment and bordered on neglect, involved drinking, and smacked of a lack of commitment.

The therapist recommended to me by a co-worker pitied me on more than one occasion, *Poor thing*. I bawled my eyes out during almost every session. Mike had me thinking that our relationship problems were my fault. His avoidance and indifference exacerbated my separation anxiety. I sought help to overcome my past and blamed myself for the lack in the relationship.

I was crippled by low self-worth, but Mike agreed to meet with my therapist hoping that this would help us...or me. My load lightened when he took this step for us. But what I believe is that he felt that this would get me off of his back.

Following his one-on-one session with her, he entered my home and radiated unparalleled panache. "You poor thing."

Mike praised the therapist for making a caustic comment about me, and then he refused to tell me what she had said. If you would like a glimpse into hell, try that hat on for size.

I had been seeing this therapist, trusting her, and then in the blink of an eye Mike alone, or Mike and the therapist, or the therapist, razed all sense of trust that I had built up. The ground beneath my feet shook. Not knowing what she had told Mike, or even knowing if he had made it all up, drove me to the edge.

I discontinued my work with that therapist and found counsel in personal development books and the bathtub. I gave up on traditional therapy and ignored my problems. I attended grad school, bought a house on my own, and lived in survival mode, wondering when love would find me.

After five years flew by, and I cycled through the same problems on an increasing scale, I somehow acquired enough hope to find a third therapist to perhaps fit my needs. Using the list of therapists associated with my health insurance plan felt fraught with challenges, as if the system had been designed in the model of the Department of Motor Vehicles rather than the guiding hand that I needed to help me. I knew way too much about myself and the area of psychology necessary to settle for a substandard therapist, and yet I found myself sitting across from one.

"Have you journaled?" This woman from the insurance list prodded me.

Okay, am I on a bloopers show? I paid this woman $100.00 an hour to suggest to me that I journal? It is official, then. I have lost my mind. How did I know more about my condition than did the professionals in front of whom I plopped myself over and over? Why could I not find the help that I needed for real change and freedom from abuse?

I am illuminating this point to save you some time. Only you know if you may become your best self by yourself. You may need support on this road to inner peace. I recommend that you trust your inner knowing. If you feel that a therapist would benefit you, it is the right choice for you.

Visit three therapists in person before deciding on one. Take with you a list of your goals, questions, and major concerns. Determine what this person's background is, and inquire how they choose their patients. You will want a therapist with whom you may have a relationship. You need a safe place to build trust.

A second direction in which you may decide to go is coaching. This may be a more expensive means to achieve your desired objective, but the results may surprise you. Coaches are not restricted in what they may provide for you. A coach may give you exercises and hold you accountable to meet your goals. For me, an investment in a coach was priceless, and working with my coach launched me off of the hamster wheel of my own indecision and lackluster ideas. Again, choose wisely. Does the coach or mentor have the relationship you want? Do they work with clients similar to you? Discern.

You also have you! You may take you with you on this journey without a therapist or a coach. With the support of self-empowerment books like this one, a circle of encouraging friends, and seeking out like-minded individuals through free or inexpensive Meetup groups or recovery groups, you may find your peace. The most important aspect of doing it alone is to ensure that you have a hand to which you may reach out if you find that you are lost inside yourself. We are not meant to isolate ourselves from others for long periods of time, though short periods are encouraged as an incubation time to listen to your needs.

If you are able to make wise choices, and have some degree of discipline, this is outstanding. If you find yourself spiraling out of control, speak up. A friend will always be there for you. On this planet full of billions of people, no matter how lost you feel, a compassionate other is always available for you.

CHAPTER 10

Easier Said than Done

(a.k.a. *Just Leave Him*)

With supportive intentions, my friends and family members demanded that I stop complaining and leave Mike, break up with him, and end this already.

From the outside peeking in, this appeared to be a no-brainer. Your relationship sucks, and you feel depressed, so end it. Could it be that easy? End the pandemonium, end the relationship. If you want a valid reason to escape, consider the fact that he cheats, he lies, and he manipulates.

All of these characterizations are true, right? You feel spurned, insulted, and undervalued. Then why are we fixated on all of his charming traits as if they are all that we see? Feeling like you can't live without him is a disturbing sign.

If you are having a hard time ending a relationship that you know is not right for you, I feel you. I have attempted to end relationships that lived on long past their expiration date. I mean *years* past. These relationships became moldy, unpalatable, and even spiteful right before my eyes.

My first adult relationship lasted for twelve years. I adored Mike... and then the bottom fell out. We broke up over and over. He cheated on me, or did he? Were we even together at that time, or did he move on though I did not receive the memo? Perhaps I felt obliged to him by the cosmic bond of physical attachment.

I should have left him early on, but I didn't. Addicted, we both played an alluring role in holding our relationship together through a decade. I received less attention each year, but it was enough to keep me in the thick of it. He forgot my birthdays, and I accepted every excuse offered. Invested in him, I stayed.

I thought that the problem had to be me. He led me to believe that I didn't understand him, or men in general, for that matter. Had growing up with three masculine brothers and a father not taught me how to communicate with men? Deemed the inferior one, I accepted crumbs like a loyal servant.

I attended social events alone and hit the town by myself. As I met people, they did not realize that I was in a relationship, since I always flew solo. Life-long friends expected me to attend events alone after I lost my cool with inquisitions about where Mike was all of this time. *I don't know! I am here, isn't that enough?* The anxious attachment and his avoidant absence had taken an obvious toll on me.

So how did a twelve-year relationship steeped in cheating and egregious psychopathy end? Well, after those years of feeling unappreciated and insignificant, no matter whose fault, I searched for answers to save the relationship. I read book after book, I attempted to talk to Mike, and I attended therapy. When I initiated a conversation about the instability of our relationship, Mike up and left for days! I suffered abandonment triggers galore. I waited up and gazed out the bedroom window waiting for his car to pull into the garage. I sent texts pleading for him to return home. With no response, I was pelted by my own worry.

Like a gift from heaven, or an insult to my integrity, I then received attention and messages from my ex, Scott. Scott and I had our own trauma-induced entanglement from when he was arrested by the police.

He interrogated me. "Ellen, how could you settle for a guy who is so uninterested in you, a man who doesn't adore you? How can you stay with him? When are you going to leave him?"

Knowing my capacity to love, Scott insisted that I deserved better.

When a man outside of your relationship impacts that relationship, fractured or leaky energy occurs. I knew that my ex should not be in the picture, but I allowed it. I opened up to him because I knew that he was right and that my love for Mike had been unrequited for too long. Though I felt shame for this, I needed help. I had allowed myself to live in a lifeless, loveless relationship, and Scott wanted me to see the shambles that I had endured?

While Scott wanted me to leave Mike and be with him, confusion won the day. My empathy toward Mike if I hurt him tore my heart open. I knew that I could not inflict the rubbish that was in my own mind on him, though I had been on the receiving end of his less-than efforts for years. I cared more about my absent boyfriend's feelings than I did my own. My needs were an afterthought, if they even occurred to me at all. I had to preserve Mike's feelings first if at all possible.

As a result, I simmered with indecision. Indecision is your enemy to true love. It will cause you more heartache than you may imagine. It is better to make the wrong decision than it is to make no decision.

I felt like an emotional cheater, and yet I had been dismissed for years. This was a lose/lose proposition. I could not run off with Scott, nor could I contemplate one more night with my absent partner. Not a nibble of wholesome and refined love could be found in this storm of my own making. Corral the courage, and steer the ship away from rough waters. You are, after all, the captain.

Burdened with indecision and crippled with fear, I retreated to Mexico alone for a month! I could not handle one more moment in this horror show.

I fled the scene with my tail between my legs so that I could see and make sense of my love life. I missed Mike while I was away. After all, we had been together for twelve years. But I could not go on with him disappearing for days on end. I could not go on with him ignoring me at night. I could not go on with him leaving dirty dishes in the sink when the dishwasher was a foot away.

I needed clarification about my life. At 38 years old, I could not believe that we had not started a family by now. Bitterness and resentment filled my body, and I could no longer hold it in.

The Mexico escape felt like the antidote that I needed. I coasted around in a fog, attempting to make sense of my life. Leaving a twelve-year relationship felt next to impossible for me. Committed to Mike and co-dependent on him for emotional regulation, I had invested my time, my heart, and a boatload of tears in us. How could I ditch the investment and leave with nothing to show for it?

I believe that this is what made it so hard. Love did not keep us together, pride held us in place. I identified as Mike's girlfriend. I identified as an achiever who did not give up or throw away a relationship.

Anxiety about losing Mike was stifling, but I had already lost myself. Not who I wanted to be, I was living a constricted and apologetic life. I lived in constant fear of abandonment, with an overactive nervous system locked in fight/flight/freeze mode. I had not learned the pedestal practice at the time, but in order to end the relationship, I had to get serious. That relationship felt like a fantasy, a cover up. It did not resemble the relationship that I had made it out to be in my heart. In fact, it was over long before now, and I lay broken, alone, and done.

I summoned the courage to let Mike know that our relationship was over, but he already knew it. While I was in Mexico, he helped himself to a few valium in my bathroom cabinet, left over from my broken wrist after a snowboarding fall. He admitted to wanting to dull his pain and his shame at our mutual participation in a toxic relationship.

He then made some real efforts. Surprised to have him home more often, I recall a time when he mentioned to me that we could get married, with the same intonation as if we could order a pizza. His passionless demeanor wearied me. I felt like a consolation prize, not the grand prize.

He suggested that if he didn't make it with me, he wouldn't make it with any woman. Unimpressed by his too little, too late, insignificant gestures, we broke up. Within a month, Mike was dating a younger woman, who seemed to adore him as I once did. I ran into him one day and inquired about her, with shame pouring out of me in buckets.

According to Mike, she partied a great deal, and she threw a landscaping rock through his car window because he wouldn't acknowledge her texts. He depicted her as unstable, but I knew the truth.

I cried. A part of me wished that I had thrown the rock through that window, but I knew that I could never have survived the indignity of such an act. Regardless, these dangerous stories showed me that leaving the relationship was a fortunate gift to me. I felt so glad to be free to rebuild my self-worth. I could see now the extreme situation in which I had been living.

Don't blame yourself for being less than judicious. These relationships are all-consuming. It is not easy to see through muddy waters, and I have hope in my heart that Mike and his girlfriend found clarity and peace for themselves.

The three-year relationship with Ryan, whom I believe had narcissistic personality disorder, followed six months after I ended my relationship with Mike. As I struggled to build myself up, Ryan tuned in to my vulnerable state like a shark to blood.

Ryan and I also had an on and off relationship. Breaking up with him felt more dramatic than it had been with Mike, and it was never mutual. One of us always kept it going, a co-dependent dance.

I broke up with Ryan often because I sensed trouble in the air. These breakups fell around times of infidelity, which, of course, made sense. The distance that I insisted on lasted long enough for Ryan to feed off of the attention from whoever the flavor of the month was. The wise women called him out, and he hastened to make amends with me.

How embarrassing. I can't say that I knew that he acted this way at the time, but as the pieces of the puzzle fell into place, I discovered that Ryan lied to me and cheated. This left me feeling like a fool, a girl who did not trust her own intuition.

So, why couldn't I ever make the breakup stick? Well, similar to what Mike had done, Ryan fed me crumbs when I was starved for attention and affection. He held my face in his hands, peered deep into my eyes, and made promises to me that spoke to my most cutting wounds. He made vows related to family, to building the relationship that he knew I wanted with every cell in my body. This desire of mine made me putty in his hands. This desire clouded my perception of reality.

We broke up forever after three backbreaking years. This occurred after the recovery from anxiety with Dr. Goldmann and after Ryan ran off to Europe and slept with a woman he met at the hotel bar. He proffered a story about how he had assisted a drunk woman to her room. What a hero! What a crock!

So, why was I so blind? How could I have forgotten...or ignored... this betrayal? Get this! Somehow, after we broke up, we decided to spend Christmas day together in 2017. I planned to spend it alone cooking, and he happened to be alone, so I invited him over. *Ugh!* I know! I felt for him. Did I mention that I feel your confusion related to narcissistic abuse? This is it. This is the real deal.

We had been talking even after all of his duplicity. A potent force, our attraction lured us in. What could I have been thinking?

He arrived at my door dressed to the nines. With a gleam in his eyes, he handed me a gift. He bought me a Ray Charles album that I did not have yet. In fact, I didn't own a record player, so I did not have a use for this gift.

With scarlet cheeks, I reveled in the present. "Thank you so much! I love it! But...I don't have a record player."

With a clever grin, he darted out to the car and carried in a wrapped box. Ryan, whom I was not dating anymore and ended up spending the holiday with on a whim, bought me a record player.

Shocked, I quivered. "I don't have a present for you."

Taken aback, I hadn't realized that people bought their exes Christmas presents. The truth remains that they don't!

We drank, listened to records, danced, and fell into each other's arms. His love-bombing worked, and I ended up wrapped and tied to him with ribbons and bows. It was a tremendous day, until it turned south.

I pulled back from our embrace to chat with him about what we were doing spending the holiday together, him giving me gifts, and making out. It occurred to me that our time together had been an inconsequential moment in his exotic other life. Amidst the liquid truth that we consumed, Ryan admitted that a woman was coming to see him the next day to spend New Year's Eve with him.

I lost it! I kicked him out of my house. I skyrocketed into the most anxious, angry state of my life. How could I have been so stupid? How could he be so manipulative and bold? I thought that I had left this man behind. How was it possible that he entered my house and twirled me around his little finger? Ryan was the Oscar winner in a demented performance. My life mimicked a psychological thriller and, as if viewing the show on TV, I was irritated with the woman character who wouldn't leave her abuser.

After deceit, lies, manipulation, infidelity, and discarding, Ryan and I were in a relationship whirlwind. This was the lowest point in my life.

The next day, knowing that his visiting girlfriend had arrived, I packed my car with all of the items that he had left at my house for five months after our breakup. He used to stop over when he needed attention with the excuse that he needed to pick up a few more things. He always left behind a valid reason to return. He had his next visit planned. It makes me sick to think about this now. My mind does not work that way.

I stuffed all of his junk into my car and headed to his condo, aware of the scene that I could act out there. I would be the raging lunatic ex prepared to dumbfound him and myself. I imagined that Ryan would open the door, and his gobsmacked and nearsighted guest would hear me handing his trivial garbage to him. I wanted her to know about me. I wanted her to be scared off. In fact, I later looked her up on Facebook and sent her a message telling her that he had been with me the night before.

I spoke to this earlier, and I don't advise doing this. I figured that his visitor would see me as a jealous woman, since she was now ensnared in his web and a victim of his lies. At the time, I felt that I had to do this out of respect for women. Regardless, I wanted to cause a scene, and I wished to reveal his lies. I felt like a woman on one of those believe-it-or-not shows where the star of the show snaps. While great for TV ratings, this sucks in real life.

As I drove to Ryan's place in this defining opportunity for vengeance, a voice in me (yes, you know the one) whispered to me. As if the voice projected straight from my heart and rose around me in the car, I felt filled with light and silence. *Look for a sign.* This voice wanted me to stop my pursuit but appeared wise enough to know that I would not listen to a direct command or comply with an order not in support of my goal. Set on this mission, my ego had no intention of letting up.

After hearing the voice, though, my heart and I scanned for a sign while my bewitched mind kept an eye on the road to Ryan's. As I turned off the highway and on to the exit that led to his house, my brother sent me a text. I don't remember what it said, but it slowed me down. Then my friend, Will, sent a text. My phone had been silent up to this point. These two acts were enough. I plucked myself out of my trance and called Will.

In fact, Will was friends with both Ryan and me. This friend knew the whole picture. I filled him in on the latest story to date. I admitted that my car was filled with Ryan's belongings and that I intended to go to his place to crash his party of two.

Will's voice of reason rang through to me. "I don't think you want to do that."

I burst into tears and knew that he was right. I turned the car around. Once I arrived at my house, I placed Ryan's stuff in a corner of the garage as tears streamed down my face. I later dropped his belongings off on a day when I knew that he would be at work, so as not to make a scene. Though ashamed and depleted, somehow grace found me. Somehow, I was not all lost or hopeless or even alone, for that matter.

This is what leaving a narcissistic man looks like. When kindhearted friends and family members enjoin you to *Just leave him*, they have no idea what this will take from you. Tears well up in my eyes as I acknowledge the loss of control and my fears related to rejection, which caused me to hold on to this horrific relationship with a death grip. *Let go or be dragged* is a quote that reverberated like a bell ringing in my heart.

I am here to assist you with making your breakup less dramatic and save you some face. Re-building from this low point was difficult and profound for me. Leaving a narcissistic or abusive man may be the most challenging thing you will ever do.

The Mind-Maze

Let's first identify the tricks that one's mind plays that mislead one into believing that senseless and co-dependent relationships are salvageable.

- *What Ifs.* I filled my head and my heart with *what ifs* about these relationships. *What if* Mike changes his mind and wants to marry me? *What if* Ryan is just stumped? *What if* I stop giving Mike a hard time? *What if* I change how I talk, act, or dress? *What if* all relationships are difficult? *What if* Eric is the last guy on earth who will love me?

- Extending the Honeymoon. This is when your mind hamstrings you to the rapture of the relationship as it was when you first met. You live in the beginning of the relationship and refuse to see that the honeymoon period is over and will never return. Beware of exciting relationship jumpstarts that run out of gas in three months, and *I love you forever*'s that meant *I love you right this minute.*

  The fantasy of who you first met may not be the man standing in front of you today. When I made Ryan my knight in shining armor, I took the blame for perpetuating the fantasy in my mind. The fairy tale, in fact, had been him being the wolf in sheep's clothing.

- Staying for Potential. *We had such potential. If Mike would commit, we would be an exemplary couple. If he would rush home after his nine-to-five, we would be happy together. If we stopped drinking, if we communicated better, if Mike talked about his feelings, if I learned to relax, this disaster would be a success.*

  Mike was smart, attractive, and fun, but we were incompatible. Making excuses for your man's behavior or your own is an act of falling in love with potential. It is not reality, and it is a dead end street that we drive down if we are not careful.

- Feelings. *No man has ever made me feel this way before. This man must be special. This man must be the real deal. He must be the one. We are kindred spirits.*

These feelings and emotional bonds are a dangerous pitfall. True love does not fantasize or exaggerate itself. True love does not require fabrication. True love is consistent, reliable, and certain. It will not leave you whirling, up one second and down the next.

Please do not fall for the hype that sells love to us in commercials and in movies. No filmmaker has yet to portray true love in an hour and a half-long movie. This movie has yet to be seen, and it wouldn't sell, anyway. True love is not a drama or a psychological thriller. True love is a feeling of peace. Be wary of the intense feelings, as you may be in a danger zone.

- Believing Words Over Actions. Word seduction is one of the tools that a gifted manipulator may use. He knows what you long to hear, and he knows the secrets of your heart. It is possible that you shared your desire to have a family with your perceived soulmate early on, and now he has all of the ammunition he needs to keep you in a state of wishful thinking.

  He doesn't have to do much. He keeps you satisfied with romantic words that become foreplay for your future with him. You are smitten and under his spell. When you realize that his actions don't match his words, it is too late. You are already duped. To save face, you may excuse his actions and rely on his words. He uses words that do not hold up, words that don't back up his actions, which leaves you disappointed and resentful.

  Believe his actions. For a man of integrity, his actions are his word, and he will never have to defend them. You will not feel let down because his intentions are clear.

When you are having a hard time leaving him, see if you are snagged in the mind-maze of making sense of his words and his actions. The act of reading about these lures is sending an awareness message that is landing in your subconscious. We are reaching in and pulling out what needs to be seen to gain clarity in order to make lasting changes.

 SOULutions

SOULution #1:
Save Yourself

At some point, you will have to save yourself from this inferno. No hero or friend is going to fly in to rescue you, and no therapist is going to understand your inner experiences or how you relate to others in this world. Each individual life is inherently unique. I had to shoo out my perceived saviors. I could not discern the integrity of who I welcomed into my life. My entire being decided that the gig had to be up.

It is this breakdown time when you feel like you don't care at all that brings a sense of grounding. I didn't care what friends or family thought of me. Seeking outside validation halted with a screech, because it wasn't serving me.

Ryan called to reveal that his latest woman thought that I must be an obsessed ex for sending her the Facebook message that he had been making out with me the day before she arrived, that he had been at my house giving me gifts, serenading me with song, and dancing the night away.

He called me on the phone. "It's okay for your friends to see your crazy, Ellen, but you shouldn't show her."

For the first time in my life, a feeling grew inside of me that I could not contain. *What the hell!* No more hiding my feelings.

As if time stood still, the words exited my mouth with malevolence heretofore unknown to me. "I don't care what you two assholes think of me! Have a nice life together!"

I hung up the phone with Ryan forever.

After the intensity of what I endured with Ryan and the minimizing of my voice throughout the relationship, my friends and I now laugh at this.

Anna rejoiced at my moxie. "Well, you sure showed them, didn't you?"

She knew that it had taken all I had inside to deliver a vitriolic remark to Ryan.

I had never spoken up for myself in that way before, and I had never resorted to calling a guy an asshole, let alone the guy I idolized. I had always feared the repercussions of such an act. It served as comical relief to summon the nerve to do it to Ryan, to whom it should have been done much sooner.

From then on, mission-save-myself launched. I requested the roommates of mine move out, and they did...in a fit of rage one of the two took items of mine on the way out.

No longer would I allow this type of person in my life, and neither should you. No more Mrs. Nice Gal. This is your life. Take it.

For months, I read a postcard of Malcolm X fastened to my refrigerator by a magnet, which read, *No one can give you freedom. Nobody can give you equality or justice. You take it.* There it is. No more pondering why these messed up scenarios happened to me. No more reacting to the difficult people in my life. I wanted freedom, and I had to be the one to fight for it for me.

Lost on this island of one, I could give up and die, or I could risk it all and set off through treacherous waters. Remember, the hero for whom you are waiting is you.

SOULution #2:
Be Loyal to Your Creed

Now is the time to establish your own creed, a set of statements that will guide your actions. Your feelings are unstable. At times you will feel superior and ready to take on this healing and your life. At other times, you will feel at the end of your rope and ready to throw in the towel, apt to go home with that hot guy, or willing to accept unwanted advances out of loneliness. At times you will want to pick up the phone and call your ex.

Yes, I know. After all of the gunk that you have survived, you may want answers from him. Instead, we are going to compose your creed. In times of temptation, when you want to submit to your old ways, you are going to rely on your oath and your contract with yourself, not on your emotions, which may be dysregulated.

Some may refer to this creed as a mantra. I believe that the word mantra earned a stigma as soon as it found a place in our vocabulary. Ruining words is unfortunate, but that's us human beings.

A creed feels timeless and etched in stone. Think of it that way. Etch your creed on your heart. My heart holds these truths, and I am accustomed to placing my hand on my heart when I reiterate these statements. That way, I may place my hand on my heart at any time and feel them.

- *I keep myself safe at all costs.* I developed a wealth of coping mechanisms to survive narcissistic abuse, one of which was the aforementioned Stockholm Syndrome. Stockholm Syndrome occurs when the victim attaches feelings of safety, affection, and trust toward her captor or abuser. The attachment is familiar and, therefore, the victim is conditioned to race into the arms of her abuser, as she may have a hard time trusting her own judgment.

  She feels safe in what is known even though circumstances may be appalling. These statements brought awareness to my environment. I listened to my triggers, and I made a vow. *I protect my heart, my body, and my soul no matter what. I will leave any situation that makes me feel unsafe.* At the time that I fashioned these statements, I did not believe that I had the strength to leave a relationship if it felt unsafe. It felt safer for me to remain there, hidden.

- *I listen to my heart and act in accordance with what I hear.* My heart knew that Ryan, Mike, and Mitch were risky and dangerous prospects. I did not listen, and I did not act in harmony with my heart's desires. Sit in silence, and listen to what your heart is expressing to you. That is your authentic voice, and it will lead you to the life to which you aspire. Be audacious.

- *I have the courage to love again.* In taking complete responsibility for my actions, I became aware that I feared commitment. I was emotionally unavailable because I did not want to get hurt anymore. I failed to be honest or authentic in my past relationships because I tortured myself and twisted myself into pretzels in order to be the person my boyfriend wanted me to be at any given time.

I didn't want these empty relationships filled with cheating and lies, and yet I stayed to conform to a storyline. I had to search my soul for the courage to offer deep, meaningful, genuine love to another person, and I had to risk being seen (scars and all). I confessed to myself and the world that I wanted soulmate love, marriage, and family.

Your creed may sound different than mine. Take some time to listen to the desires of your heart. If it makes you cry, you have struck gold. *I will keep myself safe at all costs* crippled me with tears. I had no idea that I had allowed myself to go so unprotected for so long. I had allowed myself to be hurt. I had not controlled who I let into my life. I now take ownership of this control, and you can too.

This creed is your statement of influence over your own life. Repeat it aloud every morning. Keep it with you throughout the day. Erase whatever words that have been holding you hostage, and replace any false beliefs with the creed that you design for yourself.

Don't move on until you have written out your statements of truth. You need this roadmap to guide you out of the dark.

SOULution #3:
Stick to the Plan

In your official decree to save yourself and rid your life of wily people, it is important to devise a game plan along with your creed. You need to be able to rely on a structure to support you through times of indecision, temptation, and instability. We are not attempting to utilize more crutches, though we may now choose support with awareness and wisdom.

I endorse taking a break from dating. Six months is the goal. More may seem like you're stranded on a deserted island. Fewer will have you counting the days until you wrap your arms around the next best guy. Six months will provide breathing room, recovery time, and a solitude to re-build, regenerate, and restore yourself.

A strict guideline of choosing to be single for this time will become easier as you retrieve your lost self and mend your broken heart. Your heart will need time for treatment from co-dependency. A sadness may appear that you have been avoiding for years.

Draw out this game plan. Know what you are going to do with your days, and follow through. Don't overdo it, and don't live in accordance with the fairy tale or conjure up a life radically different from what you are used to. This is a time of recovery. Below is a guide to assist you:

Wake Up: Listen to positive affirmations, journal about the day's intentions, stroll with the rising sun, and read your creed aloud.

Get It Done: Attend to all of your obligations. Arrive at your job every day. Recognize and appreciate the benefits of your livelihood, whether it be your co-workers, a paycheck, or a purpose.

Take A Nap: Your soul needs to rest. Allow yourself time to sleep. Listen to peaceful music or guided meditations.

Step It Out: Move your body, even if it is not vigorous exercise. Go for a sunset bike ride, indulge in an excursion to a museum, wander in the park, or meet a friend for dancing (but do not gossip or cogitate).

Connect: Find ways to interact with loved ones. Disengage from old patterns, and establish a splendid framework for your marvelous self. If you always hit happy hour, switch it up for tea and coffee, an event, or a fitness class with a friend.

Exercise Your *No*: Let me be straight with you. Others won't care that you are reviving your life. You will have to use your *no* when you are called to work overtime or cover a shift. You will have to reply *no* to that friend who asks you out but always gossips and complains.

During my time of *no*, a man approached me at the coffee shop, and we engaged in a riveting conversation related to the book that I was reading. As we finished visiting, he asked for my phone number, and I declined to give it to him. I did this for no other reason than to remain true to myself.

Dinner: Cook for yourself. Prepare yourself delectable meals, and sit alone and appreciate the meal, your effort, and the chef (you!). Conjure up images of the man that you would like to be with and the life that you would like to have. Feel that place as if it is here now, and not out of reach.

Create: Decorate an inviting, peaceful space for yourself. Buy yourself flowers. De-clutter by tossing out items that remind you of that old life. Save money by trading decorative items with others. And then liven up your home with your favorite guests.

Plan: Schedule an activity that you love, or inquire if you may join a friend as she participates in her favorite hobby. This won't cost a dime, and these action steps will push you out of your comfort zone and allow you to collaborate with interesting people.

Regardless of what structure you install, stick to this plan. Do not waver. If you do, from that icky and wounded position of emotional abuse, you may attract more of the same low-energy circumstances.

The guy who invites you out is not the man you hope he will be. Please don't be tricked. It is too soon. You are vulnerable, and if a suitor is picking up on that, he is the same guy with a different face. Do not be fooled. Stick with the game plan no matter what.

Professional athletes do not throw away their well-thought-out game plan when they fall behind in the playoffs. They dig in and reinforce what they know will take them to the top.

Success begins with a plan and ends with the determination to follow it through despite any and all distractions. Leave yourself reminders to stick with the game plan. You will need them! You are re-training your mind and your body to act according to your standards, not your ever-changing emotions. You can do this!

CHAPTER 11

Compassion and Grief

Dear Love,

You are entering a stage that many people may not understand. Don't be upset by this stage. Sorrow may penetrate your bones and weigh you down in even the safest of settings. At some point, you may feel a heart-wrenching loss of your relationship. You may even grieve for the pattern of overreacting that is vanishing inside of you.

Your body does not know whether these attachments and clinging actions were in your best interests. Your body isn't making these judgment calls. However, your body knows the associated feelings all too well. Now that you are moving away from this familiar feeling, your ego may react as you step out of your pleasure zone and into the unknown.

Your ego, the part of the brain coaxing you to stay in the known, wants to keep you in the abuse. This part of you thinks that it is benefiting you. We have to teach it otherwise. This will take fortitude and perseverance. Your body and spirit will strive to cope as you transform, and you must have the courage to move through it.

Others in your life may not see a reason for your heartache. Friends may wonder why you struggle to let go of a destructive relationship and a man whom you may now detest. When you turn away from a text that he sent and burst into tears, know that it is okay to not be okay. Fend off defining those intense feelings as love. Please do not listen to friends and family members instructing you to forget about him, and please do not go down the road of examining why you can't get over him.

Protect your right to grieve, to miss him, to understand that this is a process of which you should not deprive yourself. Honor the parts of you that are breaking. Have enough integrity not to fall into the arms of a stranger to negate your feelings. You need this time alone. This is not only all right, it is necessary. You have permission to miss him, to remember what you loved about him, and to cry. Feel the ache inside your heart. Feel it until it releases the hold on your heart and falls to the ground beneath your feet.

Love,
Your Healed Self

Compassion

Compassion is a term used to describe a feeling of sympathy for the suffering of another person. At this time, you may feel compassion for your ex, be him narcissist, addict, or personality enriched. It is possible that you feel compassion for his plight in life over compassion for yourself.

I followed my thoughts until they rationalized a reason for all of Mitch's unacceptable behaviors toward me. At 2 years of age, Mitch's mother left his family. His dad had a drinking problem. Mitch had been hurt. I believed that he did not have the love that he needed as a child. Mitch felt like he had been left to raise himself.

Yes, these are all valid reasons to feel sorry for an ex. I want you to feel this compassion. I want us to live with empathy. I don't want you to numb out or not care. I want you to care about your ex, if just to honor your own heart. You are not going to join the ranks of the millions who do not care for humanity. You are not going to give up.

Feel compassion for him in your heart. Send it out to him. You may write him a letter, but do not send it. Burn it, and watch as your condolences rises from the ashes.

Feel your feelings, and then remember that we are keeping you safe at all costs. Feel for him, but do not take care of him. Love him, but do not lose yourself in him. Do not deny your right to feel compassion for a person even if he has hurt you. Do not allow your heart to harden, but do protect yourself no matter what.

Friends and family would not counsel feeling compassion for your abuser, but have these allies been in love with a man who isn't treating them right, now or ever?

My friends were scandalized at the thought of my adoration for Ryan, and I too found it hard to believe that I might be suffering from a form of Stockholm Syndrome. Regardless, pretending that you didn't love him, pretending that you didn't see all of the laudable qualities in him, and pretending that you don't care when you do will take you nowhere.

I promised that I wouldn't require that you deny your feelings or demand that you move on with ease. We are going to travel through this place together. I know the love in your heart. We are going to see it, acknowledge it, and give it proper recognition before we proceed. Your sympathy is a double-edged sword. It may hold you with him, or it may lead you to safety.

As we lean in toward the latter, it will be time to turn that compassion (reserved for others) inward toward yourself. Recall how easy it was for you to show understanding to him. See in yourself how you love him with ease and without judgment. This is a radical and dangerous form of affection to demonstrate outward, but mirroring this unconditional love inward toward yourself will move mountains. The time is right to take all of that love for others and give it now to yourself.

My inward journey unfolded in different ways, most of them subtle, as I have detailed below.

As Valentine's day in 2018 approached, my beguiling thoughts of Ryan lingered. I wandered into the grocery store, and I passed a display of boxes of salted caramels, each wrapped with a red ribbon. As if on autopilot, I bought a box of them for Ryan. Maybe I would see him. He had come over on Christmas, after all, and since I had no gift to give him to demonstrate my love for him on this special holiday, I should be prepared this time. (Yes, this is a much softer ride through crazy town, but we have arrived there. Please don't be alarmed. Recline, and see how the town has changed. We won't be stopping for the night.)

I held the box of chocolates in my hand. Each petite square lined up in a pristine row. I set my gift, with strings attached, next to me in the car. It was entertaining to think of times when Ryan and I were in sync. I yearned to give him this gift as a peace offering, implying that all of our love had not been forgotten. Butterflies filled my heart. I indulge in loving, and shutting off that valve had always been difficult. I want to love.

I knew in my heart that I could not give Ryan this gift. I could not even allow myself to see him, but my ego needed this waltz down memory lane. I could choose to see myself as pathetic, or I could honor the fact that I had lost what I believed to be true love. This was compassion and grief. These two emotions intertwined and produced a solemn heaviness and a true knowing in my heart.

Instead of falling prey to my own love addiction and turning right toward Ryan's house, I took a left. I remember that left turn as if I had pressed the pause button and taken a photograph. Defining moments may rest in your being as huge inner truths. I felt my heart thump.

As I later slowed to a stop in my own driveway, I picked up the box of chocolate-covered salted caramels. I pulled one end of the ribbon and watched it fall into my lap. I raised the transparent cover, took one cube from its snug home, and placed it against my lips. I savored every heartfelt salty-sweet decision hidden within its chocolatey shell. I'd rather lose him than myself, my heart decided.

As the tender bite dissolved in my mouth, I knew that I had chosen me. This felt like a turning point worth all of the struggle. I knew that I deserved the same mercy that I lavished on others without restraint. This must be the true love that I had been chasing. I discovered a love for myself that remains unshakeable to this day, and you will too.

Grief

I have no way of knowing how long you will sit with your grief, nor to what depth you will endure it. Grief is unique and personal, and yet we should never be left to face it alone. Therefore, I will stand here with you. Imagine a circle of all who have suffered abuse and overcome it here to protect you as you fall apart and lament at this time. It is safe to let your guard down and grieve. You are not alone.

Our society has become so determined to be free of neediness, and independence is glorified. I disagree. I believe that we are designed for fellowship, and a time of utmost grief is a time for renewed reliance on each other. The truth remains that stepping inside another person's soul to soothe them is impossible. Healing is an inside job. Therefore, taking a stance of being supportive is an incredible gem for the sufferer. Know that all of those who have suffered and now thrive are here for you. This knowing is critical in your recovery and your quest for freedom.

Once your friends acknowledge that you are grieving the end of your relationship, they will do what most friends believe they should do. They will offer advice. You may learn firsthand the five stages of grief: Denial, Anger, Bargaining, Depression, and Acceptance. You may find some reprieve in understanding these stages, but be careful not to tie yourself to any expectations. The stages are not linear.

You may blow the stages out of the water, take a U-turn, and move straight to a stage that you believed you had moved through. You may dive in and out of depression and experience highs of exuberant acceptance and self-empowerment. Grief is a roller coaster with twists and turns that may make your stomach lurch, your breath cease, and your heart drop. Screaming is not out of line, either. You may also be told to suck it up and find a replacement guy.

That most offensive comment delivered to me by a friend had my heart quaking. *The best way to get over him is to get under someone else.*

I offered a snarky retort. "Let me know how that pans out for you."

Please allow yourself to ache without pulling an innocent man down with you...or into bed with you. Most of us are searching for love, and when you are not ready to give love, please don't take it.

I mention this from a place of what could be shame. I did this without knowing it. I did this out of loneliness and out of a complete lack of awareness. As soon as I recognized that my loneliness had lured in men, I stopped welcoming advances and sunk deeper into grief. Unconscious hook-ups do hurt other people and yourself. You may decline these offers and sit with your sadness with the support of friends and mentors. The right man for you will be waiting when you are ready to love.

By no means am I suggesting that you opt out of all social interaction. Women need other women. When you feel like you have lost the man whom you loved (even if lust had a starring role in your relationship), you will have a visceral reaction as if your house is on fire and your family cannot escape. This is not a joke. We have a primitive biological need for bonding with others.

Do not make it wrong for you to feel this way. You are not needy or hard up for attention. You are human. Instead, cater to this need. Join with friends in a way that supports you. It is okay to call friends for encouragement. *I want to see you, but I can't socialize at a bar right now. Could we go for a mountain drive instead?* Invite a close friend over to your house to keep the energy in your space moving. Depression draws the life out of your home and invites a stagnant heaviness. Raise the blinds. Let the light in.

I attended the ballet and the symphony during my time of grief over Ryan. Alas, I felt moved to tears by the serenity of sound and the peaceful atmosphere in the symphony hall.

SOULutions

SOULution #1:
Dress to Impress

As you may recall, I could not hide my sorrow. When a co-worker inquired how I felt while in the midst of a breakup, I struggled to hold back the tears. I have always worn my heart on my sleeve, and the fiasco that was my life spelled out like a billboard across my face. When that co-worker approached me with a simple question, *How are you?*, I had to muster up every ounce of strength that I possessed to push back the tears that wanted to fall.

I stifled the truth. *No, I am not okay, and I have not been okay for a long time.* I was exhausted pretending to be all right. At this point, I would be content to never hear the words, *Are you okay?* or *How are you doing?* ever again.

That is when a ray of sunshine shown through in the form of a kind-hearted colleague. "Please, let me know what we may do to help you right now."

Delight splattered across my face. "Please don't ask me if I am okay."

I suggested complimenting me, my class, or telling a story that did not require me to explain my mournful state. Yes, I pleaded for a compliment. I longed to hear, *You look happy.* Instead, it seemed that others judged me. *Are you okay? You look so tired.* I felt depleted. Well, asking for what I needed engendered feelings such that I decided to solve my problem right then and there.

I found my solution in dresses. I realized that if I wore a pretty dress, daily encounters shifted for me. Colleagues and even strangers exclaimed, *Great dress! I love your dress. Oh, you look lovely today.*

Aside from the kind words, my dresses solved a second underlying problem for me, the slump. I suffered from the woe-is-me, I-will-never-find-a-man, white-towel-surrender salute. You can't droop your shoulders in a dress in the same way that you do in jeans. My posture straightened, and I styled my hair to match the dress that I wore that day, an up-do here and a curl and a wave there. Bed head didn't pair well with my heels, and this change altered my inner and outer experiences of life.

Determined to exit this pit of exhaustion and avoid any run-in with casual encounters that left me bemused, I swore that I would wear a dress every day for a month. And I made it happen. I decamped to my computer and ordered dresses online that would fit my hopes for my future self. Dresses with color and flair filled my cart, as opposed to the safety of black dresses that once would have aligned with my wounded soul.

Evidence that I was on the right track appeared as a result. Men complimented me, and women expounded on their own love for fashion with me. I ended up explaining my plan of action to overcome my fragile state with lipstick and heels...and new dresses...to other women who seemed defeated by life.

"You can't feel sad in a dress like this." I boasted with a vulnerable truth about what the dress covered up.

A woman sitting alone in a coffee shop approached me, and after a brief conversation, she announced that she too would try this!

One day I wore blue with white polka dots, one day a black dress with red hearts draped my shoulders, and on another day I wore bright, soothing flowers. I dressed my sadness up with love until it had no choice but to respond to the care that I provided. My sadness dissipated, and friendships grew.

I am by no means suggesting that you must wear a dress every day, if dresses are not your thing. Nor am I taking you in a time machine back to 1950. But I do want you to have the skill and ability to investigate how you make an appearance in your life from a different angle. Find what makes you glow. You are standing on stage, and you are the Star of the Show!

I also attended a yoga class in cowboy boots and tube socks. I needed to be me! Stand out. Use your imagination to dream up solutions to the problems that arise for you when you're in this funk. Consider the most difficult part of your day, and conjure up an image of the highest and best version of you. Picture yourself handling tough conversations with ease. Be gracious when declining offers to go out for a glass of wine. Practice yoga or meditation during what would be your afternoon breakdown. If dresses inspire you, go dazzle on the stage. Find the light that is you, and allow it to twinkle.

SOULution #2:
Pamper Yourself

Think of what you would do for your best friend, your niece, or your sister if they remained hobbled by the blues over the loss of love. Would you bark at them to suck it up and snap out of it? Of course not! You are not a drill sergeant. So why talk to yourself that way. Take this opportunity to do for yourself what you would do for others.

If my friend felt deep hurt, I would write her a nice card and drop flowers off at her house. So, I mailed myself uplifting cards. The act of browsing the card aisle and selecting a card especially for you, taking it home, and writing a loving note to yourself is an active way to be solicitous toward yourself. Write the words that you have always longed to hear from a family member, a man, or a friend, and give those words to yourself now. These words will be yours to keep.

I always forgot that I sent myself a card. During this time of sadness, my memory appeared fragmented. When the surprise arrived in the mail, I could read and hear the kind words that I wrote to myself. This act of self-love and self-acknowledgement of the anguish that I had experienced healed the deep recesses of my heart that I had neglected for decades.

I also bought myself flowers to cheer me up. Studies indicate that gazing at flowers releases the same endorphins as does seeing a baby. How can you not sparkle when you see a baby?

Situate yourself in inspiring environments. Find charm in acts of self-preservation. Prepare a meal instead of ordering out. Allow shopping for comfort food to be a personal ritual for your heart and soul. Require of yourself each day an answer to this question, *What is the kindest action that I may perform for myself today?* Place your hand on your heart, pause, and reflect. *What do you need from me today?* You may hear a response that surprises you. Take note of it.

I have heard a variety of responses. *Relish a nap. Cancel that meeting with the acquaintance who drains you. Take a lunchtime stroll instead of venting with colleagues.* I have also heard exclamations from my heart. *I need music!* And then I purchase a last-minute, inexpensive ticket to the symphony or listen to a local band at a dive bar.

Whatever your bliss and wherever it resides, follow it home to yourself.

SOULution #3:
Talk About It

It may feel like your head has been spinning for a decade. It may feel like you have examined your damaged relationship and your mind to death in hot pursuit of figuring it all out. You have talked it through in circles, as you searched for tidbits of truth in the chaos. Do you feel short on answers and solutions and long on self-reproof?

I suggest that you approach the subject in a different way. Imagine that you are an outsider peering in at you. What do you see happening? Find a close friend, and broach this matter in a safe place. Keep your desire to fix what appears broken at bay, and discover the hard truths about your contribution to the mess. Read on, Braveheart, to expand your awareness.

- What happened, and what meaning did I place on the event or action? He cheated on me. I made that mean that I am unworthy, that I will always be cheated on, and that I am broken beyond repair.

- What occurred in the past, and what did I believe about myself, others, and life at that time? He cheated on me, and I believed that I was in a lasting relationship. I knew what was in my heart, but had mutual consent to be in an exclusive relationship been agreed upon?

- What did I assume about myself and others when I allowed myself to be misled? I assumed that my relationship with Ryan would last forever and that the man with whom I had been involved had integrity and loyalty as a foundational truth. I placed us on the same page with mutual hopes and dreams without evidence to support this perception. I assumed that he wanted what I wanted, and the truth persisted that I had never voiced my hopes for marriage and family with Ryan.

Talking about these difficult points will bring awareness to what you believed at the time of the offenses, the breakup, the dissension. Claim power in your awareness. Can you see how you may choose a different way of communicating and advocating for yourself in the future? Can you see how having difficult conversations before you give your heart to a man may prevent some of this suffering? Tell others what kind of relationship you desire. Do not settle for less.

Explore these questions, and include a close friend or a mentor in the conversation. Do not search for evidence that you are the sole partner to blame and that you will be single forever. That is not how a strong, grounded woman handles self-reflection, and you are a strong, grounded woman. Believe this, own it, and partner with yourself now.

CHAPTER 12

"Mind Full" Mess
and Town Meetings

Right about now, you may feel like you are flipping your lid. Great! The way that your mind used to run around in circles is not sustainable for the changes that we want to make. You may feel as if the rug has been yanked out from under you, and life as you once knew it no longer makes sense. You may realize that your friends are strangers. You may be seeing the past with eyes of wisdom, and this awareness is wigging you out.

Waking up to the fact that close friends may have deceived you and that the man you thought you loved did not feel the same for you may leave you feeling trampled to death. These realizations may indicate long-denied inner wounds that have been left uncared for. Some answers as to why you always end up in dead end relationships should be surfacing. You may feel the equivalent of being pierced by a sharp, hot poker when you ruminate about the time that you have lost in relationships that were not beneficial for you. That young, vibrant girl now appears as a clinging, forlorn woman whose clock is ticking.

Please note that I stated that you *may* feel like you are flipping your lid and that the young, vibrant girl *appears* as a forlorn woman. Yes, those are real feelings that may arise, but that is not where we are going to stay. We will honor these feelings and regroup.

At the age of 38, a guy wrote to me on a dating website that my biological clock must be ticking. A second man took the time out of his life to let me know that he sought a younger woman with more fertility (whatever that meant!). Both had the audacity to pursue me and engage in conversation to turn around and crush my spirit, so I understand the fear that you may be feeling. I would never accept a man as the father of my child who would talk to a woman like that. My inner truth about that allows me to escape the limited mindset of these men and their opinions about my reproductive organs.

Do your best not to play with fear. I am not one to post pictures to dating sites of myself at a younger age in hopes that younger men will message me. I call that scarcity thinking.

Regardless of whether you are 29 or 49, time feels precious. As I brooded about the ten years that I spent from age 28 to age 38 with the same man, my heart wept for that young girl to step out of that relationship and find a clue. I bewailed the passage of time and my inability to make a decision based on myself and my own visions of the family that I wanted. I bemoaned the idea that I gave my best years away. At least that is how I perceived it at the time.

A number of obstacles may be at play during this time. First, friends, co-workers, and family members will not take a timeout while you gather yourself together, step up your self-care, fall apart, stay in bed all day, clean the house until it gleams, drink that whole bottle of wine, and detect the plethora of emotions that you're feeling and tend to them.

No, family members may place more pressure on you to conceive before it's too late. Friends may set you up with their best friend, who suffers from the same problems as you do. Co-workers may sling suggestions that you should find your man in the same fashion as they found theirs. Life will go on, and others will not gift you with a timeout.

Second, and perhaps more profound, your trauma-ridden brain will not categorize or prioritize your thoughts. They are going to flood in as if a dam broke. You may hear in yourself a poisoned soup of words that evince shame, self-doubt, fear, and loneliness. These words have been there all along, but they did not sound loud enough for you to hear them. You drowned them out with shiny objects, attractive dates, and constant activity. This is what I call the Mind Full Mess.

Mind Full Mess

I am going to be alone forever. Why is this happening to me? I am defective. I am broken. I am worthless. Will I ever find love? I think too much. I am so needy. Why did I stay with him for so long? I can't even make a decision. I don't even love myself enough to keep myself safe. What is wrong with me? I am so tired! I am so old! Who will love me now? It's too late. I think I knew he felt like the wrong guy, and I didn't listen to myself. I can't even trust myself. Who is ever going to want me? I want to give up. You think these thoughts...followed by a sigh that surely bespeaks failure.

That's it, I will be alone, and all of my problems are solved. You feel a false sense of relief. Your mind thinks that you have made a final decision, and it may then move on to solve the next pressing question in your mind. Maybe it is about your job or your housing situation, but for now the thoughts about the relationship may rest.

Alas, freedom! You then think about living life as a single person forever. And like a turning tide, five or six minutes later, the thoughts crash upon the banks of your mind, and that lethal ocean of regret pours in. It oozes down the back of your throat, burns your chest, and lands as a cesspool in your stomach. Your mind is taking joyrides with your heart.

Our minds fill up with all of the critical chatter of our caregivers, teachers, siblings, and other authorities. These comments bounce around like ping pong balls in times of increased stressed. If we are not careful, an inner battle ensues. This self-destructive talk, this place where the opinions and wounded words of others becomes our inner voice is a Mind Full Mess.

A Mind Full Mess may haunt you and keep you up all night. You may cringe when your eyes open after slumber, and then the waves of the slaughter eddy around you. You will want to combat your subjugated mind with any and all advice. You may scan the Internet to learn about narcissism or emotional abuse. You may run in circles relaying your past with a therapist day in and day out. Left to your own devices, you may vacillate until the end of time. This is a dangerous place to be, and much devastation may occur during this time.

Fretting exacerbates an abused brain and a Post-Traumatic Stress Disordered mind. Stewing about the past at this time is your enemy. It may take you out of the game and disconnect you from yourself, activities in life, and kinship with others. It may take all of your focus away from your work, your family, and your responsibilities. Chewing over the past, or making time to sit with your deliberations, which you may consider doing, may intensify the derogatory thoughts and make the pattern even harder to break.

Three stages of the Mind Full Mess are identifiable. The first is a complete unawareness of the voices in your head that are running the show. In this phase, depleting mind-chatter becomes your daily mantra to yourself. A consistent voice within murmurs that we are not enough, that we are too much, or that we are unworthy. The reasons to support these untruths are also limitless. I am not enough, because my friends are married and I am not. I am too much, because guys can't handle and are intimidated by my drive. I am not worthy of love, because men always leave me or cheat on me.

So many of us frolic around this earth unaware of this polluted background music. In fact, we may turn up the volume and rock out to it. This soundtrack meets up with and matches the soundtrack of like-minded individuals. We meet each other and bond at the level at which we vibrate. Your cryptic tune meets my cryptic tune, and together we boogie. The lack of acknowledgement of this inner melody is our demise. That which orchestrates in the background heralds the habits and patterns that are our love lives.

It is time to pay close attention to the voices in your head. Do you dream of peaceful classical refrains while heavy metal sprains your mind and pokes at your soul during the day?

The second stage is when the awareness does sink in. *Holy shit! Have I been speaking such cruel words to myself every day? No wonder I am a Hot Mess. Who can function under such ridicule and impossible standards?* Would you coach a child to suck it up, to take what that bully dishes out, to chill, or to let it go when she is being abused? No. But if you replied yes, we need to talk.

Some of us will fall into a state of depression when we tune in to the diminishing self-talk. We will hear it and believe it as our truth. Some of us will somersault onto the anxiety wheel, wondering and worrying about how to stop these unwanted harsh conversations within us. Some of us, you and I, will find a way out.

The third stage unfolds into multiple other phases of denial, heartache, and confusion. Recognizing the deafening sound brigade in our heads will promote a change within us. As I altered the frequency of my annoying internal podcast, I slid into a pit of darkness.

These vexing tapes may have been frolicking in your mind for a considerable amount of time. I found that I had to grieve the dying pattern, as much as I had to overcome it. My critical dialogue had also been a lifelong partner that I cuddled up with at night.

Any time you move out of what has become your refuge, no matter how uneasy and ill-suited you are for it, your ego is going to protest that change. Based upon my comprehensive studies, I would even go so far as to mention that your molecular physical makeup will be in resistance. In this case, it is time to shut down this noise, thank the nagging nuisance for whatever it thought served you, and sob your eyes out. Then you may move on to brighter horizons.

Weep because you will miss your negative self-beliefs and the fun and exhilarating habits that joined them. These habits might include nights at the bar, spending money with nothing in the bank, or jiving at the midnight hour with whoever arrived out to have some fun. You are going to miss that! The thought of home cooked meals and sitting for game nights may at this time make your skin crawl. You may realize that an adrenaline junky lives in you.

Alas, don't worry. We will bridge the gap from here to there with plenty of soul-nurturing activities.

Dismantling a Mind Full Mess is a process. Please do not expect to crank open your brain and dump out years and years of ingrained beliefs, false promises, and self-consumed lies. According to Buddhist texts, Buddha meditated for forty-nine days under a tree without moving. We don't have that kind of time or stamina, and I am not even sure that you can remain still for five minutes!

Tell yourself right now that you are re-wiring your brain and that this is a process. *I am in the process of changing my internal self-talk.* Draw this out in bold print on a sticky note and post it where you may soak it in every day.

Gestalt Therapy

You may be wondering why so many incompatible voices are jouncing around in your head. Some tango together holding hands, and some jitterbug in a constant state of conflict known as cognitive dissonance. Perhaps we are the sum of all of our parts, and different voices are battling to be heard.

I became determined to find out how to control the thoughts in my mind and that state of anarchy that could take over without notice because of a trigger. This search brought me to a therapist who introduced me to Gestalt Therapy. Gestalt Therapy is a technique that allows one to focus on the present while taking into account how the perceptions of the past are impacting her decisions, actions, and emotions today. This allows us to experience past events through re-enactments in a controlled setting, which often reveals the thought and behavior patterns that are causing distress.

Intrigued and seeking freedom from internal noise, I delved into the process. We all have heard that there are three sides to every story: her side, his side, and the truth. I am a seeker of the truth, and yet I know for a fact that I perceived life experiences in an uncharacteristic way due to my empathic traits. Could Gestalt Therapy uncover more truth related to what had happened to me? This sounded like the freedom from victimhood that I longed to discover.

The word *gestalt* means whole. Gestalt Therapy, developed by psychotherapist Fritz Perls, is based on the principle that *humans are best viewed as a whole entity consisting of body, mind, and soul and best understood when viewed through the eyes, not by looking back into the past but by bringing the past into the present.* After years and years of piecing myself out to others, over-giving, and then shutting down, the image of the whole-self enchanted me.

Yes! I want to feel whole. I want an organized mind, a responsive body, and a radiant soul. Sign me up!

Gestalt Therapy allows an abused sufferer to reclaim her voice by speaking to the person who hurt her through role-play in the safety of a therapist's office. The mind re-organizes the past and believes that the individual has effectively stopped the abuse. When we disregard this process, our bodies pay the price.

Hogtied by freeze mode for so long, health issues seeped into my body. Overburdened and exhausted, my nervous system went haywire. My symptoms ranged from adrenal fatigue to nerve damage, back problems, and neck soreness that pointed to stenosis.

The stress on one's body exposes itself at some point. For me, my physical ailments followed the healing of psychological wounds. With my mind in a more placid place and able to respond, my body retired from protecting me and fell into shut-down mode. All of the trapped emotions that my body had shoved into the shadows surfaced. Feeling safe enough to expel the anger and resentment that had built up in my heart and in my body produced physical reactions. These cornered emotions caused dis-ease in my body. Gestalt Therapy allows you to see your suppressed emotions as well as the different personas of yourself that have been silenced.

As with all effective therapies, some techniques may be used so that one may release past emotions in a safe environment. Gestalt Therapy is most well-known for the empty chair technique. An individual sits across from an empty chair and imagines a significant person in it. This could be an abuser from the past, living or not. It could also be a specific part of the individual's personality, perhaps the angry child or the part of her that acts jealous in relationships. She then participates in a conversation with this person or inner persona, who sits in the empty chair.

As you may imagine, the tension in the room changes as the individual speaks her truth to the person sitting in the chair. The individual then moves to the chair and responds as the significant person who sat there only moments before. Much is discovered about the individual and the relationship with the person sitting in the chair through this dialogue and the critical questioning skills of the therapist.

I first placed my perceived antagonist in the chair, per my therapist's request. I acknowledge that I reverted to being a disgruntled teenager when dialoguing with my imaginary enemy. The patterns that ran through my life where I acted immature and disempowered as a grown woman presented themselves. However, this is not all about blaming others. It is about empowering you.

Wow! I nurtured those weak parts of me to wholeness through this awareness, and that stubborn high school girl who was furious about her life no longer interfered with my relationships. Gestalt Therapy played a meaningful and productive role that changed the thought patterns in my mind.

I embraced the concept that we are a whole person based on the sum of our parts. Some of these parts of me burst onto the scene with a vivid presence. As the Mind Full Mess noise emerged, I commandeered Gestalt Therapy and transformed it into my own strategy. Granted, I dove right into my own research on the topic.

My therapist appeared taken aback by the fact that I read the book that he recommended, in one week, and others as well. He seemed frustrated by my over-willingness to save myself and my over-eager participation. Regardless of the fact that this caused a rift in our relationship, the end result felt phenomenal, and my motivation was fueled.

At first, I tried to ascertain whose voice I heard in my head. As I heard words suggesting a scarcity mindset or warnings to be more careful and not take risks, I questioned myself. *Is that me? Do I feel that way?* In this case, a distinct *no* resounded. I knew who that fear-based voice belonged to, and I sent it to that person with love in order to free up space in my mind for more of me. I am a fearless adventurer!

As the days passed, it became obvious to me that some of the defeating thoughts originated from outside sources, from coaches to teachers, from siblings to parents. I even picked up the snide remarks from Joanie, the seventh grade girl who breached my boundaries. As these thoughts surfaced, I returned the words and energy to these gift givers or consigned them to the universe to be recycled into dust.

Wherever you send these false beliefs, send them far away from you. Listen to the mental invaders that are blocking you from your dreams.

You can't go teach at an orphanage in Rwanda. It's too dangerous. You could contract a disease and die. You could be attacked and maimed for life. This fear invaded my mind as I fundraised to fulfill a childhood dream of teaching in an orphanage in Rwanda after learning so much about the tragic genocide there. I felt compelled to see Rwanda for myself, but I had been blocked by this obnoxious voice that popped up. *The world is dangerous and unsafe.* This blanket statement of fear yelped in my ear.

What? I didn't believe this at all. I see and feel a common bond across all cultures and lands, and I know that people are both safe and dangerous no matter where they are. This voice belonged to a protective caregiver from my past, not me. In an effort to keep me safe from harm and close to home, community members instilled in me a fear of travelling to other countries. I sent this fear away from me, identified it as not mine, and spent the summer in Kigali, Rwanda, with the most intriguing and happy children I have ever met.

You may hear, *You are too much.* If I had a dollar for every time this phrase appeared in my life, I could retire early. I also heard this in other terms. *You have a lot of energy. You are always going. Can't you chill out?*

In the past, teachers, siblings, parents, and friends had expressed to me that I am too much. They did this with objection or dismissive glares. I presented as a hyper, energetic child who could not stop talking. I interrupted lessons in school out of excitement, though I attempted to contain myself. Am I too much? No. Does my intensity deserve a safe place to land and be received? Yes.

As I sent away the *too much* message, tears fell. Unlike the *travel is unsafe* tidings, the *too much* notion hit me on a personal level. Believing that I am too much regulated my interactions and controlled the direction of my life.

Though my *too much* identity stemmed from others' opinion of me, I did find that I believed it also. I may be renouncing that false belief for a long time, and that is okay. I will go within and console the part of me that feels rejected and like an outcast each time that it appears before me.

Truth be told, my empathic intuitions felt like too much to me too sometimes. I wanted to be normal, until I realized that average is not what any of us are designed to be. I can now let the *too much* part of me know that she belongs and that it is safe to be herself regardless of the reactions of others. Granted, perhaps parts of me, when heard and understood, don't need to be so loud. Perhaps one part of me is bobbing up and down crying, *Listen to me!* That's right, listen to her. Peace settles in, and *too much* dissipates into the ripples of the pond.

Once you pinpoint the different voices within, you will refine the skill of identifying what belongs to you and what needs to be sent away. Then you may question your own thoughts. *Is it true that I am too much? What evidence makes me think this? What is the benefit of being too much?* Mold and rearrange these thoughts in a way that will guide you forward instead of keeping you handcuffed in a pattern of circular thinking. It is with my "too much" energy that I dedicated my time and effort into creating this book.

Personalities are multidimensional. There may be one aspect of your character or nature that you present to other people, perhaps in contrast to how you view your real character or nature. For instance, I heard on more than one occasion that I appeared confident and independent. This seemed to happen when I felt ravaged inside over my co-dependent, traumatic twelve-year stint with Mike. I allowed a confident facet of my personality to mask my true feelings.

This may be life-preserving, but is it authentic? In order to live a more genuine, radiant life, we want to dismantle these components of our character and make decisions about who we are and how we present to others.

In my most traumatized times, I recall hearing myself whisper, *This isn't me.* I felt cold and critical to myself even though I believed that I had a loving, kind, and sensitive soul. I allowed the traumas and unfulfilling associations to harden me. I wanted this to change. Iron-clad boundaries that keep others at bay are an act of disowning yourself. If I wanted to live in alignment with my true nature, I had to call off the guard dogs around my heart. Perhaps you do too.

 SOULutions

SOULutions #1, #2, and #3:
Town Meetings

I constructed Town Meetings in my head when I felt myself out of alignment or when I needed to make a decision.

To hold a Town Meeting, sit or lie down in a quiet space. It is best to close your eyes. Visualize all of the different elements of you that have shown up in your life in a circle. These are the emotional states in which you have found yourself throughout your lifetime, from the weakest, most insecure self to the strongest, most confident self. These personas are coming in and assembling together as if they are attending a town meeting. Visualize this now, and take note of who arrives. Your dynamite mind will do this for you. State the intention that you want to draw these personas out with simplicity.

Remember that the entire spectrum of who you are is invited, even the most rotten, bitter, and angry parts. No piece of you is excluded. The most obnoxious and hazardous parts of you and the most quiet, frail, and peaceful aspects will all gather together. They may appear as different ages. Whether the outcast child, the angry teenager, the jealous girlfriend, or the simmering angry mother, welcome them in to be seen.

Depending on where you are in your own life as you read this chapter, you will discover which one of you is running the show. This component of you will appear in your visualization louder, brighter, and more vivid than the others. If the star actor in your current life does not show up in your mind, welcome all by asking, *Who here needs to be heard?* Wait and listen as one steps forward, raises a hand in the back of the audience, or is ushered to the front of the crowd. This may sound wacky, but hang tight here.

After identifying the aspect of you that needs your attention, call in your highest self. All of who you are already exists on a spectrum. In this case, your higher self is your most powerful and pure self. She has your best interests in mind at all times. She is understanding and yet holds you to a high standard of excellence, because she knows that you are unlimited. She is the person you strive to be. She is your cream-of-the-crop self. Invite her in, and listen to her guidance as you soothe and aid the facet of yourself that needs care at this time.

In one of my most anxious fits of despair, I held a Town Meeting:

I wanted to call Ryan. Driven by narcissistic abuse syndrome and fueled by a peptide addiction, I wanted to reach out to my abusive ex for some palliative care. This absurd logic had driven me to him before, and it never ended well. Relief felt temporary and sporadic, and yet, my subconscious itched for it.

I called a Town Meeting! As you might surmise, my desperate-self gained the crowd's full attention. Hopeless dejection and aching bones emanated from this vision, which all in attendance felt. I called compassion and concern to the forefront. In my mind's eye, I summoned the most caring aspect of myself to soothe this flagellated part of me. I appealed to my helper self to wrap a warm blanket around my destitute self's shoulders and nurse me to health. I called for courage and dedication to remind this downcast piece of me that I did not need to call Ryan (a man who did not care about me) and that I had the love that I needed right here within.

As the inconsolable component of me felt cared for and changed from a fiery scarlet to a tranquil sapphire, my higher self nodded that all was well now. I had been saved from the dire elements of my own self.

This visualization tool combines what I learned from Gestalt Therapy with my own Town Meeting idea. It has been priceless in uncovering the parts of me that need soothing, and the practice allows me to identify the current persona of my destructive patterns. Don't allow your fears or paranoia to goad you in to thinking that you have multiple personality disorder. We all feel anger, resentment, and jealousy as well as love, kindness, and elation. Your choices and actions will define you, not your thoughts.

Explore these different parts of you through this exercise. Watch how the noise of a Mind Full Mess coordinates to construct your personal dream team, one that is ready to move in the direction of your choosing. This is how you respond instead of react, a tune that we have all heard before but for which we didn't have a *how-to* until now.

This strategy is so profound that I am offering no other SOULutions in this chapter aside from the Town Meeting. Read over this practice three times. Follow it. Draw in your primary personas that are angry, happy, and sad. Then, embrace some secondary emotions of frustrated, surprised, resentful, betrayed. These parts of you are calling you to be healed. Your loving and nurturing heart will nurse all of these parts into the wholeness that is you.

PART III

Don't Look Back

CHAPTER 13

Tunnel Vision

You have arrived at the place in your exploration where you will need to utilize Tunnel Vision. Tunnel Vision has two meanings. It may refer to a time in your toxic relationship when you felt hyper-focused on the familiar and found yourself unable to take a broader view of that relationship, or it may be a positive spin in which you have averred that you wish to change and have dedicated yourself to recovery from noxious partnerships. You have decided to forge your way out of rotten relationships forever.

The most successful people exercise extreme concentration in furtherance of their goals, not toward dead end relationships. Think of how much joy these relationships have taken from you. The propitious news for you is that you have illustrated your ability to focus, though this focus might have been misdirected toward the wrong relationships for you. It is time to flip that compulsive and ingrained script and use it to support you now.

Allow me to elaborate how strong toxic Tunnel Vision is, and then we will use that conditioned survival reaction to catapult you out of the past and into a loving future.

Recall a time when you felt up to your eyeballs in a neurosis. For me, I felt consumed in most, if not all, of my past relationships, but Ryan took the cake. When he said *jump*, I asked *how high*?

This is so sad for me to admit to now, but it is the truth, and we are being honest with ourselves. I ditched my own plans if he sent a text and wanted to spend time with me.

Another wretched example occurred with Mike. In the early dating stage, I once prepared to go out with him on a Friday night when we didn't even have plans! Based upon his previous pattern of last minute invites, I divined that Mike would phone me to hang out that evening.

As the hands on the clock ticked their singular rhythm, I fell down on my bed, fluffing the pillows around my curled hair so as not to mess it up, and fell asleep waiting for his text. Instead of calling friends, I slept alone all dolled up for a night out with Mike!

Talk about Tunnel Vision. Mike and the relationship consumed my every thought. Prioritizing myself first did not register for me then, and all other activities fell to the wayside. True to form, Mike did contact me after his drinking binge with his friends, and I popped out of bed and met him at his house. This reinforced my behavior and perpetuated my Tunnel Vision related to Mike.

Now, let's utilize the strength of this destructive behavior. In dealing with Ryan, who slept with other women and yet peered into my eyes and declared his love for me, I had to make a decision to flee his grip. Granted, I had placed myself in those hands, but I could break loose if I wanted to. So can you.

This type of Tunnel Vision requires scrutiny of yourself and others. It was time to stare down my own demons and not take on Ryan's. I needed to harness all of the ability that I had used to obsess about Ryan in order to flee his pernicious embrace.

Focus

Upon arriving home from a business trip where Ryan had slept with another woman, he graced me with a breakup talk. He explained that he could no longer be my boyfriend.

I had mentally prepared myself, as I had seen this day coming. "Okay."

Shocked, Ryan lingered around my house for a while, expecting me to want to talk it out or to convince him to stay, I'm not sure which. I did not grovel in hopes that he would change his mind.

I used an anxiety strategy that I had learned from Dr. Goldmann in Colorado. He rang a bell and instructed me to listen to the ringing until it ended. I sat still and listened to the fifteen-second tone until it died out. He then rang the bell a second time and requested that I stopped the sound before it faded. I humored him, as I knew that this would be impossible. I did not have control over the bell's momentum, and the sound disappeared in the same fifteen seconds as it had the first time.

I heard Ryan's words when he broke the news to me that he couldn't be my boyfriend anymore. Like with the bell, I remained still and listened as his words disappeared into the wind. Though my nervous system leapt to halt the sound of his voice, I had no control over Ryan's words nor the actions that accompanied those words. Complete acceptance of both opened my eyes to reality. My tranquil response threw him way off, and he retreated to make his own sense of our encounter.

Like most talented manipulators, he chose to up his game. How could I have not fallen to pieces and begged him to change his mind? He sent a text a few days later. *Ellen, can I come pick up my stuff from your garage?*

I shrilled to myself, "Why don't you stay out of my life and buy yourself some new crap?"

However, I messaged him in the affirmative, even though I didn't want Ryan anywhere near my house. I knew that he needed his belongings, or I would be tethered to him in some way forever, and then I would be waiting to hear from him, unable to move on.

I decided to take the day off of work and be home when Ryan dropped by, even though he had a key to enter the house and open the garage on his own. I did not want him on my property without me there. Ryan looked surprised to see me.

We have a tendency to equate our ex's items with strong ties that bind us together and hold us in the relationship. The truth is, however, that all belongings are just stuff. I placed a lot of meaning on Ryan's stuff, and as he gathered the tools that he had kept in my garage, I felt as if I was handing my own child over to the authorities. I was attached to our three-year relationship, and his items that were stored in my garage felt packed away in my heart as well.

However, I gathered strength and chanted to myself that this was just stuff. This reality-check statement grounded me, and I remained calm throughout the exchange. My disposition caught Ryan off guard.

Well, being a clever man, Ryan perked up. My newfound resilience allured him and disrupted his own conditioned response with me. My ability to let him go bothered him. He showed this to me by choosing not to collect all of his property at that time. I did not know it then, but Ryan left some select tools in my garage...as a way to re-visit my life, the perfect set up for hoovering.

This is where my Tunnel Vision concerning my own health had to take precedence. And, by the way, yes, I did ask Ryan to give me back the key to my house.

One day after ceasing interactions with Ryan, I was on my way to an outdoor festival with a friend, who understood what I had been through and supported my desire to move on. Ryan texted me. I received the text as my friend and I chatted and strolled down the sidewalk toward the entrance to the festival. *I am near your house with my kids. Can I come pick up the rest of my things?* I froze. My heart raced. Repellent hormones rushed through my blood stream. My face turned pale, and my feet suddenly became plastered to the concrete.

I panicked. I feared the initial and conditioned type of reaction that would keep me engaged with Ryan at my house for the next... however many hours. I feared his kryptonite control that would lure me into rationalizing leaving my friend and helping him move the rest of his belongings out of my garage.

Let's be honest here. That type of reaction had an agenda, to win him back. The trigger had been pulled, and I had two seconds in which to step out of this space or be annihilated.

Magic occurred. Given my history, we could even call this a miracle.

My friend acknowledged that haunting and familiar expression on my face and gasped as he stood back. "Oh, no."

"Give me a second to think." I solicited his momentary indulgence.

I turned away from the phone in my hand, and I gazed up. I focused my eyes on an exquisite emerald leaf swaying in the spring breeze among other verdant leaves in a massive oak tree. I channeled all of my focus on that one leaf. I grounded myself. I paced my breathing. I allowed my nervous system to experience and move through the trigger, while casting my eyes on a single leaf.

Instead of rushing to go meet him at my house or flying into a frenzy, I sent him a text, *I am not at home*. He persisted. I did not counter his move because I was busy living my best life! Ryan then texted, *Are you ignoring me?*

In fact, I did ignore him! I moved on! I did it! In real time, I overcame this trigger.

Well, when you become awesome, and you will, some people rise to challenge you. They don't want you to change, as they like who you were for them. Now, this is a man who slept with other women while dating me and used text messages to gaslight me multiple times. I in no way lowered myself to his level of behavior, nor was I pleased that he texted me.

I wanted to be left alone. Ryan's pique with me that day astounded me. His ego exploded on the scene in the face of rejection. I was tempted to engage.

But by utilizing my Tunnel Vision skill, I enjoyed my time with my friend on a stupendous day in Colorful Colorado. I didn't talk about Ryan once during the whole day, and I didn't have to leave or adjust my life to adapt to the demands that Ryan made of me. With my eyes set on the future, I embraced moving-on vibes.

Please remember, the bond to this type of man is an addiction. I was hypnotized by Ryan's charisma, intelligence, and control. The science of willpower tells us that willpower alone is not a reliable source of motivation when overcoming an addiction. Willpower depletes and runs out. It is important to rely on other resources and strategies in times like this. Do not tough it out, instead get out. This is a save-yourself situation, and you must do whatever it takes to stay out of this relationship. Do not turn back.

You are over him, and this inauspicious relationship is far, far behind you.

Building Integrity Within Yourself

One of the most rewarding acts that you may perform for yourself is to build integrity within yourself. Not reacting to kryptonite and staying present with my friend demonstrated one step that I took in building my integrity and self-esteem. I remained solid in the midst of this threat. I acted on my desire to find a life partner, not on my emotions. Your daily decisions must move you toward your dreams with laser-like, tunnel vision focus.

 SOULutions

SOULution #1:
Commitments Before Coffee

The shame that arose from placing Ryan and the others first in my life hurt. Know that you are on a mission of rebuilding yourself to be a better version of the you before abuse. The most profound way to build integrity and self-esteem within is to make a daily pact with yourself and keep it.

I write down my commitments to myself as if they are bound by my own blood. These promises to yourself should be attainable and valuable to you. Set yourself up to win!

The accords that I made with myself toward building enough integrity to stay out of relationships that didn't serve me are detailed below. *Today I will wake up at 5:20 and watch the sunrise at the park.* Imagine, before 6:00 in the morning, I had been true to myself and gazed upon an immaculate sight and felt the presence of certainty in my life. The sun always rises. It never let me down.

I could depend on the sun, and now I could depend on me. I built trust in my own abilities to show up, a trust in self that had been lost by choosing unfulfilling and disastrous relationships.

I took other oaths as well. *By 6:00 p.m. on Wednesday, I will have cleaned out the closet. At lunch today, I will eat that yummy salad that I made for myself.*

Notice that I didn't over-promise or assert that *I will eat a salad every day.* Each morning, settle on one or two guarantees that you may make, and watch how this rebuilds your self-worth. Establishing this core routine for yourself will make you more capable of not summoning up the past or being pulled into unhealthy relationships.

Start each day with attainable commitments for yourself that support your goals and aspirations. These objectives are not intentions. Intentions sound like an idea, but perhaps it is okay if you don't fulfill the intention. Intentions are movement in a direction, like a wish. A commitment is a pledge that you make to yourself and then follow through with action.

- I commit to writing three pages of my random thoughts before 8:00 a.m. today in order to free my mind and make room for inspired action.

- I commit to drinking eight ounces of water four times today before 6:00 p.m. for my overall health.

- I commit to cleaning out the junk drawer in the kitchen to de-clutter my life and throw away what no longer serves me before 5:00 p.m. today.

- I commit to signing up for that speaking class to move my business forward before I go to sleep tonight.

SOULution #2:
Be Brave Enough to Disappointment

People-pleasers, like ourselves, find it impossible to disappoint others or to be seen in a less than flattering light. As you recover from co-dependency and placing the needs of others before your own, you must be willing to disappoint. As you fill your schedule with activities and purposes that support your highest excellence, you will find that you have less and less time to meet the requests of those in your life who don't encourage your goals.

One exercise of which you might take advantage is *wait-time*. Practice this phrase, *I'll check my schedule and let you know by tomorrow morning.* Honor the timeframe that you have given this person. When a friend, co-worker, or acquaintance invites you to coffee, to go on a date, to volunteer your time, to join that class, or to hit a happy hour, practice this remark even if you think you have an answer. The idea is to make space in order to bring awareness to your decisions. What do you want to do with your time?

During this *wait-time*, sit in a quite space and feel what you would like to do. You may be surprised that what you once did not hesitate to do you are now reconsidering or even seeing as a time drain. Allow all proposed activities to percolate before you concur with them. For instance, I may love to hike, but I don't want to go hiking with a friend who chatters during the entire trek. This exhausts me.

Perhaps you love the person but want to avoid the mindless drinking and expense of her happy hour routine. Bringing awareness to how you spend your time and with whom you spend that time is crucial in moving toward the life of your dreams.

Your ego may kick out some instant guilt. *But he wants me there. But it is such a charitable cause. What will my co-workers think if I am not there?* This is your ego's attempt to keep you in people-pleasing mode and focused on others. You know how to be a people-pleaser. It is familiar. Remember, the ego loves familiar, but we are now normalizing a future centered on you!

Plow through this guilt. You may achieve success by paying attention to what happens when you set boundaries that serve *you*. Notice how your time frees up for your own life. Notice how others respect your time and your purpose in life, even if that purpose is your own recovery and peace of mind. Notice how you feel when this unearned culpability subsides.

While this will be challenging at first, it will get easier with time. The worst strategy that you may employ is to be wishy-washy. Be apprehensive about this sabotage. You don't want to sway to and fro. *I don't know. Well, maybe I can make that event.* This leaves you tethered to indecision and keeps your mind and energy tied up with multiple *maybes* that deplete you, regardless of whether you are aware of this.

SOULution #3:
Ground Yourself

Find ways to ground yourself. Well, what the heck does that mean? For those of us with strung-out nervous systems, we must ground ourselves in the most physical sense. Take your shoes and socks off and place your feet on the ground. Wiggle your toes in the dirt, and let the grass tickle the bottoms of your feet. Do this until you feel one with the earth. Do this until you realize that you belong here and that you are connected to all living creations.

Allow the earth to draw you in. The sheer force of the earth is undeniable. I don't even have to debate this with your ego because, as a human being, we all innately hold this understanding. It is a fact that the earth, the wind, water, and fire are healing, as they are also lethal forces outside of ourselves. These forces may both slay us and bring us to life!

Feel the range of this gravitational pull. Toss an item like your car keys into the air, and watch how gravity slams them to the earth. Then toss a leaf into the air. Notice how it flutters down to the earth and lands in the grass.

Our precious earth doesn't destroy the light of our spirit, and it hasn't destroyed you. Neither has a broken heart. While the earth is a force beyond measure, it offers a soft place to land. What an awesome protective security blanket we have surrounding us.

Rely on the grounding that is the earth in the same way as I relied on the rising and the setting of the sun. Take a long hike in nature. Leave the house every single day. Throw open the shades to let the sun in.

Find the closest body of water, and drop your fears and anxieties into the water. Dip a toe or your whole body in, and allow the liquid to wash your past away. The water in your shower or bath is that same water! Establish daily practices of grounding in the earth and refreshing yourself in the water.

On my sunrise mornings, I did what I call a walking meditation. My body had lived in fight/flight/freeze mode for so long that it did not relax well and could not stay still.

With my German Shepherd, Thurman, by my side, I wandered around a lake at the park as I announced on replay to myself, *I release the fear of being in a destructive relationship.*

You may voice any intention you wish. I dispatched this fear to the water and allowed it to cleanse self-doubt from my being. In this same park, I found a stream in which I discovered river rocks the size of loaves of bread. Upon each sunrise walk, the weight of the rocks drove me further into the earth as I raised them out of the water and stacked them on top of each other. I felt like a child, and with that feeling, I requested balance in all areas of my life, including my mind, my body, my heart, and my soul.

I then climbed to higher ground. I released the weight on my shoulders and walked up a hill, symbolizing a step toward my higher self. I discovered the perfect setting at this park near my home in Denver, Colorado. A bench squatted next to a giant oak tree, and with the panorama of the Rocky Mountains in the distance, the sun whispered hello to a bright blue sky.

Next, I strolled through a garden of roses. I serenaded myself with ideas that united me to the miracles of life. I became aware of the rose bushes all at different stages of growth, some with petals wafting on the breeze, some fresh and vibrant, some dry and falling to the earth. You and I are a part of this marvel and this cycle of life. In the right environment and with proper care, you will flourish.

Warning: Leave your phone in the car. Participate in these activities without recording them and posting them online. Social media is the opposite of Tunnel Vision. Please trust me on this one. With your phone out of sight, you gain clarity and awareness in order to open your heart to the wonder and peace around you. You may even meet and make eye contact with others along the way.

CHAPTER 14

Burn the Ships

In 1519, Hernán Cortés de Monroy y Pizarro Altamirano, 1st Marquess of the Valley of Oaxacaset, set sail to Veracruz, Mexico, with his crew. Legend has it that his men were weary and scared and had hopes of turning back home to their old life and old ways when they breached the shore. The commander ordered that they burn the ships, allowing for only two outcomes: either fight and win or die trying.

The burning of the ships represents the need for great change in order to move into new ways of thinking and being. This is a risk-it-all-to-have-it-all mentality. You are at war for your life. Forsake the old. Act as if your life depends on this change, because, Angel, it does!

By now, you have built up enough strength to make some tough decisions in your life. I made some radical changes in my internal world during this time of recovery. What are you holding on to that is keeping you moored in place? Chances are, you are not even able to see what is holding you back. Walk with me as we unload and burn off the old ways of clinging to the past and move to a freer, full-of-possibility new you!

Healing in a Labyrinth of Pain

You cannot sober up at an open bar, and you cannot heal while being surrounded by memories of your ex! If you are like me, it may be time to go cold turkey. Brain research indicates that it takes a great deal of mental energy to manage moderation in addictions. We are going to use that same mindset to set you free and open your mind, body, and soul to a new way of being. We cannot make that happen when you have one foot caught up in the past. When you move forward into the life of your dreams, you will need both feet under you.

Take a look around. Do you have a memory chest or a photo album? Most every woman does. Perhaps it is crammed into a closet or is ensconced safely in the basement, and yet it is there somewhere in your environment. Are you willing to let go of letters from your past? Are you willing to discard those items that make your heart burn? Remember, that is not love, that is regret over love that did not work out. Are you willing to open up and establish breathing room in your love life?

I had to be extreme, even for me, on this move. I burned pictures and offered the past up to change with all my love and intention for a brighter future. There I sat, amidst writing this book, and with tears streaming down my face, I burned more than ten journals. These journals captured and froze in time my loss. I had written words of losing friends to sudden death, of being left in the lurch in relationships, of longing for love that always felt one step away from me. The most crushing writings that I relegated to the trash heap were from my young and innocent heart, which yearned to live in a loving world.

These journals were filled with dark poetry depicting failure, anger, and depression, and yet my words felt familiar, like my sanctuary. These journals housed my soul. As sailors might be heartened by the familiar yet harsh conditions of life at sea, these letters, pictures, and words, which reminded me of my past, consoled me.

Letting Him and the Events that Bind You to the Past Go

I was 22 when my boyfriend went to prison. We were carefree and careless, and then it happened. Now here is a lesson for the young and invincible and in love.

I was gutted, confused, and triggered most of the time! This experience had the same effect as when my friend died after she left my house, with the added component that Scott was alive and yet out of reach. Similar to how I wanted to talk to my friend, Angela, one last time, I needed to hear from Scott. I needed to know that he was safe. If he was okay, I could breathe again.

(Does this sound familiar? I later felt like I could breathe when my ex, Mike, decided to come home after I felt marooned by him also. I diagnosed myself with separation anxiety.)

My triggers compounded, and I was in a constant state of anxiety. Being present felt like a huge challenge. When I lay my head down on the pillow at night, I wondered if Scott had a pillow. When I woke up to go to work, my heart burned with longing to hear Scott's voice. I waited for his phone calls at a friend's house and paid her hundreds of dollars a month for the phone bill. Yes, I drove to her house because I had moved back in with my parents. I did not tell my parents about his imprisonment. I hid it deep inside my heart, and it jostled around in my brain.

Keeping this a secret was an irrational move on my part. I believed that my mother would not survive such news. I kept it from her to protect her. I kept it from my pops to protect myself from feeling that he would be disappointed in his baby girl. I was a people-pleaser and a parent-pleaser above all else, even above my own health and stability.

A decade and a half later, it proved time to relinquish the death grip that I had on these memories. These memories felt so charged with energy that trauma bonded me with Scott. He was now living his life as a loving and caring man with a great job. It was not necessary to carry on with this adolescent heartache. I knew this, and so I took action.

I had an entire trunk of letters that he had sent to me from prison, two-years-worth of exchanges between his trapped heart and mine. We shared our dreams and our deepest feelings, but most of all, we cared. These letters, written on a yellow legal pad, were keeping our love suspended in time and deemed me unavailable to move on with all my heart with my current partner Mike.

While freed up to travel during a spring break from teaching, I packed up the letters and drove to Mike's work. Yes, this part is going to be difficult to delineate and oozes with self-shame. I told Mike, with whom I had been together for ten years at that time, that I had to take Scott the letters that he had sent to me from prison. I told him that these letters had been holding me back. I told him that I needed to give them back to the person who had sent them to me. Mike was not pleased, and he did not understand.

It didn't matter, though. I felt so broken that I couldn't let his disapproval stop me. I fought for inner peace, and if this was the route that I needed to take, then I had to take it.

I cried a lot. Think of crying, and then add six hours of crying from Denver to Albuquerque, New Mexico and back to that. Add hysterical weeping to that while I told Scott that I was there to give him back the letters that he had sent to me from prison. Add bawling when he shared that he had no idea that his imprisonment had impacted my life in such a profound way.

He had had time to process his experience. I had locked myself and my life in prison with him. I had never dealt with any of it. I had been trussed to the grief and the pain.

This event, this letting go, impacted the trajectory of my life, similar to the crew members who had to fight for theirs. It place-marked the rebirth of my life, a new chapter.

 SOULutions

SOULution #1:
Change Your Space

"Everyone out! Everything has got to go!" I proclaimed.

I owned a house, and I grew accustomed to opening my home to anyone and everyone whom needed a place to stay. I corralled the courage to ask them to leave. I needed to be alone. If you haven't experienced living alone, I recommend it. As an empath, solitude may be the one way for you to know who you are outside of the influence of others.

As I looked around this home that I had decorated for myself (but really for others), I realized that I didn't like it! I had two cushy couches for watching movies. I don't even watch television! As I transformed, I realized that this was not my happy home.

Making a physical move could not happen since I owned the house, but it was time to reclaim my space. This is how you do it...

- Grab a trash bag or a box, and start small...or large! Pick a room. Get to work. Look at each picture, each trinket, each piece of furniture, each article of clothing, and make a decision. Does this item bring me joy? Is this item aligned with my future dreams? (That picture of you smiling during that picnic with your ex hanging over the fireplace is not welcoming to a new life. Take it down.)

- Rearrange the furniture. Take yourself out of the same old patterns. It is time to change your brain and your habits. Switch things up. If you can afford it, buy new appliances that look better in your kitchen. Adjust your before-work and after-work routine.

- Head to your bedroom, and clear out that panty drawer. Yes, I said it. Include the bras too! Do you need an explanation for this one?

- Donate or sell clothes that scream *this is the old me*! Use that money to shop for the new you!

- If you have children, separate their items from yours. Allow all members of the family to have a place for their own miscellany.

- If you can't let go of an item, move it to the garage or a storage unit. If you do let it go, be patient with yourself. I sent my sister a box of childhood mementos that I had been keeping safe for her!

SOULution #2:
Fire it up!

A primitive energy exists around our need to burn away the old. Don't be afraid to let go in this way. The most powerful moment I had was when I browsed through old pictures that I had clung to like a security blanket for more than a decade. I also placed love letters in the fire pit, all from people who were meant to be passersby in my life. I had saved it all, as if this smorgasbord was evidence that I was lovable or at least that I had been loved by men. These items were, in fact, an energetic anchor, holding me back from true love.

Please don't feel callous about burning what no longer serves you. It does not erase the beauty of these people or the experiences that you had with them. It simply makes space for more love to come into your life and breaks the ties that bind you to the past.

Notice, too, the commitments that you may have sealed deep in the pockets of your heart or subconscious mind. At the age of 18, my friend, Angela, had pleaded for my help with her drinking. In college, drinking was popular. Well, Angela drank too much one night, and a beer bottle that she held broke when she stumbled against a wall. Small shards of shattered glass became lodged in her hands.

I didn't know how to help her. I was a kid also. Every solution that I could think of involved telling on her. Three days after she solicited my help, she died in the car accident.

Though that had happened when I was in college, and this soul cleansing was happening a decade and a half later, the commitment that I made to her was still in the present.

As I rested Angela's picture on the flames to release our bond, I realized the profound promise that I had made to her in college. I felt guilty for not acting in a way that would have helped her, and from this place of shame I blamed myself for her death. I then issued a subconscious edict to myself to help anyone and everyone who needed my help. This included staying in relationships with men dependent on alcohol or drugs to help ease their suffering and perhaps love them enough to help them quit and free them from addiction.

I also stayed in relationships well past the maximum advantage because the man did not die, which meant that we could talk and work it out. I developed unhealthy attachments, and after my friend's untimely passing, I stayed glued to the past. Burning away these attachments and releasing the responsibilities from the past was such a healing experience.

Are you married to vows that you made to an ex-husband well after the divorce? Have you been loyal to a friend who has betrayed you? Perhaps you are miserable in a job that your parents wished for you to take. Is your present benefitting you, or is your energy geared toward a past partner?

I also burned those journals. Now, this is coming from a woman who is writing a book right now. I didn't set out to write a book, but I had an inkling that it might happen. Here I stood burning my content away. Why? Holding on to that material and keeping myself chained to the pain would not result in an empowerment book worth reading. In fact, the heavy writing that I had done in the past drained the energy that I needed to write a book today. I let it all go and stepped into the faith and belief that the stories lived inside me and that I could retrieve them at any time.

SOULution #3:
Give It Back!

Give others back their energy and the items that they may have dumped on you. Stagnant energy is trapped in our bodies and in our houses. It is stashed in the closets and is rotting away in chests and drawers. If this seems reasonable and will not cause any difficulty for yourself or others, send items that don't belong to you back to their rightful owner.

You may also donate or sell things that remind you of your exes. This means ex-roommates, ex-boyfriends, ex-co-workers. You may be surprised at the mess in which you are living as you take on this project.

If an item you own comes with an explanation or a story that conjures up the past, let it go. Shop for a replacement, and change that story. Your possessions may be possessed!

I can't tell you how many relics I have collected to help others through their adversity. These curios were accumulated in loving ways. *My dog died, do you want this water bowl that reminds me of him? I am moving and can't take this with me, can you hold on to it for me? Can you store my bike? You have the space.*

If you are holding on to other people's belongings, clear these items out of your personal and energetic space! Now! Okay, maybe not now, but schedule this time for yourself. This is an important act of self-care in recovery. Be kind to yourself, and let go of these things in a loving way. Allow your emotions to come up. Express your anger, resentment, sadness, and remorse. Watch as the burning ships sail out to sea and the past fades away. We will win this battle.

CHAPTER 15

Identity Crisis

Down in the quagmire of recovery, the strong, passionate woman I once knew, at least on the inside, appeared now as a capitulating, out-casted, and underachieving adult child. The righteous and *party-until-you-drop* hot mess now ducked out of invitations like a girl afraid of her own shadow. The awareness of my abusive love life kicked in, and this was a direct hit requiring self-preservation and time alone.

My self-worth had diminished beyond recognition. Self-care, if I had ever embraced it, took a back seat. I avoided and isolated. I wavered between the two. I called avoidance my time for myself, and I labeled my isolation as recovery time. The truth is, I hid out, wrapped in shame.

The image that I saw in the mirror was a dull, pale, sad version of myself. My eyes were clouded from the storm brewing within, and the corners of my lips turned down in a perpetual frown. My social media posts resembled a cry for attention, not a real attempt at vulnerability or making friends.

I believed myself to be more, to be better. I believed that I held qualities of kindness and care for others, but I couldn't even show up as a friend. I didn't have it in me to assist others. I strained to drive myself to my job teaching and taking care of the children who needed me. When I did meet friends, I exhausted them with stories of emotional abuse. From an outside perspective, my words rang of complaints and disdain for my ex-boyfriends.

I was self-absorbed. I admit it. Enmeshed in these excruciating stories, I petitioned the gods to make sense of my love life for me. Whether the relationship was a decade long or a year long, it had ended now, and I refused to accept these conclusions. Wrestling with the happily ever after fairytales in my mind, I had never had closure and did not bury the past. The romances in my mind longed for a story that ended with wedding bells.

Falling victim to re-telling these stories, I shuttered myself to the past and stunted my growth forward. My empathic self could no longer handle inflicting my life-drain upon others. I retreated into seclusion. At the least, I had to protect my friends from me! My brick wall built up. No one could get in, and I could not get out. I lived in my own personal penitentiary. Isolation became my safe haven, and I did not intend to leave.

As a shadow of my former self, I knew that I needed help.

Time for a complete investigation! I researched personality disorders as if hired to do so. I analyzed myself to the point of grappling with the idea that I must be the one who had the problem. *Am I a narcissist? Am I a sociopath?* My abused brain had been so wired to believe that I must be the problem that I now mistrusted myself. I turned on myself.

This self-absorption and taking time to isolate and recover birthed the notion inside my mind that I had been selfish and self-serving, like my abuser. Yes, I nose-dived into this pattern of distorted thinking, and I believed it about myself.

I pleaded for a diagnosis from therapists and doctors. I completed self-assessments online. It turns out that all human beings require a healthy dose of narcissism to maintain boundaries and to live an authentic life. My score evidenced a serious level of lack in this department. I even beseeched friends and strangers to decide for me whether they thought I had earned the label of narcissist or sociopath or psychopath.

Now that is a stellar conversation starter!

The bottom line is that I searched for hope! *Who am I? Why did I go from an independent, confident woman to seeking validation from strangers to decide who I am? And, what is true about this life that I am living?*

The Flash Flood

Heavy rain burst from the sky, and the questions poured in, some valuable, some enervating, and all drowning out my ability to foresee a future.

Let's take an insider view at who you think you are and clear up this identity crisis. Do your current friends know you, or have you been adjusting and fitting in? Do you speak your truth in all areas of your life, and therefore, live a life that is most authentic to you, your goals, your dreams, and your ambitions?

Let's take time to answer these questions. Let's take stock of all areas of your life and dive into the deep end of the pool of reality. Grab a magnifying glass, and examine how you have behaved in the past compared to how you would like to be living.

Below is an example borrowed from my self-audit:

At the top of my journal page I wrote, *Decide what needs to change in your life.*

Identity: Who do you want to be?

- I want to be a supportive, kind, and uplifting friend.
- I want to be a grounded, responsive, loving, and understanding wife.
- I want to be the woman who brings joy, light, and love to the table.
- I want to be a woman of resilience and abundance.
- I want to be a responsible, caring dog owner.
- I want to be a healthy, active individual.

Environment: Where do you want to live, work, love, play, and laugh?

- I want to live where the air is clean, the sky is open, and nature and wild flowers surround me.
- I want to have access to water and open space.
- I want to work where my skills, talents, and heart may have an impact.
- I want unlimited access to my potential.

- I want to love wherever I am.
- I want to play in the river, on a field, at my job, anywhere.
- I want to laugh until my sides hurt.

Well, this thoughtful list is also quite general. Step two of this process guides us to delve a bit deeper.

Who do you want to be?

- I want to be a supportive, kind, and uplifting friend.

How does that look and sound?

- I listen to the goals and dreams of my friends.
- I receive permission before exporting my knowledge or offering assistance instead of giving unsolicited advice to unreceptive parties.
- I have faith in the ability of others and voice that faith to them.
- I allow friends, family members, and co-workers to have their own experiences and lessons, and I respect their process. I meet others where they are!

Who do you want to be?

- I want to be a grounded, responsive, loving, and accepting wife.

How does that look and sound?

- I understand what to expect in a relationship with my partner.
- I define my boundaries and have integrity with myself.
- I take care of my needs first and foremost.
- I stay in tune with my feminine essence and spirituality.
- I comprehend interdependence and act from that place.
- I accept my flaws, my past, and my mistakes as well as those of my partner. I take full responsibility for myself.
- I treat my husband like my friend.

Who do you want to be?

- I want to be a woman who brings joy, light, and love to the table.

How does that look and sound?

- I arrive with my needs already met.
- I meditate to generate love and light from a place within me.
- I monitor my exchanges with others and discern what is the best decision for me.

Who do you want to be?

- I want to be a woman of resilience and abundance.

How does that sound and look?

- I carry the torch for myself and keep my fire lit so that others will see that this is possible for them.
- I face my fears. I take risks and act outside my comfort zone daily. I solicit help, if necessary.
- Resilience prevails. Giving up is never an option. I do whatever it takes to keep moving forward, no matter the speed or the pace at which I move.
- I am a source of abundance. I know in my soul that I have infinite resources from which to pull. I have inner wealth and do not need to dull my light.

Who do you want to be?

- I want to be a responsible, caring dog owner. (I felt like a delinquent because my dog, Thurman, needed more training, and I was too sad and worn down to provide it.)

How does that look and sound?

- I tell Thurman that he is loved. I thank him for being in my life.
- I solicit others to assist with dog care when needed.
- I buy Thurman toys so that he is not bored when I am not at home.

Who do you want to be?

- I want to be a healthy, active individual.

How does that look and sound?

- I will listen to my body and eat clean and organic foods.
- I will take vitamins and minerals daily.
- I will hydrate with hot water, lemon, and apple cider vinegar in the morning.
- I will exercise five times a week.
- I will pay attention to what I read or listen to. I will be selective about the people with whom I spend my time.
- I will participate in yoga and meditation or spiritual practice.
- I will plan and implement activities with friends or join groups to engage with like-minded, growth-oriented people.

From this process you may complete the third step, which is an action plan. These are the steps that you will take daily to become the person that you have described. Don't overwhelm yourself. Choose one category, either your identity or your environment, or select one question from each category to implement today. Easy wins will build momentum. It is a whole lot easier to buy some dog toys than it is to exercise five times a week.

Break the grander goals down into digestible steps. Today, I am going to go to the gym, inquire about purchasing a membership, and receive an overview of the equipment so that I feel comfortable on the workout scene. Dwelling on how far you are from your goals will stop any progress that you might make. You can do this!

How did this process feel for you? The level of shame that you may feel for not being the person you want to be is the distance that you will have to travel to meet your authentic self. You will forgive yourself. You have to.

As you stand in this space between emotional abuse and a life free of abuse, many ideas, thoughts, and illusions may pass through your mind and heart. Let them pass without impediment. Be aware that thoughts and memories will beckon you to the sea in hopes of drowning you. We burned the ship. No refuge for you exists in your past. Proceed with vigilance.

Many victims of psychological abuse catch themselves up in the lies and betrayal of the abuser, so much so that they believe that any resulting hurt is all their fault. This causes a battle within. The stories take over their lives. Post-Traumatic Stress Disorder and an inability to be present and move on to craft an extraordinary life after abuse may occur.

As the person on the suffering end of betrayal and lies, you may have acknowledged times in which you had had enough and lashed out with vicious words. Would it benefit you to beat yourself up for this? Will that change the past? Please, reflect on the times in which you retaliated as the abuse reached the door to your authentic self and you cried out, *enough*!

If you discover that you have been unkind and vindictive because of psychological turmoil, it is your responsibility to change. Blaming others or claiming that you are a victim will propel you deeper into the past and not forward into your future. Let's take responsibility and move on. Do not call the abuser and apologize. Forgive. Live and let live.

Unable to Receive and Not Feeling Like Enough

During the time that I gathered information about how I presented myself to others and myself, it occurred to me that other people entered my life and nudged me to see my authentic self. However, self-blame and other turbulence flooded my mind so that these gifts of encouragement offered to me could not be received.

Scott re-surfaced in my life during the time that I lived with Mike. In my mid-30s then, Scott left me a voicemail stating that he had had a dream about me. His voice was soothing, like a warm hug. He wrote me e-mails expressing his feelings for me and reminiscing about how I made him feel when he suffered alone in the constraints of a jail cell. *There is no other feeling like being loved by you.* His heart made confessions to mine. These words echoed within me as if Scott could read my war-torn and wounded heart.

The girl who I had been, cowering and disheveled, perked up and stood tall, finger pointed in the air, and cried out, "He's right, you know!"

I felt it. I felt the person about whom Scott spoke. I had pushed her aside in order to protect myself. This girl who loved life and all of the people in it had led me astray. Though she felt fool-hearted, she was also wise and caring. I re-connected to that authentic self, that vibrant young girl who loved with all of her heart before the abuse. Scott's e-mail was long, but his words reminded me of my true self in a split second. *There is no other feeling like being loved by you.* Buried among so many words that passed by me like strangers in a crowd, his one loving phrase became the parent that held my truth.

You will hear what is true for you. Our inner truths are always available to us. We are at one with our authentic self no matter how lost and detached we may feel from her. She can and will be found, and we will call to her from a place of truth. We will find her where our heart feels free. She is living in the activities that inspire joy.

All of us may engage with our authentic self no matter what has happened in the past. I will always believe this for you. This partner lives in you. It is you. It is real.

Examine Your Price Tag

Aside from the gift of uncovering my hidden self in a few words, Scott gifted me a second time in 2009 when he sent me an expensive present for Christmas. Divorced and in the dating world, perhaps he hoped to re-kindle our flame. Not knowing his intentions, the experience is burned within my memory, as it mirrored to me my actual value over the discounted price for which I had been giving my love.

Taking advantage of my winter break from teaching, I drove from Denver, Colorado, to St. Louis, Missouri, to visit my family. Scott must have known that I intended to spend Christmas with my parents without Mike, as Mike had driveled his latest excuse not to spend a holiday with me. In the delusion of an exclusive relationship and feeling isolated and alone, I made the twelve-hour road trip to my childhood home by myself. My wheels spun on both the open highway and within my mind.

Weary from the many hours on the road, I arrived and swung open the front door. Welcomed by mauve-colored lipstick kisses and the lingering scent of Estée Lauder, I leaned into my mother, wondering if I could stay there forever, held up by her love. As my father closed the door behind us, I knew that I had arrived home, protected and now safe.

After a long winter's nap under the peach comforter that my mom and I bought when I was a tween (the one for which I had been sworn to secrecy not to tell my dad the price), I awoke and trudged downstairs.

My mom sang out, "Oh, I almost forgot. A package arrived for you."

How exciting. Mike sent me a present since he couldn't be here with me. My foolish heart fantasized about Mike's love for me. I believed that he would redeem himself for forgotten birthdays and cancelled vacations.

I sat on the couch lined with pillows in every shade of mauve and opened the present. My heart dropped into my stomach when I noted the name of the sender. The gift was not from my boyfriend, but from Scott. The trigger set, and the room narrowed in on me, as did an audience.

My mom and my sister-in-law, whom had arrived, now gazed in anticipation, as they must have spotted the UGG label on the box.

I felt nervous, hesitant, and trapped. Guilt filled my veins and my heart. Though Mike had attended few to zero holiday gatherings with me, or any significant event for that matter, I couldn't help but feel grave responsibility to the one-sided relationship and to Mike. He was hundreds of miles away in both distance and affection, and I knew how he might feel to learn that I had received an extravagant present from my ex. No value could be taken from this experience. In my mind, this felt like cheating and deceit pure and simple.

As I opened the box, my mood shifted. Perhaps I picked up on the delight of the ladies around me. I felt present, and an overwhelming sense of importance flowed over me. A pair of leather and wool designer Ugg hiking boots with a cashmere scarf and Ugg gloves nestled inside the box. I had never hinted for such a gift, nor had I foreseen this gesture.

I felt honored. I felt that princess feeling, a tingle of magic. I felt as if Scott knew me and could see me. The tangible object represented his love for me, and it felt palpable. Like Cinderella, my foot fit snug and perfect into my glass slipper, also known as lambskin-lined boots.

After giving and over-giving in the past, it felt like my turn to receive.

The occasion couldn't sustain itself. I felt exhilarated for a split second, and then I paused and dropped my head.

The flood gates opened. "I can't keep this! Why did he send this present to me? What was he thinking? I am with Mike."

Then my primitive mind exclaimed so much more. *I can't take this gift home with me. Mike will know, and I will have to explain.* Mike, however, had sent me no holiday gift, and during each year of our relationship, I had had to remind him of my birthday or let it slip by unnoticed by him.

I felt shame for receiving this gift and anger for allowing myself to accept less in my relationship. I felt unworthy of the surprising and incredible gift and afraid to admit that I might deserve it. If I deserved this gift, it meant that my life as I knew it would have to change.

I did deserve this gift from Scott, whom I had loved with all of my innocent heart in my youth and during the traumatic time of his imprisonment. *Lapse-in-judgment* screamed through my body and congealed in my veins.

I left the gift with my parents and drove home to my dying relationship and mediocre life, but the impact of this incident planted a seed, a seed deep below a dry, rocky surface cracked with pain and darkness. However, in time, water found its way through the cracks, and fresh life climbed its way out.

 SOULutions

SOULution #1:
How The #&@$ Do You Learn How to Receive?

Answer: You find a way.

Here is how I did it. Though I once shied away from accepting help or gifts out of fear of being controlled by others, I now receive with grace and in a way that makes the giver feel appreciated and honored. I arm myself with the daily mantras that I deserve wonderful gifts. I receive with dignity and gratefulness, and I am a generous giver. With these mantras, I set out to accept help and be willing to receive.

To proceed, you must possess a willingness. You must decide that you are willing to learn to receive. Your willingness to receive is the invitation, the welcoming letter. Your gratitude is the love that you provide yourself and the giver.

The word grateful has a dynamic personality and may light up a room or a heart. Gratitude is contagious, and we all wear it well! As I write these words, I feel thankfulness gush through my cells. It is warm and soothing, not frigid and cold. Appreciation is the heart of receiving and giving.

If you feel on edge when you receive help, coach yourself into knowing that you are giving the gift of gratitude in exchange for help. Embrace this notion, and know that your thanks is enough. No other debts are owed. Giving and receiving is a profound exchange between two people.

In the past, I couldn't receive because I thought that this meant that I owed the giver money, an action on my part, or my friendship. I had many relationships where this idea could be justified.

You don't owe a man or a friend a thing except gratitude for a compliment, for paying for dinner or a drink, or even for a gift. Yes, we should receive all tangible and intangible gifts with a genuine *Thank you*. Look the person in the eyes. Deflecting a compliment due to our low self-worth is normal for abuse victims. Let's change that. A compliment is a gift. You are a gift. Be grateful in return.

A strategy to assist you in receiving is to stay out of your head. Envision the compliment, the giver's words, floating straight into your heart. Place your hand on your heart as you respond with a *Thank You*, locking this gift or compliment inside. Our disheartened mind doesn't believe that we are worthy of hearing kind words. After years of ridicule and harsh words, compliments feel like invaders to our nervous system and we bat them away. After all, we are conditioned for and accustomed to hearing demeaning words.

Keep the compliments away from your analytical mind. Don't let your head over-process the gift, not even for a second. When a compliment is given to you, set your hand on your heart and reply *Thank You*. Imagine the compliment, the love and the kindness, and the effort that it takes from a person as healing energy for you. Practice this feeling of receiving in the mirror right now. Compliment yourself. Feel your own words penetrating your heart. Use every act of kindness toward yourself to heal your past wounds.

On the other hand, if you give a compliment to your over-active mind, you will hear rubbish. *He didn't mean that. She thinks I look pretty tonight. Does that mean that I don't look nice on other nights? I like your hair that way.* But I never wear my hair this way. I like it curly, not straight. *People don't like me the way I am.*

Need I go on? This is such a sad way to process a compliment, and it is a specific indicator that you have lived in the muck of verbal abuse. Your mind has been conditioned from the slights of others. *Are you going to wear that tonight? Have you always styled your hair that way?* You were all dressed up and feeling swell until you heard condescending remarks that knocked you off balance.

The stress is showing. I like it better when you... (enter the complete opposite of what you are doing at the moment). These are subtle manipulative digs at your self-worth. They are disturbing, and exposure to them will disrupt the harmony within you.

In this SOULution, you must step away from that space and place your focus on your heart center. All compliments are stored there, and no contemptuous words are allowed in. All gifts are received with the heart, not the head. Don't attempt to make sense of this at first. Place these presents where your suffering once lived. The gifts from others are meant to help you. They are powerful. Let them in.

Dear Over-Givers, you are going to love this! See, I didn't forget about you. You will offer a heartfelt *Thank You*. Your gratitude cannot be the dismissive *Thank You* that the ego would dish out. Please don't side-step a sincere thank you with *Oh, you shouldn't have. But I didn't bring you a gift. Oh, my goodness, this is too much.* No, it's not, it is the right amount. It is perfect, thank you. Here is the trick to making it all worth your while. Here is the difference between an ego *Thank You* and a heartfelt *Thank You Very Much*.

Make eye contact with the person. Wait for it, or even request it if the giver of the gift is fumbling around and avoiding your response. State this person's name until he acknowledges you. If you feel safe, place your hand on his hand, his arm, or his shoulder. Yes, your eye contact and touch are compelling. With admiration and awe, offer a sincere *Thank You*.

Now, I have done this while a date signed the credit card receipt for the dinner that he paid for. I have slowed down, stopped him, and invited him to turn toward me. The act of breaking the routine, of not allowing my date to rush to pay out of a sense of obligation, solicited appreciation. These men remembered this.

Sometimes I received an abrupt ego reaction from the man. *No problem. It's not a big deal. Sure.* Disheartened by this, I then took a risk and explained, *Here is my thank you, and I want you to place it in your heart so that your head doesn't mess with it.*

Others shift, you shift, and giving and receiving is re-born, and the fatal take, take, take evaporates from your life. It is almost too overwhelming to articulate into words. Learning to receive is a piece of your recovery from injurious relationships. Do it, and I will thank you from far away because this act will heal the people of the world and you. *Thank You* from the bottom of my heart.

SOULution #2:
Disown Your False Self

Oh, my, I was the number one culprit when it came to acting from my emotions. Some of us believe all of our thoughts. I believed all of my emotions. I had countless and intense emotions. I had primary emotions, and then I had a wide range of secondary emotions, followed by the merging and overlapping of emotions, and of course a few nuances of emotions sprinkled on top.

My nervous system of emotions felt like New York City on the 4th of July. Together we packed the streets, bumping into each other, dodging around corners, placed on the shoulders of friends, floundering around, held up by street poles in a drunken stupor, or screaming at the sky. Yes, all of that erupted within me during any given time of day, most often when I needed to be focused on a particular job or teaching a classroom of students.

How did I overcome this inner storm and soothe my soul? How did I guide the sad, mournful, and frail traveling with me down those streets of emotions?

I did what any rational person would do when faced with such an incendiary crime scene where no voice of reason could be heard. I had a nervous breakdown, of course.

True story. This landed me on the couch of that anxiety therapist, Dr. Goldmann, claiming that I would do whatever it took to turn down the noise.

The solution: Disown My False Self. Stop giving attention to these emotions. Ignore the internal child turning over chairs to gain attention. Do not concentrate on your unsettling emotions. Focus your attention elsewhere. *Focus on what, though?*

It is time now to sculpt your future self. I cannot do this for you. You, and you alone, know who this person is. Tap into the truth about yourself, and design your life. As always, I will give you a glimpse into how I molded myself from the inside out.

At the time of my breakup with Ryan in 2017, I called in sad to work, often. I did not feel sick. I felt melancholy and gave this sorrow my undivided attention. This attention gave my sadness power over my life, and my true self and my emotions conflicted.

I taught kindergarten at the time, and I neglected my teaching to nurture my woebegone self.

I had to get tough with myself. The interrogation process unfolded. What did I value about being a teacher? Did I believe that a teacher should be there for her students? Did I believe that in some way my students' success depended upon my presence and my teaching? Did I believe that 5-year-olds needed consistency so that they could be resilient? Did I believe that my students, many of whom had learning challenges, parents in prison, or early childhood trauma, would flourish without me?

Oh, my! My students need me, and I am a dependable, responsible, and present teacher. Time to act like one!

Despite my stirring emotions around the breakup, I re-committed to being present and there for my students until the end of the school year. At night, I prioritized my recovery.

To what do you need to re-commit in order to move in the direction of the person you wish to be?

Design a plan for your future self to step into today. List the traits that you embody and the actions that you will take in the areas of work, love, family, friendships, finances, health, and purpose. This list is not devoid of emotion. Have your emotions, but also question them.

For example, my current down-hearted self believed that I had to work hard for money. As a result, earning money posed a challenge for me, and my money tended to slip right out the back door, if it ever came in the front door. I decided to change that mindset.

How had I made it to 40 years old without a thought of establishing a list of my personal values and who I aspired to be? All of this time I believed that I was acting in alignment with my values, and yet I had never defined the character traits that I wished to live up to. Once I did this, my life changed.

I had been impulsive and reactive with my emotions in most, if not all, of my prior relationships. I texted or called my boyfriends when I had a feeling that our relationship felt off. I brought up conversations based on my feelings alone. I clung to attachments at any price, and this drove men away.

Now, I sit with my feelings. I gather data related to my body triggers and soothe myself. I recognize my desire to correspond, and I allow time and space to determine whether it is necessary. Today, reciprocal relationships are the goal, and I honor and nurture myself before seeking attention from others. I reach out from a grounded and empowered place, not desperation. I open up based on what my image of healthy relationships is and may be, and I live out that future feeling as if it is here now.

Determine who you want to be, and watch how you catch yourself when you act from this example. This list is your recipe for life. Similar to planning for a delectable meal, you don't want to pick up a bunch of unhealthy food at the grocery store because you are distracted or because you can't stop yourself from impulse-buying. Your future self is the most fabulous feast that you may prepare. Balance your flavors so that you may taste this sweet life like you never have before.

A note of caution: A flip side exists. If you already have strong moral beliefs, and it is your adherence to this strict or skewed belief system that is causing such a strain in your life, it is time to question your interpretations, as I did. Are these your convictions, or have you struggled to live up to your family's or an institution's standards? Discern your true self and release your false persona.

SOULution #3:
Tell Yourself The Truth, Even If It Is After The Fact

Change requires a high level of awareness. Habits repeated over time develop into our disposition. It may be difficult to catch ourselves before we act, as so many survival strategies have become automatic. For this reason, it is vital to tell yourself the truth about whether you are reacting from a limited range of emotions. Or are you following through as your highest and best self? Progress is being able to define these two states, even after the fact. Whether in real time, or in hindsight, it is time to identify the truth about your actions.

I deserve an award for rationalizing that my actions were valued-based and not fear-based. When I felt like having a glass of wine to quell the stress of an overwhelming day, I rationalized that taking a break or celebrating life with a toast was a high-value move. When I felt like staying in bed instead of lifting weights, I quieted my internal censor by justifying that I deserved to rest.

I saw the negative impact of certain friends, but my habit of pleasing others with my *yes* or out of a need for immediate validation persisted. I chose the easy way out instead of the road less travelled, and every time I did this, it slowed my recovery, and it blocked my way to the life of my dreams.

Do not beat yourself up if you have these habits to break. What is important is to remember that your environment is always going to be stronger than your ability to make decisions when you are tired, emotional, or stressed. Audit your environment.

Are your friends supportive, or do they influence you to fall prey to your shortcomings with group excuses and side comments that accept a lifestyle that you don't want? Do you prepare nutritious food in your home for the fragile times of day when you reach for chips to soothe yourself? Are you assessing your body's needs and relishing a short nap instead of a tall glass of wine? To what activity do you turn when you are anxious? Performing this evaluation and making a plan of action will change your life.

In addition to identifying habits and changing the environment to support your decision-making process, your brain may need reminders. In stressful times, when I wished to claim my *no* to ungodly relationships, and I longed to let go of relationships from the past, I wrote in capital letters in bold marker STICK TO THE GAME PLAN on a notecard. I propped the card on my nightstand in order to awaken to this message.

When my emotions took over and I wanted to reach out to the wrong person, I remembered, *I have a plan. Stick to the game plan.* When doubts loomed over my shoulder, I brushed them away. *Stick to the game plan.* When the heat is on, when the pressure mounts, stick to the game plan like your future depends on it, because it does!

As you tell yourself the truth, bring awareness to your actions, and recognize that when you stray from the plan, you must hold yourself accountable. Your game plan or roadmap regulates your behaviors as either moving toward your goals or moving away from your goals.

Throughout this life, you are going to make some wrong turns. You may feel lost. Feeling lost is acceptable, losing yourself even one more time is not! When friends beckon you from the trail, you make your way with their support. When an inner mantra guides you with purpose and determination toward your goals, you find your way to stay the course.

Be as honest as possible. If you feel off, maybe you are not seeing with a clear lens. Solicit a reliable friend, a coach, or a therapist to help you pinpoint your blind spots. If you feel triggered or uneasy, a past wound may be within your subconscious that you are bringing up in the present. Seek guidance, and remember to tell the whole story. Often we know the story. We know what we are doing wrong, but we deny it.

If you find yourself hiding part of the story, that is where your problem lies. Uncover your shame, admit it. Shine a light on the story that you are telling yourself, and make the necessary changes. So often we lie to ourselves to avoid this process, to avoid hurt.

I lied to myself. I placed the needs of others before my own needs until I implemented these ideas. I now stick to the game plan whenever I am in doubt!

CHAPTER 16

Down the Rabbit Hole
with a Headlamp

When our life doesn't make sense, it is in our nature to search for clarity. I felt ready to uncover the hard truths, and my hope is that you are ready now as well. I left no stone unturned as I searched for the reasons why I attracted manipulative, self-serving men and friends into my life and wanted to stay in a relationship with them. I attracted caring people as well, yet I felt addicted to the inconsiderate, dismissive, and selfish types.

What character traits in me kept this penchant for carnage to my heart going? I had to know. I believed that the cycle would never end if I didn't find them. In order to change these qualities in me, I had to first reveal and identify the monsters in the room. I told my friends that I needed to go down the rabbit hole with a headlamp to avoid being trapped in my own thickening plot forever.

I needed solutions. I had to understand what positioned me to be abused, demeaned, and discarded. I studied narcissism, personality disorders, and other psychological conditions. I learned about addiction and the toxicity that robs our souls of a clean, clear, crisp existence.

I learned that I attracted relationships with men who met me at my own level of love for myself. I normalized vile behavior because it felt like my normal, and it felt familiar. Of course, I asked *why* at this time.

With my mind in a softer place, I felt ready to answer some questions and strong enough to handle the facts of my life.

Why did I accept lies and deceit in my life? *Why* did I allow unfair treatment from others, so often that I didn't even notice their rude behavior anymore? *Why* did I allow these people into my life and into my home? The findings: This was my port in the storm!

I cruised way down the rabbit hole to find the reason as to why I normalized such shoddy behavior. While you will find details personal to your individual story, I have found that universal behaviors that occurred at a young age thread their way through the lives of those who become susceptible to psychological and emotional abuse. These behaviors may have left imprints on our psyche, therefore, priming us for abuse.

Family has an incredible impact, as do other authority figures in one's youth. I grew up in a family of eight and so had to develop a tolerance for personality types that I don't prefer to be around due to my own personality. As an empath, I spent my youth hiding behind my mother's leg and reacting to life around me. In fact, I formed an underlying belief that people around me were not safe.

Environment plays a huge factor. As you may imagine, in a house of eight people, five children all two years apart, two parents, and a grandmother, noise always prevailed. I learned to adapt to this. Every room had a TV in it, and every TV blared to override the noise. My siblings argued and yelled as a means to communicate. At least one family member occupied each bathroom whenever I needed it, and my siblings always invaded my space.

Hence, this launched my odyssey into a lack of boundaries and some serious stomach issues caused by frazzled nerves. If my mom wanted to be in my room, she entered regardless of whether I wanted her to. I became desensitized to loud noises, cruel words, controlling behaviors, and restrictions. As a wild child with an inclination to roam, I felt trapped in a personal prison.

Now, please listen. My parents and my family did not set out to imprison me or to hurt me in any way. This is where we take full responsibility for ourselves and stay clear of mindless finger pointing. They, all seven of them, treated me the best they could with the knowledge that they had at the time. My siblings and caregivers experienced and reacted to life in their own way, and they always came from a loving place.

We didn't wake up with intentions for the day or have family meetings about how we could add more joy to our lives. Those mindfulness resources may have existed, but we did not know of them. To our good fortune, we may utilize them now.

What else did I find in the rabbit hole of my past? Well, I found the manipulative and boundary-intruding behavior of childhood friends. I found a sport's coach who had acted so angry and verbally abusive that my skin crawled when I thought of him. I also had an inner fear that the coach had been abusive toward his own children.

These events occurred in the 1980s, when corporal punishment existed as a norm within many schools and homes. It is dismaying for me to even suggest that the actions of authority figures from my past may have been abusive. However, the long-term effects of spanking and hitting are known to cause anxiety disorders and substance abuse, as well as issues of trust, safety, and security. I find it valid if you wish to scan your past for evidence of abuse in order to move on and to acknowledge that you are no longer a helpless child.

Journal any evidence that emerges for you. Feel it in your body. At what age did you feel this fear? In what setting did you feel unsafe? Write about whatever images appear. Find the logic in some of your survival reflexes. Perhaps you have extreme anxiety before a test, and you discover that you were punished or even beaten for poor grades in school. Notice the sense that your body is attempting to make for you in order to soothe your way to confidence.

Words may be spoken in your mind's ear. Listen. Listen like a friend or a mother would. Listen to what your subconscious wants you to know, what your heart has been carrying around. Listen to the inner child who is hurt and scared, for we are going to comfort that child.

℘SOULutions℘

SOULution #1:
Move Out of Beware to Being Aware

Precious One, it should be safe for you to relax now. If you have left your ignoble relationships and made space for healing, you should be in a place to engage with others with a higher level of awareness. It is time to lower the shield and to be the observer of your life.

Bring your awareness to your present life. I would like you to pay attention to how you spend your time, with whom you spend your time, and to what you say to yourself and others.

Notice without judgment, but do acknowledge how you feel after interactions. Do these examples resonate with you?

Eek! Every time I run into that guy, I feel ill at ease. He appears nice and cordial, but I feel off. I wonder what that is about?

Uh, oh! I found myself gossiping at work. That does not feel like the person I would like to present myself as. What changes may I incorporate to change this behavior in the future?

I sometimes allowed myself to be pulled into conversations about a family member, a co-worker, or a friend. *Wow, that is not an effective use of my skills or my time. How may I initiate more rewarding conversations for myself and others? Perhaps I may make a point to have a few fascinating anecdotes on hand to direct conversations away from this kind of behavior.*

First, decide how often you may need to bring your awareness to the day's events. Is spending time musing in the evening sufficient, or do you need a few stops during the day to take inventory? My practical advice is to pause, set this book aside, and program an alert on your phone for the times when you would like to be aware.

When this alarm is heard, turn it off, and then set your timer for three minutes. Process the day's events. Take written notes of how you felt, what company you kept, and discern whether you would like more of these interactions, experiences, or opportunities moving for-

246 • *From Trigger to Happy*

ward. If you reacted from a trigger or due to lingering survival instincts, call it out by name, and visualize how you will act next time.

Do not clean up or change the day's events. They are now lessons that are sculpting the new you and defining how you act from here on. Recognize as well the times when you stop the alarm and carry on with your day as if this time is unimportant. You are giving yourself three minutes. Three minutes out of a 1,440-minute day. You are worthy, deserving, and dare I say that you require this time!

SOULution #2:
Prepare And Practice Your Response

Change does not occur in one fell swoop. The image of this idealistic vision of transformation is broadcasted to us in thirty-minute sitcoms and during coaching seminars designed to inspire action. Unless a radical event such as winning the lottery or a traumatic event such as a car accident occurs, life, for most of us, goes unaltered without change.

In order to fashion a life free of abuse, you must act in a different way every single day.

Review your notes from SOULution #1. What is causing you the most distress? Are there any reactions that you may be able to tweak? Take the time right now to write out how you will approach old patterns moving forward. In addition, feel in your body the sensations that would occur in you if you did indeed think and act in a more conscious way. Review these images in your mind. Imagine receiving that degree or promotion. Imagine declining an invitation to date an alluring but dangerous man. Better yet, conjure up the song that you will hear while walking down the aisle with your life partner. Take liberty with your imagination, and feel these events as if they are occurring today.

Now, recruit a friend on whom you may practice your new future self. Based upon my experience, you may find some of this process hysterical. This laughter is anxious energy that needs to leave your body. This comical approach may also bring light to what has developed as a heavy weight on a serious matter. You may find that situations, people, and life itself is not what your abused and battered mind made it out to be.

Rehearse the life that you want until it shines across the stage. Hear yourself announce, *No, thank you. I have plans.* Interrupt the gossip with, *I hear you, but I prefer to have a more uplifting conversation with you.*

In the most trustworthy of situations, you may gasp mid action and yell, *Wait! I am in the process of changing this behavior. That is not a thought that I want to share!*

SOULution #3:
Claim Your Throne

The days of yelling *this seat is saved* out of misplaced need to sit next to your best friend at lunch or your own mother on the couch among siblings pawning for attention are over. No longer do you need to make a mad dash to the car in order to grab the shotgun position. It is time to claim your throne.

There is a place for you in this world. You belong. The right man or woman and love is available for you. Numerous opportunities for you to thrive as the authentic woman you are exist for you. The perfect job, a lasting relationship, and a dream home are designed for you. This has always been available to you, and it is available to you now. Your past does not predict your future.

You are not taking from others. When you have more, others do not have less. There is plenty to go around. More straightforwardly, if you do not claim what is your birthright as a human being on this planet, it goes to no one else.

Step into this space now. Claim your throne. Speak up at that meeting, for no one may say what you have to say in the way that you deliver it. Follow your passion, and change careers despite the appearance of competition, regardless of the fear of change. When you are being your genuine self, the right place for you already exists.

May we agree that you have not been your true authentic self as you bent to the will of a narcissistic man, as you gave your *yes* to him while abandoning yourself?

Life is not happening to you, it is happening through you. You must act. You must assert your being-ness into your life. Take the reins, and guide yourself in the direction of your utopia. Make no excuses for speaking up, communicating your feelings, or for defining and holding boundaries. Be kind in your delivery and resilient in your mission.

You are the Queen of your life. Stand tall. Dress the part. No other woman may play this role better than you!

CHAPTER 17

Face Your Fears
or Risk Self-Sabotage

I have heard more than one acronym for the word FEAR. Future Events Already Ruined and False Ego Appearing Real are two of them. Fear is at the heart of what stops us from becoming who we are meant to be. Fear prevents us from living our most superlative life. Fear stops us from taking a risk.

As much as I dislike circulating this news, your fear may be multiplied after narcissistic abuse. This type of abuse establishes a deep fear of loving and being loved. We will have to face this fear together.

Fear is a state of the mind that we all have. Please do not be fooled or intimidated by those who seem fearless. They have fear, they happen to handle it in a different way and do not let it stop them from conceiving the life that they desire. This will be you.

Now, my fear is sneaky and manipulative, and it fakes me out all the time. At least it once did when it convinced me that a man in my life would change, that I could handle the abuse, that it felt safer to stay than to face the unknown, and that maybe I caused the problems in our relationship.

My mind offered solutions that pointed the finger at me and generated self-blame. If I talked to my abusive boyfriend in a different way, didn't call out the disturbing behavior, or solved my own problems, the relationship would be better, and he would change. As I made the modifications, read the books, and bent over backwards while tiptoeing around any number of my exes, my ego snickered. Knowing full well that change eluded me despite my best efforts, my ego seemed to be against me as well.

My ego wanted me living in fear with an illusion that real and unforeseen threats lurked around the corner. Was this true? No! This fear birthed a baby demon named self-sabotage. While aspirations had me pressing one foot on the gas pedal, self-sabotage held the other foot on the brake.

Let's take a glimpse into your fears and belief systems that are against you and not for you. Here we may build a system that is supportive and rewarding. We will fashion a different way of seeing life and facing it head on.

Let's face your fears. See my examples here.

I fear breaking up with the man I am dating because he may become upset with me. The truth is that I knew that ending relationships also hurt me. I felt attached in an anxious way, and letting go terrified me.

I fear telling my truth. The truth here is that I acted so other-focused for so long that I did not even know my own truth. I did not stand up for what I wanted in intimacy. I felt like a shadow of myself.

I fear retaliation. I felt like Ryan would seek revenge against me, and this fear lasted long after the relationship ended. The way that a narcissist retaliates is fierce. Payback seldom occurred swiftly, rather it lurked in the near future. During any type of conflict or disagreement, my narcissistic ex acted so understanding. In time, I discovered that his wound gaped wide open and that he wanted vengeance. He needed to get back at me for acknowledging that my feelings were hurt from the latest lie or betrayal that I uncovered. Instead of pangs of conscience, I earned revenge.

According to the narcissist, his betrayal would never be the problem. The problem was my revelation of the betrayal. I didn't know that a person could live and act like this. My brain could not wrap itself around the lies. My reality and my sense of self became altered.

I fear being found out. I felt weak. I felt so susceptible to abuse, and it appeared as if I allowed it. I welcomed degenerate acquaintances into my home and my heart. I was terrified that my abuser would use my weakness against me. I was worried all the time about keeping him happy. I believed that if he became unsatisfied, the abuse would be revealed, and then friends and family would know. I could not bear my shame on top of the abuse.

What if those who looked up to me or at least valued me as their equal found out that I had stayed in an abusive relationship? What if others found out that I had been the poor, worthless woman who stayed with a man who treated her like dirt? I know now that I was not weak, but this is how I felt at the time. The shame and cruel self-judgment kept me paralyzed.

I fear that I won't find a man to love me. Hello, blinders! I am sorry, but is it possible that I thought that Ryan must be the last man on earth for me? In fact, I thought that Ryan was God's gift to me and the answer to my prayers. I believed that I deserved this gift and that I could not reject it. Sucker-punched by lust, I saw Ryan as the best man that I could find (even though we did not want the same type of relationship at all). I even thought that he seemed too extraordinary to be true. Gulp!

I fear facing my own unhealed wounds that matched me to an abusive relationship. Enmeshed and entwined with Ryan's fantasies, lies, and gaslighting, I had no time to sort out my own inner wounds or even think about life. It is ironic then that I did not have to face any of my own shortcomings because his problems oozed into every conversation. I realize now that he kept me busy with these distractions to cover up his deceit. However, I feared the responsibility of looking at my own past. Perhaps that is why I stayed with Ryan.

What did you or do you fear? Take some time to write it out.

After I ended all relationships with men, I feared my addiction to Ryan and the overwhelming pain associated with it. I feared that I would go down in flames. I longed for him, and wanting him in my life made no sense. I feared my own sanity. I thought that maybe I had been narcissistic, and I sought out a diagnosis. I feared for my health and well-being, as I felt that I had slipped into a darkness out of which I would never be able to extricate myself.

I feared ever being in a relationship with a man. I feared social media. I even feared the notification sound of a text message. After all, one glance at a gaslighting text message could send me plummeting to the depths, and all of the harmony that I had earned through my no-contact plan disappeared. I feared places where we might meet and mutual friends. I feared running into Ryan somewhere...anywhere. I feared going out or being seen.

I feared my reliance on crutches (name yours here: food, alcohol, over-exercising, binge watching TV shows). I feared being alone with my own thoughts because they felt aberrant in nature, and I did not know how to stop them from pouring in.

I feared therapists because of the gaslighting experience of Mike meeting with my therapist in the past and because of what happened when I went to the therapist that Ryan chose for us.

I feared telling my primary care physician too much out of fear that he might think that I was unstable. I feared that all of my friends would bolt, and I accepted that this would happen because I could not stop re-living the trauma. I believed that no friend could or should have to handle that.

Isn't it miraculous that I have friends who stood by me and family members who love me? I am amazed and impressed. I did not see myself as worthy at the time.

The insidious part is that these fears were valid then. I experienced physical, emotional, and psychological abuse. My cause for alarm and protection made sense. The problem is that these fears do not let any light in, nor do they foster recovery of any kind. You cannot heal while in a victim mindset. These fears have to fall away. You have to face them.

The act of bringing your fears to the surface is progress in itself. Once you dismantle and disarm these fears, you may spend time acknowledging that not all men are manipulative, that both men and women may be trusted, and that someday you will be held and safe in the arms of a man.

I will warn you, though, tough girls cry hard. Scream and cry, and let it all out. Admit that you are scared to love. It is okay to be in this frightened place. It is okay to see the truth of what is happening. Be spunky. Square up to your terrors.

If you had the resilience to stay with a narcissist, you have the strength to face your fears. You are more gritty than you think, so don't think. Be lionhearted without any knowing of how this will turn out or what will arise in you. Believe that you can, and act as if the standoff has already occurred. Act as if you will never be in an abusive relationship again. Tell yourself that this is a thing of the past and that you will never engage with such a loathsome man in the future.

Disregard that part of you and your story. That victim is not you and will never be you. Pretend that you are in a safe and loving life. As the old adage goes, fake it till you make it.

❧ SOULutions ❧

SOULution #1:
Deconstruct Outdated Beliefs

You know the routine by now. Grab that journal and your sword, also known as your favorite pen, because we are going inward. Write without restraint.

What do I believe about love after abuse?

Example of Old Beliefs: Love equals pain. Love is unsafe. Love is difficult.

Flip the Script: Love is unconditional. Love is safe. Love flows from me and to me with ease.

What do I believe about men after abuse?

Example of Fear-Based Beliefs: All men are manipulative. All men cheat. Men want to use me. Men are dangerous. Men can't be trusted.

Re-Write: High-value men seek loving relationships. Men may be loyal (look for evidence of this!). Men are protective and trusting, safe and kind.

What do I believe about women after abuse?

Example of Blanket Statements: Women can't be trusted. Women are two-faced and talk about you behind your back. Women are jealous and competitive. Women are not to be trusted around your man.

The Other Side of the Coin: Women may be trusted. Women have integrity and are loyal. Women are supportive, caring, and understanding. Women have strong boundaries around your man and respect relationships.

Please, write out your findings to these questions and then follow the pattern of changing the dialogue about relationships and people for yourself. In addition, look for evidence to support your newfound beliefs. Acknowledge the men in your life or in your friends' lives who are loyal and faithful. Look at the friends who have always been there for you. Seize this positive evidence as you renovate your belief system and turn your focus on the good.

SOULution #2:
Dig Deep

Don't stop now, your journal is your new best friend. I want you to tell yourself what you are most worried about as you step into your future.

I am worried that I am too messed up for a relationship.
Go for it! I am worried that...

Truth: We all deserve love, no matter in what stage of emotional growth we find ourselves.

I am worried that the next man will cheat on me.
Your turn. I am worried that...

Truth: Not all men cheat, and I will take the time to get to know the men I date. I will control the pace of the relationship and open up as I feel safe to do so.

I am worried that I am too old and that my best years are behind me.
Go big. I am worried that...

Truth: Thank goodness that those years that have passed were not your best years, My Treasure! My life is unfolding as it should, and love is available to me at any age.

I am worried that the man I like will not accept my past and will run from me because I have a history of emotional abuse and drama.
You can do this. I am worried that...

Truth: No person's life is perfect. The right man for me will love me for who I am and see how resilient I had to be in order to overcome my past. He will know that those men are missing out on a phenomenal woman...me!

Excellent! Doesn't that feel sensational. I once thought that I would be rejected if the guy I liked found out that I don't talk to my sister.

Then, a mentor enlightened me. "Your healthy man won't judge you for that. He will know that she is missing out on having you in her life."

As a perspective that I couldn't see from the clouded lens through which I peered then, these words enriched my life. The doors of my heart swung open, and I believed that this could be true for me. I want you to feel this for yourself.

SOULution #3:
Do What Scares You

I know what you may be thinking. *Wait, I pulled up all of my fears, and now you want me to seek out opportunities that petrify me.* I do.

Make a list of what you have always wanted to do but were too overwhelmed with fear to try.

I have chin-rattling stage fright due to ridicule in my youth. While I can now read a line or two with poise, I believed that I would be booed off stage if I tried improvisation or recitation in public. Well, as you may have guessed, I navigated myself into a position to face this fear and claim my voice.

I joined Toastmasters, an international organization that teaches public speaking and leadership skills. I was awed by the elite speakers and moved to tears when I attended a speech competition for speakers with disabilities. I spoke up a few times and introduced myself in these meetings. These baby steps felt like monumental leaps as my chin quivered with the sound of my own name in my introduction. The point is, I did it, anyway!

I also attended poetry readings at a local bookstore in Denver called the Tattered Cover. I attended and watched other intrepid souls stand up and speak from the heart. Some poets seemed trained, some were naturals, and some joined for an evening to escape the cold blustery streets of homelessness. Children skipped in encouraged by parents and teachers, while elderly men and women embraced the podium in order to hold up their frail psyches. One retired man paused for a period of time and then apologized that he could not remember his next line. It became clear that father time wanted to steal his memory, and he stood in valiant effort to retain it by reciting poetry.

Who am I not to be brave among these warriors?

With this, I advise you to follow your fears. Follow your fears to the edge of your oasis and then take one more step.

Writing this book, joining self-improvement groups, seeking help to stop drinking, building a business, asking my sister to work on our relationship, and reading my own poem aloud to an audience are my feats of faith along my sojourn of self-discovery. What are yours? Step toward them with your head held high.

CHAPTER 18

Happy

Happy: Feeling or showing pleasure or contentment.

When you can't sit still, you gasp for air, your heart races, and you pause and take a long deep breath and feel the sunlight on your face, know that you are moving toward happy.

When your chest is pounding and a burning sensation ignites like a wild fire inside you and you place your hand on your heart and profess, *Don't worry, I am here for you*, please know that you are claiming your happy.

When your mind is fixed on an impossible mission to figure out a confusing interaction and you choose to surrender to the unknown instead of fretting through the night, know that you are determining your path toward a future of happy.

When you freeze up in the moment and then allow yourself space to relax, become immune to suspicious visual cues around you, and then soothe your internal mind with affirmations that you are safe, you are experiencing the happy after abuse.

When you inquire of yourself, *What wonderful gifts may I receive today?*, know that you are in the happy grip of psychological freedom.

When you stay present in a loving way with those around you, and your mind is fixed on thoughts of building a future, know that the part of your brain called the amygdala that held you back is now at rest and out of the way.

Happiness is not a destination to which I may guide you. Happy is a state of being within you. It is the most authentic parts of you being heard and seen. It is the true you shining through. Happiness is your light, your gifts, and your love that you may experience, embrace, and share with yourself and others.

No sleazy family member, no manipulative man, and no distant partner may take this happy away from you. They can't beat it out of you. They can't scare it away. They can't dismiss, devalue, or disown it. Your ability to generate happiness has always been there, and it always will be there.

This part of you is untouchable and shatter-proof. You are filled with unlimited potential.

It is time now in your journey to tap into the infinite resources within yourself that have been nudged into every tiny crevasse within your being. Draw them out. Coax them out. Allow your happy to be seen.

You are safe now, and it is time to express the joy that is within you.

Will I still experience triggers?

Feeling triggered is a part of the human experience. You have not lived a full life if you have avoided being triggered. The difference now is that you have coping strategies, healing rituals, and the tools and means to handle what life throws your way.

What if I react?

Bank on it, you will. All humans react to frightening situations and blurry boundaries. Spend some time in silence, phone a confidant, or re-read any part of this book, and then respond with kindness. Set the parameters, ask the hard questions, and correct your course. You have what it takes.

Will my negative self-talk return?

Meditation and the re-wiring of your subconscious is not a one-and-done trick. A consistent and persistent routine is necessary to effect change. Do your morning meditations, listen to your affirmations, set your goals for your future self, and journal. If you miss a day, start over. If you miss a week, begin once more. If you miss a month or even a year and then wake up to the sound of that old chatter criticizing you, go back to this work. Say to yourself right now, *I will do it.* That is all it takes, as many times as it takes.

Will I have the strength to love again?

Absolutely. A knowing within me makes this undeniable. You have the courage to produce love wherever you go. You have the ability to love and nurture all life. You have the capacity to be a friend and receive friendship and trust. And yes, you have the wisdom to open your heart to the right man for you. I have no doubt about this.

Many make changes when it is easy. We commit to jobs, romances, ideas, and then change our minds when the pursuit is too hard or doesn't turn out how we expected. Few invest in lasting change. But you have made yourself a full, profound, constant promise to change your life for the better. Our egos are designed to keep us stuck in old patterns, and it takes effort, accountability, and support to re-wire the neuropathways that keep us locked in the past. You are rising to this challenge.

It takes considerable effort and healing to move our bodies out of fight, flight, or freeze mode. It takes an understanding of the direction in which we are leading ourselves, and it takes compassion to nurture our overactive minds and feeble hearts. My hope is that this book has provided a way out for you to follow, one to which your heart may scream an extravagant *Yes!*

Allow yourself a 100 percent *Yes!* Commit here and now. Commit to yourself over and over. The responsibility is yours. Don't expend any effort hoping that the trials will cease. Don't live in the *why me* space. Assimilate the indisputable ability that you have to take on whatever turbulence comes your way.

Some vows you may need to proclaim for yourself. *My old relationship patterns are in the past, and I focus on the truth of my life and love now. I will listen to my intuition, feel my feelings, and act in accordance with my needs.*

I will claim my Yes *and state my* No.

I am eternal love. This is who I am. What I seek in a partner is already in me. I do not have to go outward. I am love, mutuality, passion, and grace. I am whole.

I listen to and fulfill my emotional needs. I realize that the partner I desire is already chosen for me. I am one with all of the abundant love of the universe. I recognize, accept, and embody this perfect action, and I allow it to unfold.

I never chase love. I generate love. I give thanks with every breath of my being for this awareness and move forward in action with this knowing. I face and embrace the changes in my unfolding story with resilience. I always have a choice.

Love is action. Your resolution is a daily action in love.

Psychological abuse and emotional abuse breed a fear of love. How may you combat and conquer such a fear? You act.

As scary as it may be, you open your heart. It will open, and then it may contract as soon as you sense danger. Be strong, it is safe to love and be loved. You are unbreakable. You will keep your heart safe at all costs.

As this book ventures to a close, I have two wishes for you. One, if you slip this book into a drawer, I hope that you move on to your next best step. I am satisfied with being a hand that you may have held and a cheerleader in your corner even for a short while.

My second wish is that you see in you what I see. I know that you are deserving, worthy, and a force for good. I know that we need you to rise up into your authentic self and spread your love, gifts, and talents like the spectacular person you are. We need the love that is you to shine bright.

With that, I will leave you with one final love letter from your higher self.

Dear Love,

Don't dim your light. You have traveled so far. Set aside the time to acknowledge all that you have overcome. Take inventory of the efforts, the consequences, the triumphs, and the traumas through which you have evolved throughout this time. Celebrate every accomplishment with yourself and with others.

When you find yourself feeling lost, return home to your heart and pull your energy in. Further solidify your commitments by taking steps, drawing a hard line in the sand to stop any sabotaging, and hold your boundaries as you would hold an infant.

Sit down. Notice the actual results in your life and the impact within your soul and psyche for the work that you have accomplished. Celebrate out loud the strong sense of self that has developed! Rejoice in the satisfaction that you find in your new self! Commemorate the freedom from emotional abuse and the immense courage that you have to live the life that you are designed to live! You are living proof that you are unstoppable. You have taken yourself from triggered to attuned with your own happiness.

You are here now. You have arrived. You are prepared for your next chapter. You decide the title!

Love,
All of You

I am so happy that this book does not have a Hollywood ending!

Though this may not have been my intention, this book is closing in the right place. I am proud to pass the following information on to you and to other heart-centered souls.

I am 45 years old and single. I live alone in an apartment after having just sold a home that I owned. I have decided not to have a baby alone at this time. No other man, woman, or institution is telling me that I am lovable, worthy, or enough. The real-life happy ending is that I am. I am lovable. I am worthy. I am enough. Right here. Right now and as I am. I have never felt more powerful than I do right now. I am self-partnered.

This, Sweetness, is true paradise!

Know that you are the hero for whom you have been waiting. You give yourself the love that you have longed to feel. You comfort yourself. You parent yourself. You nurture, coach, and forgive yourself. No person may do this job better than you. You are made for this.

Though there may be other purposes in your life to accomplish, you have one purpose of which I am certain. You are made to love and accept yourself in full. You were designed to receive the gift that is your life. You have been given the space in this world to be a unique you, and you don't have to prove it. You may choose to sit on the couch all day and read a book or volunteer holding babies in the newborn intensive care unit. You are loved no matter what you do and no matter what you look like. It does not matter how much money you make or if your body is maturing. You are loved at any age. Love is available to you now and always.

You are significant.

You are worthy.

You are a gift.

It is with deep contemplation that I finish this book and in essence let you go now. My goal has always been for you to be free. My hope is not to simply inspire you, but to empower you with the skills, the heart, and the established self-worth to move forward in your life.

This is it.

This is where your new life begins.

Sources

Craig, G. (2011). *Eft Manual*. Energy Psychology Press.

Hebb, D. O. (n.d.). *The organization of behavior: A neuropsychological theory*. s.n.

James, M., & Jongeward, D. (1996). *Born to win: Transactional analysis with Gestalt experiments*. Perseus Books.

Levine, P. A. (1997). *Waking the tiger: Healing trauma: The innate capacity to transform overwhelming experiences*. North Atlantic Books.

Merriam-Webster. (n.d.). *Peace definition & meaning*. Merriam-Webster. Retrieved June 8, 2022, from https://www.merriam-webster.com/dictionary/peace

Pert, C. B. (2003). *Molecules of emotion: Why you feel the way you feel*. Scribner.

Schank, J. R., Ryabinin, A. E., Giardino, W. J., Ciccocioppo, R., & Heilig, M. (2012, October 4). *Stress-related neuropeptides and addictive behaviors: Beyond the usual suspects*. Neuron. Retrieved June 8, 2022, from https://www.ncbi.nlm.nih.gov/pmc/articles/PMC3495179/

Wikimedia Foundation. (2022, June 2). *Dark Triad*. Wikipedia. Retrieved June 8, 2022, from https://en.wikipedia.org/wiki/Dark_triad

Wikimedia Foundation. (2022, May 19). *Cognitive dissonance*. Wikipedia. Retrieved June 8, 2022, from https://en.wikipedia.org/wiki/ Cognitive_dissonance

Wikimedia Foundation. (2022, May 21). *Hernán Cortés*. Wikipedia. Retrieved June 8, 2022, from https://en.wikipedia.org/wiki/ Hern%C3%A1n_Cort%C3%A9s

Xplore. (n.d.). *Maya Angelou quotes*. BrainyQuote. Retrieved June 8, 2022, from https://www.brainyquote.com/quotes/maya_angelou_383371

Resources

Website:

www.EllenMalan.com

Contact:

Rise@EllenMalan.com

Now that you have freed yourself from the grip of unhealthy relationships, please look for the companion book to *From Trigger to Happy* coming in 2023. Author and teacher, Ellen Malan, will guide you through the next stages of healing and rebuilding a strong sense of self after abuse.